"Garling's book transports us into the intimate and remarkable life of the most important Buddhist woman nobody knows—mother of the sage and first Buddhist nun. From a cache of newly discovered lore, Mahaprajapati inspires all women to awaken, undaunted by hesitancy or obstacles."
—Judith Simmer-Brown, Naropa University professor and author of *Dakini's Warm Breath: The Feminine Principle in Tibetan Buddhism*

"This is an important historical corrective, examining the early Buddhist world through the lens of one of its most powerful women, Mahaprajapati Gautami—the Buddha's aunt and foster mother, wife of the Buddha's father, queen of the Shakya republic, and initiator of the order of nuns. Garling has written a page turner. Her deft handling of the materials and insightful readings offer a compelling 'herstory' and a fresh look at the Buddha's life and legacy."
—Andy Rotman, Professor of Religion, Buddhist Studies, and South Asian Studies at Smith College

"A brave, extraordinary, and powerful rendering of the life of the mother of the Buddha, this remarkable book is eye-opening and heart-opening."
—Roshi Joan Halifax, Abbot, Upaya Zen Center

"*The Woman Who Raised the Buddha* tells the story of Mahaprajapati, who enjoyed not only a familial relationship with the Buddha as his stepmother and aunt, but also shared a treasured Dharma connection as his closest female disciple who helped him to establish and educate the Order of Bhikkhunis (fully ordained women). As both a scholar and Buddhist practitioner, Wendy Garling skillfully weaves the story of Mahaprajapati's life, sometimes through the eyes of a historian, other times inviting us to imagine being in the presence of these holy beings, hearing their conversations and witnessing their personal exchanges. A delightful book, like no other."
—Ven. Thubten Chodron, founder and abbess of Sravasti Abbey, Dharma teacher, and author of *Buddhism for Beginners* and *Working with Anger*

"The Buddha said, 'Still there are fools who doubt that women too can grasp the truth. Gotami, show your spiritual power, that they might give up false views.' How good it is to see this book appear now in our world. How welcome. How timely. These stories need to be told. For all those who have wanted to know more about the awesome lady who was both the mother of the Buddha and founding woman elder of the ancient Buddhist monastic order of awakened women, the Bhikkhuni Sangha—this book is for you."
—Ven. Bhikkhuni Ayya Tathaloka Theri, founding teacher, Dhammadharini Sangha

"Using numerous and varied translations of Buddhist texts, Wendy Garling has here reimagined and reconstructed a rich and inspiring life story of Mahaprajapati, the Buddha's foster-mother and the first Buddhist nun. By doing so, Garling has proven her superb skills as a storyteller and writer."
—Jan Willis, author of *Dharma Matters: Women, Race, and Tantra* and *Dreaming Me: Black, Baptist, and Buddhist*

"This narrative rendering of Mahaprajapati's life gladdens the heart, illuminating the silence that has concealed her remarkable achievements."

—Karma Lekshe Tsomo, professor of Buddhism and World Religions at University of San Diego

"How precious to have a deep look into the life of the most important woman in the Buddha's life. Usually we just hear her name and know she was turned down in her first attempts to receive ordination, but other than that we have had little information. Now, through Wendy Garling's masterful research into redacted sources and her beautiful writing, we gain a full portrait of this fascinating foremother of Buddhism. *The Woman Who Raised the Buddha* adds a precious missing link to the history of women in Buddhism."

—Lama Tsultrim Allione, author of *Wisdom Rising: Journey into the Mandala of the Empowered Feminine*

"The contemporary revival of the bhikkhuni order makes this beautiful and compelling book especially timely. Mahaprajapati, the first Buddhist nun, emerges as a strong advocate for women on a spiritual path, a wise and beloved teacher, and an accomplished practitioner with emotionally rich and caring relationships. Weaving together stories from multiple traditions, Garling invites us to reimagine the foundation and qualities of these traditions, with women at the heart of Buddhism."

—William Edelglass, Director of Studies, Barre Center for Buddhist Studies and Associate Professor, Emerson College

"Wendy Garling's *The Woman Who Raised the Buddha* is spell-binding. It is magnificent the way she uses extensive research to piece together the life story of Mahaprajapati, the sister of Buddha's birth mother, Mayadevi, and the actual mother who took over his nursing and raising when her sister Maya passed away seven days after Buddha's birth. It may be that it has always 'taken a village' for any individual to make a profound transformation of any society and even the world, and it definitely is the case that the women of that village are the too often unacknowledged drivers of the transformation. The men later tell the story as if the individual man did it all along, and they write it that way as history. What Garling has done in this, and in her previous work, is correct that picture, showing how the 'network of angels' (*dakinijala*) of the brave and intelligent women of a community make the life of the community possible. Reading this book, you are transported back into the Buddha's life and the real herstory of how the sangha movement launched the social revolution that he sparked. This book is a delight, an illumination, and a must-read."

—Padma Shri Robert Thurman, Professor Emeritus, Columbia University

# The
# *Woman*
## *Who Raised the*
# Buddha

### THE EXTRAORDINARY LIFE OF
### MAHAPRAJAPATI

## WENDY GARLING

#### FOREWORD BY
## H.H. THE DALAI LAMA

SHAMBHALA

SHAMBHALA PUBLICATIONS, INC.
4720 Walnut Street
Boulder, Colorado 80301
www.shambhala.com

© 2021 by Wendy Garling

Cover art: Roland and Sabrina Michaud / akg-images
Cover design: Kate E. White
Interior design: Greta D. Sibley

9  8  7  6  5  4  3  2  1

First Edition
Printed in the United States of America

♾ This edition is printed on acid-free paper that meets the
American National Standards Institute z39.48 Standard.
♻ This book is printed on 30% postconsumer recycled paper.
For more information please visit www.shambhala.com.
Shambhala Publications is distributed worldwide by
Penguin Random House, Inc., and its subsidiaries.

Library of Congress Cataloging-in-Publication Data
Names: Garling, Wendy, author.
Title: The woman who raised the Buddha:
    the extraordinary life of Mahaprajapati / Wendy Garling.
Description: First edition. | Boulder, Colorado: Shambhala, [2021] |
    Includes bibliographical references and index.
Identifiers: LCCN 2020015265 | ISBN 9781611806694 (trade paperback)
Subjects: LCSH: Mahapajapati Gotami. | Gautama Buddha—Family. |
    Buddhist women—Biography.
Classification: LCC BQ933 .G375 2021 | DDC 294.3/63—dc23
LC record available at https://lccn.loc.gov/2020015265

*May All Beings Benefit*

# CONTENTS

THE DALAI LAMA

In the more than three hundred translations of classical Indian texts existing in Tibetan we find little about the lives of individual practitioners during the Buddha's time. The main content of these texts is the Buddha's sublime teaching.

Mahaprajapati and her five hundred fellow Shakya women practitioners were the first to be ordained as nuns (bhikshunis) by Buddha Shakyamuni. Mahaprajapati lived more than 2,500 years ago and resources that might shed light on her life are rare. I therefore commend Wendy Garling for her extensive research, putting pieces from multiple sources together with her personal reflections to write her book *The Woman Who Raised the Buddha: The Extraordinary Life of Mahaprajapati*.

Mahaprajapati forsook the comfort of palace life to pursue the path of liberation, inspiring five hundred fellow women to follow her. I pray that all, and particularly women practitioners, find inspiration in her life story.

September 18, 2020

# FOREWORD BY TRACY COCHRAN

In the British Library, there is a gorgeous illustrated Burmese manuscript that includes a scene not portrayed in later written accounts of the life of the Buddha. Mahaprajapati, the woman who raised the Buddha after the death of her sister Maya, who was the Buddha's birth mother, is depicted on the day of the Buddha's birth with Maya in Lumbini's Grove, deep within a forest. It is a sacred place for women, under the protection of the goddess Abhayadevi, who dwells in a sacred *sal* tree. That tree is depicted lowering a limb to Maya as Mahaprajapati offers her sister a human hand. Into this scene of divine feminine love and mutual support, the Buddha is born. But this beautiful story and the deeper truth it conveys disappeared over time. All the women attending the birth were replaced by male gods.

"It's fortunate indeed that we have early Buddhist art to serve as a counterpoint, if not a corrective, to literary narratives," writes Wendy Garling in this engrossing and essential book. "Unlike written records generated more or less contemporaneously, artistic images—some literally chiseled in stone—could not be altered or redacted over time to suit Buddhism's evolving androcentrism."

The earliest Buddhist women, including the extraordinary Mahaprajapati, were erased or cast in deep shadow in the literature. What a loss to Buddhism's legacy, and what good fortune it is to have this invaluable new work, which builds on the author's previous book, *Stars at Dawn: Forgotten Stories of Women in the Buddha's Life*. Drawing on over a decade of study and research, Garling weaves together stories from diverse sources, restoring an ancient line of teaching that is very different in tone and substance from the male-centered monastic teachings that most of us know. She reanimates the life and world of a great queen and mother, along with the first generation of Buddhist women who looked to her as a teacher and leader in the face of patriarchal oppression and great social unrest.

The author calls this book a "crazy quilt" of different fragments and textures, woven together with threads of instinct, intuition, and common sense. Yet what emerges is far greater than a collection. As we learn about Mahaprajapati, we glimpse a model of leadership that feels completely new, not hierarchical but collective. The stories Garling offers reveal a teacher and leader who doesn't assume power over the nuns who follow her. Instead, like the mother tree in the forest, she gives of the fruits of her wisdom and rich life to affirm that every tree is part of the living body of the dharma.

As mother to the Buddha, Mahaprajapati does not claim special privilege but guides the women who turn to her to affirm the depth of their own aspiration, their own part in a great collective journey of awakening. She leads them as a body to ask for what is rightfully theirs. Throughout the book, in stories of her life as wife, sister, and queen, Mahaprajapati emerges as an example to lay women as well as nuns, supporting their dedication to the dharma, leading their struggle against sexism, bringing to fruition the Buddha's intention to bring the dharma to all people, lay and monastic, including women.

It is fascinating that Garling compares this book to quilting because there is within these pages an extraordinary story of Mahaprajapati weaving a golden robe for her son. The Bodhisattva has gone forth and the great queen doesn't know what will come. She doesn't just weave, which would be radical enough for a great queen. She tends carefully to every detail, the growing of the cotton, the carding, and the spinning. The resulting robe is beyond beautiful. It is an offering of great love. But she could not have predicted what a gift it would be to the future. Wendy Garling has given us such a gift.

## ACKNOWLEDGMENTS

This book has arisen through the kindness and contributions of many. First, from the field of Buddhist Studies, I want to acknowledge with deep gratitude the pioneering contributions of three brilliant women scholar/translators of the nineteenth and early twentieth centuries: Caroline A. Foley (aka Mrs. T. W. Rhys Davids), Mabel Bode, and Isaline Blew (I.B.) Horner. Their inspirational work—forged separately within the intensely androcentric milieu of emerging Buddhist scholarship in the West—was the first to foreground early Buddhist women and introduce their stories. These largely forgotten trailblazers laid the groundwork for what is today a burgeoning area of Buddhist scholarship, where studies of women and women's stories have never been more relevant and needed.

I am deeply indebted to my long-ago graduate school professors in the Department of South and Southeast Asian Studies at the University of California, Berkeley: Padmanabh Jaini, the late Barend A. van Nooten, and the late George F. Dales. With lasting fondness, I am grateful to my dear friend, the late Indologist and cultural historian Elinor Gadon, who always encouraged me to write a book about the Buddha's mother. Many thanks to Kaia Fischer, translator extraordinaire at 84,000.co, who was a true ally during the course of my research and who generously shared many unpublished stories of Mahaprajapati. While we have not met, I offer a deep bow of gratitude to Venerable Analayo, whose brilliant scholarship and advocacy of women in Buddhism—past and present—has been a constant source of inspiration and appreciation during my research and writing. My heartfelt thanks also to Geshe Thupten Jinpa for the very kind assistance he extended to me in support of this book.

Words fail to express my deep gratitude to Professor Charles Hallisey at Harvard Divinity School for his exceptional brilliance, generosity, and friendship in supporting me over the course of producing this book. His creative ways of reading sacred literature have vastly changed my own practices, always illuminating my understanding and pointing me in new directions. I also owe the deepest thanks to Bhikkhuni Tathaloka for her knowledgeable, in-depth responses to my many e-mail queries including help with Pali translations and excellent edits and comments on my manuscript. Many thanks also to Karma Lekshe Tsomo, who generously offered many valuable insights and edits on my manuscript. I am deeply grateful to Bhikkhu Bodhi, Upali Sraman, and Georgia Kashnig for translation assistance, and to Tracy Cochran and Jonathan Walters for their kind willingness to offer feedback on my manuscript. Special thanks also to Trent Walker, Karen Derris, Deepak Anand, Ben Gleason, and Sheila Levine.

My deepest affection and gratitude go to the dedicated women practitioners in my Lam Rim study group for their loving support over many years: April Stone, Faith Johnson, Francie Nolde, D'Anne Bodman, Helen Lyons, Nina Nielsen, and Shannon May. Many thanks also to my wonderful editors, Liz Shaw and Audra Figgins, and the exceptionally talented team at Shambhala Publications, with a special shout-out to Lora Zorian who set all this in motion years ago.

Many dear friends have supported me throughout my writing journey in seen and unseen ways. To all of them I offer loving thanks: Connie Hershey, Zuleikha, Lama Palden Drolma, Todd Lapidus, John Whitehead, Rebecca von Bachelle, Richard Snyder, Olivia Hoblizelle, Shabda and Tamam Kahn, Jan Surrey, Cynthia Browne, Mary Moffat, Marcia Lawson, Carol Hamilton, and the fabulous women in my book club. Heartfelt thanks, too, to Nick Sleeman and the Tibetan Buddhist Society sangha in Australia for their abiding friendship and support.

I want to take this opportunity to celebrate the tremendous work taking place in dharma communities to include and integrate women teachers, women's stories, and the sacred feminine in Buddhist teaching and practice programs, with personal appreciation for the visionary leadership of Roshi Joan Halifax at the Upaya Zen Center in Santa Fe, NM; Lama Tsultrim Allione at Taramandala in Pagosa Springs, CO; and William Edelglass at the Barre Center for Buddhist Studies, in Barre, MA. The international organization Sakyadhita must also be mentioned for its extraordinary work advancing gender equality and the empowerment of Buddhist women, at this writing under the intrepid leadership of Jetsun Tenzin Palmo.

With palms together I offer the deepest gratitude to my dharma guides and teachers, of whom there have been many, in particular His Holiness the Karmapa (16th and 17th), Gyumed Khensur Rinpoche, and my incomparable kind root lama, the late Venerable Geshe Acharya Thubten Loden. There are no words for the many blessings I have received from His Holiness the Dalai Lama, who has been a lamp on the path for me since our first meeting in India in 1979. May the precious dharma teachings continue to flourish and benefit all beings.

Finally, my life has been blessed by a loving family. To my father, siblings, in-laws, nieces, and nephews, I love and thank you all. To my three wonderful sons and their families, there aren't words for the joy you have brought to my life. Whit, Caleb, Mia, Brett, Lara, and my precious grandchildren, Rio and Zephyr: I love you and cherish the countless ways you illuminate my life with humor, music, kindness, wisdom, wit, and ceaseless love and support.

# INTRODUCTION

This book tells stories of the Buddha's adoptive mother, Mahaprajapati. While she is the only mother he ever knew, those familiar with his biography know that his birth mother, Maya, died shortly after childbirth. Mahaprajapati, her sister, took the infant to her breast, nurturing and raising him to adulthood. There is a lot of ambiguity overall in the Buddha's biography, but not in this case. The detail of his having two mothers remains consistent across all Buddhist traditions and literature. Since it can't reasonably be argued that either of these women was more or less his mother, this book will refer to both Mahaprajapati and Maya as the Buddha's mother, except where clarification between the two may be necessary.

Previously I wrote about women in the Buddha's life, drawing from lesser-known Sanskrit and Pali sources in which many underreported or altogether forgotten stories, particularly about his two mothers, came to light.* This effort pointed toward the need for more work to be done, not just to uncover additional narratives but to continue to explore the first generation of Buddhist women, their lives, and their untold contributions to the birth of Buddhism. No one stood out more than Mahaprajapati in the course of this extended research, particularly as new stories opened windows into the past, revealing just how exceptional her role once was and how deeply early Buddhist populations respected and revered her across all stages of her life.

It has been a great loss to women's history—*herstory*—as well as the Buddhist faith that twenty-five hundred years later we know barely anything about Mahaprajapati. In traditional Buddhist literature, she takes prominence only in the story of the formation of the nuns' order, where she is credited with spearheading that effort on behalf of women—a tremendous

---

* See Garling, *Stars at Dawn.*

I

achievement, of course, but not an isolated contribution separate from the significant roles she played throughout her life. Further mentions of her are rare and fleeting, and they center almost entirely on her senior years as a monastic. Within these accounts, she is sometimes labeled the Buddha's aunt or foster mother—terms, however technically accurate, that silently devalue the depth of her lifelong relationship with her son. In this book, forgotten and lesser-known stories from primary sources will shed light on the profound ties that endured between Mahaprajapati and the Buddha, ties that shaped their individual lives and achievements, as well as the course of Buddhism.

It must be noted that no one—*no one*—had a ringside seat at the dawn of Buddhism like Mahaprajapati. First of all, no one knows a child in the same way as a mother. She raised the infant Bodhisattva*—then known as Siddhartha—through childhood and his rebellious years before he went forth on his religious quest at age twenty-nine. He grew up with nannies and an attentive father too, but stories uncovered here reveal a close, loving bond between Mahaprajapati and her son during his early years at home.

She was also queen of the Sakyas, wife to Suddhodana, with her finger on the pulse of her people, especially the women, and the social changes wrought by her son's disruptive rejection of his royal inheritance for the religious life. In later years, as the foremost nun and leader of the women, she was the key player in clearing the way for her son to fulfill his stated mission of establishing an equal, fourfold religious community of nuns and monks, laywomen and laymen within his lifetime. The Buddha's intention, in other words, was to bring the benefit of his dharma teachings equally to both women and men.[1] It's very difficult, if not impossible, to imagine how he could have achieved this goal alone, without the avid facilitation of a committed female co-creator. Besides being in the right place at the right time, no one was more qualified, trustworthy, and beyond reproach than Mahaprajapati. Indeed, she was the woman who, wittingly or not, assumed this role and helped her son establish the very foundations of Buddhism.

With some certainty we know Mahaprajapati lived a long life (according to her own autobiographical narrative, 120 years), perhaps only predeceasing the Buddha by a matter of months.[2] Thus, over her lifetime she bore witness to the entire arc of first-generation Buddhism, falling just short of witnessing

---

* *Bodhisattva* is the term used for a buddha prior to reaching enlightenment.

her son's *parinirvana*. That she was a key, seminal influence during this time makes it all the more dismaying that we know so little about her. Mother to the Buddha, mother to early Buddhist women, mother to the Buddhist faith, Mahaprajapati's importance to the founding of Buddhism cannot be overstated. The overall absence of her voice and stories, not to mention her dharma teachings, can only have skewed the course of Buddhism as it has come down to us.

In world cultures, especially world religions, it is nothing new or surprising that women have been erased or devalued in historical accounts. Buddhism's version of this travesty speaks similarly to millennia of patriarchy and misogyny. With the Buddha's death around 400 B.C.E.,* male monastics took control of his legacy. Needless to say, this was bad news for early Buddhist women, who were largely marginalized, if not erased, from original narratives as potent androcentrism came to dominate the emerging literature. On this, the venerable nun and scholar Karma Lekshe Tsomo has said,

> The positive attitude toward women evident among the early Buddhists seems to have declined sharply around the time written Buddhist literature began to appear. These texts contain contradictory statements on women, who are portrayed as capable of enlightenment on par with men and also as sirens luring men from the spiritual path. These ambivalent attitudes toward women persist today in the minds and institutions of Buddhist Asia.[3]

Influential women such as Mahaprajapati and their participation during the Buddha era—as well as notions of the sacred feminine that proliferated culturally in India at the time—appear to have been better reported, if not celebrated, in the early oral traditions as evidenced by surviving feminine elements found mostly outside canonical sources. While nothing can be known for sure—and yes, this is exceedingly controversial territory—the premises that underlie both this and my previous book draw from years of reading hundreds of early women's stories translated from Buddhism's first written languages, Sanskrit and Pali, and further translations from Buddhist

---

* His dates are not known with certainty, but about 480–400 B.C.E. is used in this text.

cultures such as Sinhala, Chinese, Tibetan, Burmese, Korean, and Thai that assimilated, retranslated, and often elaborated this earliest literature.

The bottom line here is that seeds from early androcentric influences sown millennia ago brought us to the Buddhism we have today: a complex, multilayered, thriving faith system still weighted heavily toward patriarchy, often misogyny. Much work remains to be done to fulfill the Buddha's intention of creating an equal, fourfold community of lay and monastic women and men. My aspiration in writing this book is to make a contribution toward that end.

Note that there is a critical exception to this assertion that early Buddhist literature is essentially androcentric. Sequestered deep within the *Khuddaka Nikaya* of the Pali canon, we find a startlingly anomalous pocket of women's literature.*[4] No other major world religion has recorded such a trove of women's voices that date from its beginnings. Here we find the *Therigatha*, seventy-three poems or songs of Buddhism's first nuns that flowed from early oral traditions, as well as the *Theri-apadana*, forty nuns' first-person hagiographies testifying to their spiritual attainments over many lifetimes.† While literal authorship of this literature remains subject to scholarly debate, one only need read it to feel the authenticity of women's voices shining through the words and themes. Of this, the early twentieth-century Indologist Maurice Winternitz has said,

> There can be no doubt that the great majority of the [songs of the *Therigatha*] were composed by women. First of all, the monks never had so much sympathy with the female members of the community, as to warrant our crediting them with having composed these songs sung from the very hearts of women. . . . It would never have occurred to the monks to ascribe songs to the women, if an incontestable tradition had not pointed in this direction.[5]

Pali scholar Caroline A. Foley, who published the first translation of the *Therigatha* in 1909, described the songs as "direct utterances" that were

---

* Skilling notes that monks would have been involved in later stages of editing.
† The *Khuddaka Nikaya* also contains the *Theragatha*, consisting of 264 poems, and the *Thera-apadana*, consisting of 550 biographies of monastic men.

handed down orally for hundreds of years.[6] Similarly, Winternitz notes that the song ascribed to Mahaprajapati may have been sung by her.[7]

The content of the *Therigatha* and *Theri-apadana* is exceptional for the glimpses it provides into the lives—lay and monastic—of early Buddhist women. It also displays an early Indian imagination for the soteriological expanse that leads one eventually to the attainment of nirvana, where this potential is not gendered and absolutely includes women. Within these chapters we find invaluable first-person testimony attributable to Mahaprajapati and other first-generation women. We can't know just how this slim but exceedingly consequential collection of women's literature was recorded or survived, but—just as women were sequestered in the harems or women's quarters of patriarchal households—it remained isolated as a separate entity, unseen and not integrated into Buddhism's larger scriptural corpus. Thus, the charge of extreme androcentrism in early Buddhist literature stands, albeit with this caveat. The voices and stories of women found in the *Therigatha* and *Theri-apadana* are sourced throughout this volume.

Sanskrit spelling is used predominantly in this text, although Pali spelling may appear in discussions and quotations from Pali texts. For example, the Sanskrit spelling "Gautami" is used except when quoting or referencing Pali sources, in which case the Pali spelling "Gotami" is used. Translated passages are reproduced retaining original transliteration, spelling, and punctuation except where clarification may be needed. Although many excellent lay and monastic scholars and readers have assisted me with this manuscript, all views, statements, errors, and inaccuracies are entirely my own.

### *What Do We Call Her? Mahaprajapati's Name*

Here we will segue to address the meaning and usage of our protagonist's name. Her full name, Mahaprajapati Gautami, has generated diverse explanations from translators and commentators over time. Texts (like this one) often use the shortened forms, Mahaprajapati, Prajapati, or Gautami,* favoring one over the other or alternating those names according to context. For example, in the *Mahavastu* her full name appears followed closely by "Gautami" when her husband addresses her directly, suggesting that Gautami is the more intimate or familial usage.

---

* Pali: Mahapajapati, Pajapati, Gotami.

Mahaprajapati Gautami appealed to King Suddhodana, saying, "Your majesty, if it is agreeable to you, let the Exalted One eat at my house." And the king replied, "Gautami, let it be so."[8]

Similarly, in the Pali canon, narrative passages typically use her full name, while the Buddha and others normally call her Gotami in direct address. From the *Anguttara Nikaya*,

Then Mahapajapati Gotami approached the Blessed One, paid homage to him, stood to one side, and said to him:

"Bhante, it would be good if women could obtain the going forth from the household life into homelessness in the Dhamma and discipline proclaimed by the Tathagata."

"Enough, Gotami! Do not favor the going forth of women from the household life into homelessness in the Dhamma and discipline proclaimed by the Tathagata."[9]

Conversations between Mahaprajapati and her son prior to his enlightenment are virtually nonexistent (or yet to be discovered). A single example found here appears in the *Lalitavistara,* where Siddhartha as a young toddler simply calls her "Mother."*[10]

What does Mahaprajapati Gautami mean? The designation *maha* meaning "great" or "mighty" is familiar and straightforward.[11] *Prajapati*, on the other hand, is somewhat curious, as was noticed by the nineteenth-century Indologist R. L. Mitra. The Sanskrit usage predominantly appears in masculine form, meaning "lord of creatures" or "protector of offspring."† It is found ubiquitously in Vedic literature as an epithet for male gods, particularly the creator god, Brahma. It is also used as a designation for a patriarch such as a father or king.[12]

Mitra points out that it is doubtful a masculine term would be used for a female and suggests that the feminized *Prajapati* is a conversion from an earlier *Prajavati*, meaning "prolific in offspring," denoting a mother or matron.[13] He cites examples in the *Lalitavistara* where the

---

* Sanskrit: *amba*, also translated as "mama."

† *Praja* = "creature" or "offspring"; *pati* = "lord" or "protector."

name Mahapraja*vati* appears instead of Mahaprajapati.[14] Her name as Mahapraja*vati* also appears in the Sanskrit *Adhikaranavastu*.*[15] Mitra's observations on this are shared by scholars Edward Thomas[16] and Herman Oldenberg.[17] In Pali her name appears as Mahapajapati; however, the Pali Text Society's Pali-English dictionary cites the feminine *pajapati* deriving from the Vedic *prajavant*, with the meaning "wife," particularly "chief wife," or "chief queen,"[18] definitions that now make sense with regard to our subject.

Mitra further suggests that Western translators, accustomed to double names, incorrectly read Mahaprajapati as her personal first name and Gautami as her *gotra*, or patrilineal clan name, a name she only could have assumed at marriage since her father's clan name was Vasishtha, not Gautama. He points out that women seldom used clan names since they would lose their father's at marriage and their husband's would not be distinctive since every woman in the family would then have the same name.[19] In this way Mitra would appear to disagree with the fifth-century Indian commentator Buddhaghosa, who said Mahaprajapati was so called because soothsayers at her birth prophesied that she would have a large following and that Gotami was her *gotra* name, an explanation that remains prevalent today.[20]

In contrast, Mitra concludes that Gautami was her personal name and the preceding Mahaprajapati was an epithet. Understanding it more as an honorific, her full name could be translated as something like the Great Queen Gautami or the Venerable Mother Gautami. This explanation is borne out in the *Iheri-apadana* where Gautami (Gotami) is said to be the wife or queen (*pajapati*) of King Suddhodana.†[21] While the original, intended meaning of her name cannot be known with certainty, this might explain why her husband, the Buddha, Ananda, and her monastic disciples normally call her Gautami in familiar or direct address. Out of respect and for purposes of brevity, this text mostly uses Mahaprajapati rather than her double name, although exceptions are made according to context.

---

* Mitra notes, however, that the reading is Mahaprajapati in Tibetan, Chinese, Sinhala, Pali, Burmese, and Thai.
† Pali: "Suddhodano maharaja, gotami ca pajapati." With thanks to Ven. Tathaloka for pointing out this passage.

## The Journey to Awakening

Returning to stories of Mahaprajapati's life, it is important to understand the greater Buddhist context within which a lifetime is understood. Here, we go into the heart of Buddhism where the entire purpose centers on realizing our human potential to "wake up," or become, like the Buddha, a fully awakened being. According to most (not all) Buddhist traditions, this soteriological process begins in a distant past life and unfolds karmically over a trajectory of many lifetimes until the goal is finally reached. Buddhist biography then, as we shall see in the case of Mahaprajapati and others, is generally a treatment of this lengthy enlightenment journey, beginning with an individual's past-life aspiration to awaken, typically made in the presence of a former buddha, and eventually concluding—many lifetimes and good deeds later—with complete release from the cycle of rebirth, the result known as nirvana.*

It is important to bear in mind that this complex, even mystical, karmic process, said to be temporally beginningless, takes place within an infinite expanse or web of sentient life, where all beings are interconnected and profoundly influenced by one another over the course of respective, evolving lifetimes. Huge notions indeed, but the point here, and one that is clearly demonstrated in Mahaprajapati's own story, is that the path to enlightenment is not a solitary journey but one closely interwoven with the lives and journeys of others. This can also be said of the Buddha and his awakening, although his journey, normally related in individualistic, heroic terms, is rarely described that way. A trope especially prevalent in the women's literature is that those who make an aspiration to awaken in the same assembly before a buddha will wind up traveling the karmic road together over however many lifetimes it takes, eventually attaining nirvana collectively, if not simultaneously. In this way, as a girl in a former life, Mahaprajapati aspired to awaken in the presence of the Buddha Padumuttara amid many spectators, including a throng of many other young women.

---

* Different Buddhist schools differentiate the soteriological meanings of "nirvana" and "enlightenment"; the former term is used in Theravada and some other early schools, while the latter is used in Mahayana schools. Similarly, "arhatship" (the attainment of nirvana) and "buddhahood" (the attainment of enlightenment) are generally understood and used differently by these groups.

From the premise of the karmic web of life flows an understanding that over time we have all appeared in different human (also animal) forms and circumstances; further, we have been in relationship with one another in countless different ways. This is vividly illustrated in Mahaprajapati's words from the *Therigatha*:

> I had already been a mother, a son,
> a father, a brother, and a grandmother,
> but not knowing things as they really are,
> I was reborn and reborn,
> never having enough.[22]

While both she and Maya appear in past-life stories of the Buddha—a literary genre native to India known as Jatakas—either as his mother (where Mahaprajapati is often cast as his birth mother) or presaging that future role, it is interesting to note that in this literature, from a karmic standpoint, the Buddha had additional former mothers. It is further noteworthy that mothers and motherhood are generally esteemed in Jataka stories, contrasting sharply with the treatment of Mahaprajapati and Maya during our present Gautama Buddha era,* in which the androcentric literature largely and dismissively sweeps them under the rug.

### Stories of the Buddha's Previous Mothers

Several of the Buddha's past-life mothers warrant mentioning here. One who appears in his present-life narrative is Sujata, the young cowherd, wife, and mother of a newborn son, who feeds the Bodhisattva a nutritious bowl of rice cereal as his last meal prior to enlightenment. Pali sources abound with motherly imagery telling this story, in which she prepares the special porridge from the finest milk drawn from the finest cows, ultimately boiled down to a potent colostrum-like elixir that will sustain him over the forty-nine days of fasting that span his enlightenment experience.[23]

Sanskrit sources go much further, framing Sujata's motherly role in feeding Gautama as a continuation of their relationship in past lifetimes when she was his mother. In the *Abhinishkramanasutra*, milk streams from

---

* Referring to the present Buddha, the latest in a succession of twenty-eight buddhas.

her breasts as soon as she sees him, just as a lactating mother often exudes milk when seeing or hearing her hungry infant.* In the *Mahavastu*, he asks her why she is giving him the rice porridge. The text reads,

> She who had been the mother of this pure being in a hundred births sweetly replied to him, "It is my wish. Let me have it so."[24]

Elsewhere in the *Mahavastu*, Sujata tells him of the anguish she experienced as he neared death practicing austerities. The Buddha responds by affirming that she was his mother for five hundred births, and as a result she would attain buddhahood in the future.

Another variant in the *Mahavastu* tells us that buddhahood was Sujata's intention all along. To that end she provided a meal of rice porridge to all previous buddhas just prior to their awakening. The text recalls her aspiration to awaken:

> She tendered him the strength-giving food that was exquisitely flavored and fragrant of smell. Then greatly stirred she formed a resolution saying, "May I become a Buddha accoutred with the (thirty-two) marks. . . ."[†25]

Reading stories of Sujata across the texts we find motherhood as an intentional, soteriological path. In a man's world it is not easy for women to become buddhas, but the accumulated merit of mothers (at least mothers

---

* Streaming breast milk is an image that appears in early stories to authenticate a mother's relationship with her child and normally occurs after a long period of separation. For example, in the *Mahamayasutra*, Maya's breasts stream with milk when she hears the words of her son, who has traveled to the heavenly realms to convert her to the dharma (Durt, 257).

† This is a very unusual reference, not just because a woman is asserting an aspiration for buddhahood but even more because she acknowledges that she will need the thirty-two marks of a buddha to achieve this. Normally only males are described as eligible for buddhahood, and females may only attain this goal if they take birth as a male to do so. There is no mention here of Sujata needing a sex change to attain buddhahood. See chapter 1 for further discussion of the thirty-two marks.

of buddhas) potentially leads to breaking that glass ceiling, according to this narrative thread.

A similar theme of motherhood tied to spiritual advancement is found in the story of Kacangala, who was the Buddha's mother in five hundred past lives according to multiple Sanskrit sources. However, in this somewhat humorous tale, the karmic door swings both ways. Kacangala's misdeeds ultimately caused her to lose her place in line to Maya as the most worthy candidate for being Gautama Buddha's mother. Apparently her past bad acts were so egregious that in the present story she is born a slave. The following summary draws from several accounts, particularly the *Avadanasataka*[26] and the *Karmasataka* in the Tibetan Kanjur.[27]

One day the Buddha is walking with his disciples and notices an old woman (Kacangala) drawing water from a well. As the Buddha is thirsty, he asks his attendant Ananda to request that she offer him a drink. "I will bring it myself," she tells Ananda, and so, having filled her jug, Kacangala approaches the Buddha. Immediately upon seeing him, she is so overcome with maternal emotion that milk streams from her breasts. "Oh son, oh son," she cries out as she tries to embrace him. The monks move to restrain her, but the Buddha stops them, saying,

> For five hundred births without interruption when she was
> my mother,
> She embraced me in her arms on account of her love for her
> son. . . . Having recollected gratitude, having seen her longing
> for her son,
> Out of compassion I allow an embrace by she who is worthy
> of sympathy.[28]

Kacangala goes on to receive dharma instruction from the Buddha and soon attains the level of stream entry, the first of four levels leading to awakening. Now she asks to join the monastic order, and the Buddha refers her to Mahaprajapati, who ordains her and becomes her preceptor. Soon enough Kacangala's profound insight "crushed ignorance like an eggshell," and she quickly attains arthatship.[29] So spiritually adept is Kacangala that she excels in explaining the teachings to other nuns, thus the Buddha dubs her Foremost of Those Who Interpret the Sutras.[30]

Sounds like a great outcome, so what were her misdeeds? Like many early narratives, this story is framed by a conversation the Buddha later has with his monks, who ply him with questions. In this case they are curious about the karma that caused Kacangala to attain arhatship on the one hand but to lose her long-standing position as his mother on the other. They ask,

> Lord, if she was the Blessed One's mother for five hundred lifetimes, why is she not your mother, now?[31]

At this point the story gets pretty amusing. (Mothers take note, as this is a cautionary tale.) It turns out Kacangala bungled motherhood along the way, so much so that the Buddha in a past life became distressed and prayed that she would *not* become his mother again. Apparently, she hindered her son constantly as he attempted to pursue his bodhisattva destiny. Whenever he wished to give a gift, she blocked his giving; when he wished to leave home, she prevented him. The Buddha explains,

> Monks, . . . bodhisattvas delight in renunciation and love to give, and she continually created obstacles to my renunciation and charity. This is why she caused me distress.[32]

Kacangala's bad parenting coupled with Maya's ardent prayers and positive merit sealed the deal, and Kacangala fell on disadvantaged lifetimes. Her eventual spiritual success was attributable to parallel past-life karma when, in the presence of Buddha Kasyapa, she once aspired to become a foremost nun and attain arhatship in a future birth. Unlike Sujata, it was monasticism rather than motherhood that advanced and ultimately fulfilled Kacangala's soteriological purpose.

A little-known story from Sinhala popular literature takes us much further back in the past lives of the Buddha and his mother, to a lifetime before there was a known buddha. Traditionally the ascetic Sumedha is named as Gautama Buddha's first appearance as a bodhisattva; at that time he aspired to attain awakening in the presence of Buddha Dipamkara, who predicted his eventual success. But in a striking departure from classical Buddhist doctrine, the following story goes back eons before that. Here we learn it was the Buddha's mother who predicted her son's buddhahood—in fact, buddhahood might (arguably) have been her idea.

This story has a number of variants that feature the mother's role to different degrees, her influence sometimes assigned to the god Brahma.[33] The summary that follows is taken from the *Manopranidhanaye Sivpad*, oral poetry of unknown origins with possible antecedents in the *Mahajanaka Jataka* of the Pali canon, as discussed and translated by the eminent Oxford scholar Richard Gombrich.[34] The narrative, about an incident occurring countless eons ago, begins with the poet's words, "Now I shall expound who gave Buddhahood."

A young man from a merchant family boards a ship loaded with cargo to be traded for gold. Taking along his widowed mother, he embarks on an ocean voyage. Disaster strikes on the seventh day when the ship breaks apart in a violent storm. Treading the massive waves, the young man puts his mother on his back and begins to swim. Along the way, she asks him when they will reach land. The text then reads,

> To such a son, what did she give? She gave not sky, earth or sea but Buddhahood.[35]

Miracles kick in as the goddess of the sea notes their predicament, and the god Indra conjures a convenient sandy beach in their path. When son and mother arrive on land, the son asks how the miracles came about, to which his mother recounts past acts of great merit. The implication appears to be that he did the swimming, but it was her merit that ensured their safe arrival to the shore.* Now the son resolves to become a buddha and asks his mother for her blessing. The text reads,

> He received Buddhahood by the blessing his mother gave him.
>
> On the day when mother and son went down a lonely road, that day they swam seven days in the sea; that day the hero exerted himself; and the mother went away having arranged [his] Buddhahood, did she not?[36]

Elsewhere,

> From that time on the Bodhisattva practiced Buddhahood.[37]

---

* Gombrich acknowledges that the grammar is ambiguous.

In his own words, he later says,

> Thus I came carrying my mother; by the blessing my mother gave me
> I attained Buddhahood.[38]

Gombrich suggests that the role of the mother in promoting buddhahood is this story's raison d'être, a theme that did not appear in an earlier literary version, not because monk editors were unaware of it, he claims, but because they "would not write anything so flagrantly inconsistent with doctrine."[39] While centering a woman—the Buddha's mother no less—at the heart of a Buddhist origin myth may have been a lightning rod for male monastic misogyny, the same notion apparently accounts for the story's widespread appeal and popularity among lay populations in Sri Lanka.

The Buddha's mother goes unnamed in this extraordinary story of the shipwreck. On the one hand she is described as giving "the milk of her two breasts," while on the other she goes to "Tushita heaven." Perhaps too literal a reading of this "myth based on a metaphor,"* however, these details suggest a conflation of Mahaprajapati and Maya. As far as we know, Maya never nursed her son before her death and departure to Tushita heaven. Both mothers gave of their bodies—Maya her womb, and Mahaprajapati the milk from her breasts.

### Reading Women's Stories

It is a delightful, if not joyous, task to read stories of the first Buddhist women, learning of their relationships with the Buddha and his teachings, their lives, their personal soteriological paths and methods. Indeed, reading intertextually it becomes evident that the Buddha's promise of freedom was as appealing to women as it was to men—there are just far fewer surviving stories of women, especially intact (not fragmented) stories, and stories not blighted by misogyny (which provide insights of their own). Peering deeply into these early women's stories, there is much to see and learn from Buddhism's foremothers, particularly in this case, the Buddha's own mother, Mahaprajapati.

---

* The metaphor here is of the Bodhisattva helping others to cross the great ocean of samsara (Gombrich, 92).

That said, it has to be noted that there is no satisfactory Buddhist "history" per se, and almost everything we have—including *buddhadharma*—flowed from the time of the Buddha's life via oral transmissions that migrated for centuries across India and the early Buddhist world before being written down at different times in different places. Even then, writing processes—including editing, amplification, and redaction—were repeated in many languages and traditions until we have what we call today Buddhist literature.* The progression has been likened to the game of "telephone," where a message is whispered from ear to ear around a circle, and by the time the original message reaches the last person it has become completely altered. In this way, there is much we don't know and likely will never know with any certainty about the origins of Buddhism, including the first generation of women.

Instead we have *stories*, not *histories*, from that time. Rather than narrowing our view in search of literal or "provable" truths, stories of early Buddhist women invite us into the expanse of imagination, where we can apply the tools of instinct, intuition, and common sense. To be sure their lives were vastly dissimilar from the lives of women today, yet in many ways the timelessness of women's experiences shines through, inviting us to relate to the women in these ancient stories rather than sit on the sidelines as detached observers. The commonality of women's experiences is a powerful connector across time and place, one that has given rise to this and other contemporary herstories in which women's narratives have been salvaged from patriarchal sources and reimagined and retold by women.

Imagination as an investigative tool further helps us understand the mindset of those who would tell and hear the stories. In other words, who might have been the storytellers? Who were their audiences? Why was this story told? Why did it gain traction and survive when others did not? Considering questions such as these can bring insights into the sociocultural values and conventions that held the stories or even generated them in the first place. What could be further apart, for example, than the stories of brilliant, empowered nuns found in the *Therigatha* and the degrading, misogynistic stories of these same women in accounts of their quest for ordination, both found in the Pali canon? Good money is

---

* Epigraphic and artistic records, which have proved invaluable complements to the literature, notwithstanding.

on different storytellers and different audiences for these two sets of stories. All this demonstrates that there was no one way the stories were told or understood—not then, not now.

Assembling the stories of Mahaprajapati for this book was like making a crazy quilt, with swatches of different sizes, colors, patterns, and textures, some tattered and torn, others like new, spread out on a table then pieced together with threads of the aforementioned instinct, intuition, and common sense. By no means a conventional—and certainly not an academic—approach, but one that allows for each piece to take its place in a whole that would be greater than the sum of its parts. Too, this method allows for new ideas, patterns, and stories to emerge. That said, many gaps and inconsistencies in Mahaprajapati's story persist despite my best efforts to present the arc of her life and at least begin to color in those areas that have been neglected, such as her years as a sister, queen, and mother before she ordained as a nun. As always in the vast and fascinating corpus of Buddhist literature, there is plenty of room for further research, translation, and discourse. May this book provide a helpful resource. May it also provide an entry point for a deeper understanding of the subjective layers, such as mother's love, that became woven into the foundations of Buddhism.

# Prologue: Her Story Begins

*And so the nuns gathered in the assembly hall and conversed quietly among themselves. Silence quickly fell as their beloved preceptor—Mahaprajapati Gautami—entered, made three prostrations before the simple altar, and took her cushion at the front of the room. Together the women sat in lengthy meditation for what seemed like hours. A distant gong finally sounded, and the room stirred again.*

*Rising from her seat, Venerable Ksema slowly approached their teacher and set a sweetly scented jasmine wreath at her feet. Sitting to one side, she spoke the words rising in all their hearts: "Venerable Gautami! Always you have been our guiding light, our beloved mother on the Buddha's blessed path. There are no words to express our love and gratitude to you."*

*Mahaprajapati smiled and considered Ksema's words. Slowly, with careful attention, she gazed around the room, her eyes resting briefly on each of the five hundred nuns seated around her. With warmth and affection flowing from her words, she spoke: "Gentle daughters! Indeed, our lives have been closely tied for a very long time. We share many memories and stories. How glorious it has been to share the Buddha's path, this journey to awakening together. It has been my greatest joy to be mother of the Buddha and mother to all of you."*

*No one stirred. Finally, the Venerable Mitta stood up and spoke. "Venerable Gautami! Please tell us the story of how you came to be the Blessed One's mother.*

*In your own words, relate to us again stories of your life as queen of the Sakyas and your long journey to Vaishali to request ordination on our behalf. Dearest One, please tell us stories!"*

Nodding her head with more seriousness now, Mahaprajapati replied "Gentle daughters! Some stories you may remember, and others you will not. But my stories belong to all of us! I will tell you these stories now.

"Recall how many of us, as girls in Devadaha, played together in my family's garden, weaving flower garlands with my sweet sister, Maya. Recall the grand procession as Maya and I departed for Kapilavastu to become brides of the handsome young prince Suddhodana, with Maya as his senior wife. Recall how we gathered in Lumbini's Grove, to assist her, now our queen, in childbirth as she brought the Awakened One into the world under the protection of the blessed goddess of the sal tree. But then, how quickly joy changed to grief! Together we wept when Maya died, while celebrating her short life and the holy child she gave over to me to raise as my own. I became the Bodhisattva's mother as I took him to my breast, my sister gone, and his father, the king, and I left with his fate in our hands."

She fell silent. Spellbound, the nuns waited for more. Finally, the elder nun Kesini broke the silence: "Oh yes, I think of Maya often! Each day we all played in the garden, braiding each other's hair with laurel vines and lotus blossoms. Remember how muddy we got picking them from the pool? Remember how we all celebrated her marvelous wedding to the prince? My heart broke with grief when she died! I still miss her so!" Tears glistened in Kesini's eyes. Her sadness touched the hearts of all who listened.

After a pause, Mahaprajapati continued: "Recall the joys many of us shared as young mothers drumming, dancing, and singing as we raised our children together in the king's palace. Then suddenly our lives changed again! A shadow fell over the Sakyas when my son, the young prince, left home for the homeless life. The entire kingdom shook with fear. Recall those dark years of grief and uncertainty! I could only dream of seeing him again. Long I hid my tears as I toiled at weaving a worthy cloth for him, a fine monk's robe of shimmering golden thread to present as an offering when he returned. But nothing could be more brilliant than the Buddha himself! My eyes opened as if for the first time when I saw him again; always my son but now too the Buddha, bringing all of humanity the glory of the dharma."

She went on: "Recall the joy of hearing the Blessed One's marvelous teachings for the first time, in the Nigrodha Grove when he returned home to

*Kapilavastu! (And remember that nonsense from our husbands about women being unsuited for the dharma? Ha!) Recall the happy years many of us shared practicing as laywomen together before we lost our husbands and donned these robes of homelessness. But by then we already knew, didn't we? We already knew our hearts were inseparably tied to the Blessed One and his teachings. We knew we wanted to dedicate ourselves to lifelong practice of the dharma."*

*Mahaprajapati paused again. The room grew restless as each nun reflected on her own life before ordaining as a nun. Swept up in memories, they recalled the pain of losing and leaving their families. Husbands, children, and household life were once all they had known. It seemed very long ago, yet still so raw. Tension turned to agitation when Venerable Patacara suddenly spoke out:*

> *My husband died along the side of the road, and I gave birth alone in a huge storm! My children perished before my eyes as a hawk carried off my newborn and my young son drowned in the river. I returned to my parents' home to find it had burned to the ground and they were dead. Mad with grief, I became a naked wanderer, only wanting to die! One day I wandered into the Jeta Grove where the Blessed One was teaching. "Help me!" I cried, and his kind words restored my mind. I requested ordination then and he brought me to you, Venerable Gautami. For that I am ever so grateful.[1]*

*Unable to contain herself, Mutta now spoke:*

> *I was in an arranged marriage with a dreadful old man! Life was nothing but cruel drudgery. My unhappiness became unbearable until finally he granted me permission to ordain. Now I am free![2]*

*And so the nuns spoke in turns, sharing their stories, some shouting, some weeping, some reaching for one another for comfort—stories of poverty and privilege, marriage and children, grief and loss. Former beggars, noble ladies, housewives, slaves, prostitutes, and harem consorts all spoke and listened to one other. Pain and release washed over the room, the past flickering briefly in the present. Everything was different now. In their new lives as religious women, they were equal daughters of the Buddha and sisters to one another, living a simple, contemplative life in community together.*

*The room settled down as one by one the women slipped into meditation.*

*The afternoon stretched on. Finally, Mahaprajapati spoke again. "Yes, my daughters, we came to the dharma from many different struggles. Recall the struggles of ordination too! The hardships of homeless life were difficult enough, and then we were not welcomed—abused even—by some petty monks when we arrived in Vaishali. It was not easy having our voices heard! The Blessed Buddha always intended to grant us ordination, but it took patience for the causes and conditions to ripen fully. The religious path for women is difficult. Due to the immense blessings of our great Teacher, with gratitude to Ananda for his kindness, we sit here together now as monastic women, having achieved our goal."*

*She paused again and now became very serious. Her words were both gentle and firm. "Daughters of the Buddha, we have arrived at our final destination. Through the Buddha's compassionate wisdom and guidance, we are practicing the path that brings freedom as the definite result. Without question, all of you will achieve nirvana in this lifetime."*

*Crows cawed from the treetops outside, as leaves rustled and long glints of sunlight dappled the assembly hall. The nuns sat in silence, their hearts suffused with peace. After some time, the gong rang again.*

*"Oh, there are more stories!" Mahaprajapati called out as the nuns began to stir. "We'll get to those next time."*

*And so Mahaprajapati continued: "Today I will tell you our stories from a different time. These come from long ago, long before any of you can remember. Indeed, it is true. We have traveled the path of awakening for a very long time. So now I will tell you these stories.*

*"Gentle daughters! We have been bound by friendship through a timeless web of existence, our lives interwoven through countless lifetimes. Why? Because long ago each of us aspired to supreme awakening, and since that time we have traveled the journey of awakening together.*

*"It began one hundred thousand world cycles ago, during the era of the blessed Buddha Padumuttara. At that time, in the village of Hamsavati, I was born into a noble's family. We were quite wealthy and prosperous, with many servants. One day I was out walking with my father, attended by a retinue of five hundred female slaves. At that time the Blessed One, brilliant as the autumn sun, like the king of gods, was raining forth a cloud of dharma teachings to all the townsfolk and a retinue of female and male monastics. My mind was instantly gladdened, uplifted by his voice.*

"*Seated directly in front of him was an elderly nun who was his aunt, his mother's sister. She was speaking softly to him in words I could not hear. What he then said set my heart ablaze. His words pierced me like an arrow. Addressing all of us, the Blessed One deemed his elderly aunt Foremost in Seniority and appointed her the chief of nuns.*

"*A clear, joyous aspiration awakened in me, and in that moment, I vowed one day to acquire that rank and distinction for myself in the service of a future buddha. For one whole week I made heartfelt, generous offerings of clothing, food, and medicines to the Blessed One and the monastic assembly, all the while fervently praying for the realization of my aspiration. Finally, trembling but determined, I fell prostrate at the Blessed One's feet and voiced my aspiration directly to him. Once again he was addressing a gathering of all the townsfolk and monastics. Turning to me, Buddha Padumuttara reached down and, taking my hand, lifted me to my feet. I can still hear his voice and feel the reverberation of his words as he affirmed my aspiration and announced the following prophecy:*

> *I shall tell you of [this] young girl who has fed the World's Leader and his assembly for seven days. Hear my words:*
>
> *One hundred thousand world cycles from now, there will be reborn in the world the Teacher who will be named Gotama through his lineage, a descendant of the Okkaka clan.*
>
> *At that time there will be a disciple of the Teacher named Gotami who will be an heir to the Doctrine, a legitimate offspring of the Doctrine.*
>
> *This one will be the aunt of that Buddha, a foster mother [his entire] life, and she will obtain preeminence for long standing among the [nuns]."*[3]

"*How I rejoiced when I heard his words! For the rest of my life I piously served blessed Buddha Padumuttara and his assembly and carefully guarded my virtue.*

"*So you see, dear sisters, after countless lifetimes of prayer and good deeds, my aspiration has finally come to fruition. And so has yours. You were my father's five hundred slaves, who witnessed Buddha Padumuttara's consecration of his aunt as chief of nuns. You were there too when he made the prophecy that one day I would achieve that position and become aunt and foster mother of the future Gautama Buddha. At that time all of you too made the aspiration in your hearts to awaken and be free, and so our journey together began. How fortunate that we have achieved our goal! Here we are now, sharing the precious dharma in this era of the glorious Gautama Buddha."*

The assembly hall was abuzz now as throngs of laywomen, hearing news of Mahaprajapati's storytelling, poured in from the village. They too were devoted disciples of the Buddha and looked to Mahaprajapati for teachings and guidance. Chief among them was the wealthy patroness Visakha, who had built the nuns' monastic home and seen to their well-being with food, clothing, and medicines. A respectful hush fell as she stepped forward, saying, "Thank you for this beautiful story, Venerable Teacher! Please, do continue!"

Mahaprajapati smiled at the eager sea of faces and adjusted her robes. Gazing across the room, her eyes were radiant, although her body was now very weary. With warmth she spoke again. *"For many lifetimes after I made my vow, the earth was dark, for there was no buddha to teach the precious dharma or assemble the fourfold community. Still, I continuously practiced charity and morality, with fervent prayers to quickly meet a buddha again.*

*"Finally, I was born into a family of slaves in Deer Park, near Benares, where I was the chief among five hundred women water carriers. Each morning at dawn we left the city bearing water jugs on our heads to walk a treacherous path to the river, and each evening we returned, bringing water to our masters' households.*

*"I remember what happened one evening very clearly. Five hundred hermit buddhas descended from their mountain caves to our village. Wearing ragged mendicant robes, they went from door to door seeking alms. Because it was the rainy season, they asked the townsfolk to make huts for them. But doors were closed in their faces. 'Be gone!' shouted one wealthy merchant. 'There is no time for this!' And the five hundred holy ones left our city.*

*"At that time I was returning from the river and met them along the path. Placing my water jug to one side and covering my face out of modesty, I paid proper homage to the holy ones and asked, 'Why, venerable sirs, have you entered our city, and why are you leaving again so soon?'*

*"'We came to ask that a dwelling for the rainy season might be built for us,' they replied.*

*"'Have you succeeded?' I asked.*

*"'We have not succeeded, daughter,' they told me.*

*"'And these huts that should be built,' I queried, 'can they be built only by*

*wealthy merchants, or would it be proper for them to be donated by a slave like me?'*

"'Anyone may do so, daughter,' they replied, 'regardless of gender or caste.'

"'Very well, venerable sirs,' I said. 'We slaves will do it. Meanwhile, tomorrow receive your food from me.'

"Having invited them, I picked up my water jug and went away. Waiting along the path, I stopped the women water carriers returning from the river. When all five hundred were assembled, I spoke to them. 'My daughters,' I said, 'do you always want to do the work of a slave, or do you desire to be freed from slavery?'

"'Oh yes! We would be pleased to be free this very day, Mother!' was their earnest and unanimous reply.

"'All right then. Get your husbands to labor for one day to build huts for these five hundred holy ones, that they may have proper dwellings for the rainy season.'

"And the five hundred women slaves told their husbands that evening when the men returned from working in the forests. The husbands agreed and gathered at the door of their leader, Nandaka, chief of the male slaves."

Mahaprajapati continued, "At that time I addressed the men, explaining my intention and saying, 'My friends, give your labor for one day to these holy ones, that they may have proper dwellings for the rainy season.' Several of the husbands were not of generous mind and ignorant of the unsurpassed benefits of making such a valued offering. At first, they did not agree to help, but I scolded them and persuaded them to perform the task. Finally, they agreed.

"The next morning I offered food to the five hundred holy men and gave instructions to the men how to build the huts. Swiftly they went to the forest and cut down trees. Dividing into groups of one hundred, they made fine huts connected by an enclosure of walkways. They built excellent furniture, beds and chairs, while we women provided for everything beautiful with flowers and soft bedding. We filled the water pots for each dwelling with fresh drinking water. The five hundred buddhas accepted our offerings and vowed to remain for three months.

"I set up a daily schedule such that the slave women took turns providing food for the holy ones. If some poor woman was unable to provide food on her appointed day, then I gave her the necessary provisions so she could make her offering and accrue the merit herself. Three months of the rainy season passed this way.

*"Before the holy ones were to depart, I asked each of the women to weave one piece of cloth, which I exchanged for five hundred fine robes and gave these to the hermit buddhas. Receiving the robes, they rose into the sky and returned to their cool mountain caves."*

*Once again Mahaprajapati fell silent. Closing her eyes, she entered into deep meditation. Or had she fallen asleep? The women remained seated in rapt silence. After some time, Mahaprajapati stirred and spoke again. "My daughters! You were the five hundred water carriers, and I was your chief! Our good acts providing the five hundred buddhas with food, shelter, and robes freed us from future slavery. Since then our lifetimes have been inextricably linked by the karma of our shared good deeds. Long have we journeyed together, practicing generosity and moral conduct with the goal of complete liberation from the slavery of samsara. Now in this last lifetime together, we have attained the supreme good fortune and precious human conditions to be disciples of Gautama Buddha. He alone teaches the way to the final freedom we seek."*

*Overjoyed, hanging on every word, the women waited for their beloved teacher to say more. Warmth and harmony filled their hearts. With a smile and a twinkle in her eye, Mahaprajapati stood up, slowly gathered her robes around her, and departed.*

# I

# Growing Up in Devadaha

Mahaprajapati was born to a *kshatriya** family in the small town of Devadaha in southern Nepal, not far from the Buddha's childhood home of Kapilavastu. The date was about 500 B.C.E. Legends describe a lush pastoral region dotted with deep forests and fertile farms planted with rice, banana, and sugarcane set within the foothills of the Himalayas. A tribal group known as the Sakyas flourished there, a proud and insular people ruled by petty rajas within the larger kingdom of Kosala, set along the northeast fringes of India's emerging brahmanic culture. By all accounts the Sakyas lived peacefully, and their lands prospered. Even wild animals lived in harmony.[1] These were Mahaprajapati's people, and this is where she grew up. Her closest companion was her beloved sister, Maya.

Unlike Kapilavastu, seat of the Sakya ruling patriarchy, Devadaha is rarely mentioned and not well described in the Buddhist legends—an unfortunate casualty of recordkeeping, since it is the Buddha's matrilineal home. One source says that it was founded after Kapilavastu outgrew its

---

* The *kshatriya*, or aristocratic, ruling caste, protected the lands and people as benevolent regents in peacetime and fierce defenders in times of war.

natural boundaries, and inhabitants were drawn to settle around a beautiful nearby lake that had been enjoyed for recreation:

> The princes of [Kapilavastu] were wont to go and sport on the water of a lake somewhat distant from the city. They at first erected a temporary place of residence in the vicinity of that sheet of water, and finally built a city which received the name of Dewadaha.[2]

Elsewhere we're told Devadaha was an auspicious site chosen by a *deva*:

> When [the population] had become very numerous, a deva pointed out another spot, on which they built a town, which they called "shown by a deva" or Devadaha.[3]

While the texts tell us little about the Buddha's mothers' side of the family, we do know from both canonical and noncanonical sources that he never forgot his roots. As a bodhisattva shortly before his enlightenment, he was asked by King Bimbisara in Rajagriha about his family, and he said,

> There is, O King, a country on the slopes of the Himalayas, rich in wealth and heroes. . . . They are descendants of the sun by clan, Shakyas by birth. From that family I have come, O King.[4]

## The Koliyans

Devadaha played a significant role in Sakya history because it was here that a distinct clan within this tribal group—known as the Koliyans—was centered. Mahaprajapati's family was Koliyan, her father allegedly the regent of this group at the time of her birth. The *Mahavastu* explains their origin as follows.

Long ago, many generations before Mahaprajapati was born, a Sakya princess in Kapilavastu became stricken with leprosy. Despite all their efforts, physicians could not cure her. Concerned about an outbreak, the king, her father, sadly decided she must be banished and instructed her brothers to take her away. After traveling some distance, they arrived in a deep forest and lovingly set up their sister in a cave with food, water, and comfortable bedding before sealing it with a large boulder. Meanwhile Kola, a powerful rishi devoted to ascetic practices, lived nearby in a leafy hermitage. Through years of arduous yogic effort, he had achieved superior super knowledges and the highest levels of meditation.

Now, a tiger roaming for food smelled the princess in the cave and began to snarl and claw at the boulder. The princess cried out in terror. In true fairy-tale fashion, Kola chased the tiger away and was astonished to find a beautiful princess inside the cave (we're not told just how, but she was now cured of the leprosy). It's not hard to guess what happened next. From the text,

> Though a man live a chaste life for a long time, yet the latent fires of passion in him are not put out. But once again will the poison of passion break out, just as the fire that is latent in wood cannot be suppressed.[5]

Unable to resist their mutual attraction, Kola abandoned his vow of celibacy and went on to marry the princess. They lived happily in his forest hermitage and eventually had thirty-two sons (more precisely, sixteen sets of male twins), all described as strong and handsome, wearing antelope hides, with long braided hair.

When they came of age, their mother decided it was time for them to meet her Sakya family. She said,

> Go my sons . . . to the great city of Kapilavastu. A Sakyan of such and such a name is my father and your grandfather. That Sakyan's sons are your uncles, and almost all the Sakyan nobles are your kinsmen. Such is the family to which you belong. They will provide you with means to live.[6]

To ensure that her sons presented themselves well, she carefully instructed them in Sakya customs, manners, and lore. With the blessings of their parents, the thirty-two brothers respectfully took leave and departed for Kapilavastu.

Crowds gathered and gawked as they entered the city. No doubt these feral-looking young men were a dramatic sight as they strode silently in sixteen pairs, comporting themselves with the grace and nobility of their Sakya bloodlines. "Who are you?" "Where do you come from?" was the cry from all around. An assembly of five hundred kinsmen quickly convened to receive them. After paying proper respect, the brothers repeated the stories they had learned from their mother, demonstrating detailed knowledge of their Sakya ancestry, including the account of her leprosy and banishment. The king, their grandfather, was still alive and absolutely delighted to meet thirty-two new grandsons. An added reason for his jubilation was that he knew their father, Kola, had previously been the king of Benares and was distantly related to the Sakyas through ancestral bloodlines. Afflicted by leprosy, Kola too had gone into exile, eventually becoming a great rishi known throughout the land for his yogic powers. No riffraff brahman hermit, Kola was the son-in-law of his dreams.

Thus the Sakyas welcomed their thirty-two new male relations, offering their daughters in marriage and giving the young men rich tracts of land across the river for farming. And so, named for their patriarch, Kola, the Koliyan branch of the Sakya tribe was founded, and its capital city became Devadaha.[7] A boundary river, known as the Rohini, was the natural divide between the two territories.*

This story[†] is important because there is a trope in Buddhist narratives that Sakya men (from Kapilavastu) marry Koliyan women (from Devadaha). It is often believed that these are two different tribal groups, but as we've just learned, they are both Sakya.[8] This distinction does not mean anything today, but another trope repeated throughout the legends is that the proud Sakyas never intermarried with outside populations. The emphasis on pure bloodlines is related in the *Digha Nikaya* in reference to the Buddha:

---

* The Sakya region in its entirety fell within the Kosala kingdom, with its capital in Sravasti.

† The Pali canon's version of this legend presents a much cruder, if not appalling, account of the founding of the Koliyan clan. Here, instructed by their mother, the thirty-two young men kidnapped and raped young Sakya women as they were bathing in the river, carrying them away by force. When the Sakya patriarchs heard about their daughters' fates, they shrugged; said, "Let it be, man, they're our relatives"; and kept silent (Bodhi, *Suttanipata*, 837).

As for the monk Gotama he is of high descent from both the mother's side as well as from the father's side. He is of pure birth as far back as the seventh generation.[9]

The Sakyas'* stubborn insularity is reported throughout the literature and has been suggested as the single greatest factor contributing to the kingdom's eventual downfall.[10]

Returning to Mahaprajapati, we now know that she was Sakya from the Koliyan side of the family. Following tradition, she and her sister Maya were betrothed to Suddhodana, a prince (later king) in Kapilavastu, just as a generation later Yasodhara, likely Mahaprajapati's niece, was married to Siddhartha (later the Buddha). While only Devadaha is named in the biographical narratives, the Koliyan territory extended to include numerous other towns and hamlets, some of which are noted in canonical literature as sites where the Buddha taught during the course of his itinerant ministry. To hear their names again, some of these were called Sajjanela, Sapuga, Kakkarapatta,[11] Haliddavasana,[12] and Uttara[13]—all places and peoples now erased by time.

It is significant that the Buddha never forgot the people of his matrilineal homeland. He delivered several sermons in Devadaha, including one known as the *Devadaha Sutta*.[14] In one story (related in detail in chapter 7), he once returned on personal matters to mediate a family dispute over water rights. After averting a bloody clan war between the Koliyans and Sakyas, he made a point of traveling to villages on both sides of the Rohini River to give public teachings, in a show of impartiality. He also returned to his birthplace of Lumbini's Grove, where it is said he delivered a dharma discourse as an offering to the grove goddess in gratitude for her protection at the time of his birth.[15]

## Family Life

Although we don't find stories of Mahaprajapati as a girl, we learn about her family through accounts of her sister Maya, who is better remembered. Their father (the Buddha's maternal grandfather) is described as a local raja or

---

* From here on this term includes Koliyans unless stated otherwise.

wealthy landowner, whose name appears variously as Anjana,[16] Suprabuddha (or Mahasuprabuddha),[17] and Subhuti.[18] Her mother is mentioned far less frequently and also by different names: Amita[19] or Yasodhara,* and Queen Sunatha in the Thai account.[20] Of particular interest are the Sanskrit accounts, in which her mother's name is Lumbini. In these stories we learn that the Buddha's birthplace, known as Lumbini's Grove—one of the few details in his biography that is consistent throughout Buddhist literature, as well as according to epigraphic remains and modern science[21]—is named after his grandmother. The Kanjur relates the following:

> [King Suprabuddha] married a woman by the name of Lumbini, who was exceedingly fair; and in her company he was in the habit of visiting a beautiful grove near the city, which belonged to a wealthy citizen.
>
> The queen took such a fancy to the place, that she begged the king to give it to her. He told her he was not able to do so; but he had her one made more beautiful still, and it was called Lumbini's grove.[22]

In her own words just prior to her death, Mahaprajapati reported that her mother's name was Sulakkhana.[23] A detail appearing in most early records reveals that the two sisters probably also had two brothers, Dandapani and Suprabuddha.†[24]

The Pali commentaries tell us that Mahaprajapati was Maya's younger sister and that both sisters were married to King Suddhodana, with Maya being the principal wife or queen and the future mother of the Buddha. Mahaprajapati is firmly cast as the king's second choice and junior wife, a little sister forever relegated to her big sister's shadow. The Pali canon does not mention her early life at all, as either Maya's sister or co-wife, or that she gave birth to two children by the king. It is similarly silent about her role as the young Buddha's mother, mentioning only that he had "nurses" growing up. Not until late in life, when she was an elderly widow requesting monastic ordination from her son, is Mahaprajapati introduced into the canonical narratives as his aunt and foster mother.

---

* Not to be confused with Siddhartha's principal wife, also named Yasodhara.
† Typical of name confusion in the early texts, Suprabuddha appears as both her father and brother.

But what do other Pali and Sanskrit traditions tell us? Forgotten textual fragments reveal mixed accounts of the two sisters. Some even tell us that Mahaprajapati was the eldest and the king's first choice as bride. Both sisters were augured to become mothers of great sons, though it's not always clear from the prophecies which sister was to become the mother of the Buddha. While it is impossible to sort out inconsistencies in the earliest accounts, they warrant separate scrutiny and shed light on alternative views of Mahaprajapati's significance in the Buddha's life and to an early Buddhist audience.

### Twin Prophecies

Several Sanskrit texts report that Mahaprajapati was one of seven (or eight) sisters, sometimes the eldest. This account is found in the *Mahavastu*, in which the Buddha's father-to-be, King Suddhodana, chooses the youngest daughter—in this case Maya—to be his bride only to be told that her six older sisters have to be married off first (youngest to oldest, they were named Maya, Mahamaya, Atimaya, Anantamaya, Culiya, Kolisova, and Mahaprajapati). The enterprising king selects the oldest and youngest for himself—Mahaprajapati and Maya, respectively—while the remaining sisters are promised to his five brothers.[25] A variant of this story from the *Abhinishkramanasutra* tells us again that the king chooses the youngest sister, but here the youngest, his first choice, is Mahaprajapati.[26]

In the Kanjur there are two sisters, Mahaprajapati and Maya, and Mahaprajapati is the oldest.* Suprabuddha offers both daughters to Suddhodana; however, the young prince (not yet a king) can accept only one because of a tribal law—an anomalous detail not found elsewhere—stating that the Sakyas were monogamous and allowed only one wife. He chooses the younger Maya but winds up with both sisters after a governing council of Sakya female and male elders make an exception in his favor.[27] Note that in two of these three variants Mahaprajapati is the older sister, and in one she is Suddhodana's first choice as bride.

The *Dipavamsa* specifies that Mahaprajapati and Maya were born of the same mother—a useful detail that should not be taken for granted given the prevailing *kshatriya* culture of harems and co-wives. It throws a curve ball

---

* Adding to the confusion, Mahaprajapati here is named Maya, and her sister is Mahamaya.

into this discussion by further saying that the sisters were co-natal, or twins, a reference not found elsewhere.* In this text we find that Mahaprajapati is revered both as the Buddha's co-mother and for her accomplishments as a practitioner of the dharma.

> The younger[†] twin-sister of queen Maya, born from the same mother, kind like a mother, suckled Bhagavat.
> [She was] called Mahapajapati, known by the name of Gotami, renowned, an original depositary [of the faith], possessing the six supernatural faculties and the high [magical] powers.[28]

But why all the attention to these two princesses, especially when there may have been other sisters to choose from? It turns out that their marriage desirability had everything to do with auspicious prophecies rendered by soothsayers when they were born. This was an era when divinations were de rigueur and carried a lot of weight, especially at the time of betrothal when a woman's prospects for bearing children were an essential consideration in a marriage contract. Based on an examination of bodily marks, the best possible prognostication for a *kshatriya* girl was that she would become the mother of a *chakravartin*, or "wheel-turning monarch," the apogee of worldly kingship according to *kshatriya* values of the time in this region of ancient India. For a *kshatriya* boy, of course, the hoped-for prophecy would be that he himself would become a *chakravartin*. Such a divination was exceedingly rare and highly valued by noble families.

What is a *chakravartin* king? No ordinary monarch, a *chakravartin* is supreme in virtuous qualities, ruling his people and vast lands ethically and benevolently. While the physical signs on a future mother of a *chakravartin* are not described, those on a male include thirty-two marks—best understood idiomatically. For example, the *chakravartin* will have flat feet (that he would encounter no obstacles); a long tongue (that he would speak kindly, his words commanding respect); soft, unwrinkled skin (that he would be generous and nurturing); and so forth.[29] The birth of a *chakravartin* monarch is further confirmed by numerous co-natal births; for example, his future chief minister, mount, and wife are born simultaneously amid an

---

* Pali: *sahajata*.
† Birth order is important even in the case of twins.

elaborate display of miracles. The appearance of a *chakravartin* in the world is very rare and augurs an era of universal justice, peace, and prosperity. Every *kshatriya* king or nobleman naturally wanted such a marvelous son and heir, thus a judicious selection of wife and queen was paramount.

The notion of *chakravartin* kingship is likely pre-Buddhist in origin, but it was adopted by early Buddhism in ways that created a parallel between the ideal secular and ideal spiritual worlds, more specifically between the perfect king and a perfectly enlightened buddha. The term *chakravartin* came to be used as a descriptor for the Buddha since he reigned supreme as the "wheel-turning monarch" of dharma in the world. As a marker of equivalency with *chakravartin* kings, the Buddha's birth was said to have been attended by spectacular miracles and co-natal births.

Whether destined to become a great king or an enlightened buddha, all *chakravartins* exhibit the same thirty-two bodily marks at birth. As explained in the *Lalitavistara*,

> Someone with such [thirty-two] marks would become one of two things. There would be no third option.... If such an individual would live as a householder, he would become a universal monarch with a four-fold army. He would become a conqueror, a righteous Dharma king....
>
> If, however, he leaves his family behind and becomes a monk, he will become a buddha. Relinquishing the attachment of desire and without relying on anyone else as a guide, he will become the teacher of gods and men.[30]

Whereas we might recognize that a buddha would be the far superior of the two possible outcomes, kings in ancient India definitely wanted a secular son and heir. Either way the *chakravartin* monarch is an upholder of dharma virtue and leader of a fourfold "army."* That the two career paths differ vastly explains the later confusion and quasipanic when the baby born to Maya and Suddhodana displayed the *chakravartin's* thirty-two marks at birth. Auspicious indeed, but was he destined to become a great king or a great saint? One was to remain home and rule the kingdom, the other

---

* For a buddha, this would be the fourfold community of laywomen, laymen, nuns, and monks.

would forsake the kingdom altogether. This remained an open question, setting up tension in the palace that persisted until the Bodhisattva's destiny became obvious when he left home at the age of twenty-nine to pursue the religious life.

This returns us to prophecies regarding the two sisters who would be his mothers. A similar conundrum took place at their births because Mahaprajapati and Maya exhibited identical bodily marks that augured a future *chakravartin*. Talk about mixed messages. According to the attending soothsayers, a future *chakravartin* (or two?) was definitely in the cards, but which sister would be his mother? Both perhaps? Was the future *chakravartin* to be a king or a buddha?

We see from variants of the prophecies that the sisters' fates as mothers at times appeared shared, even merged. Given the premium placed on *chakravartin* sons, the ambiguity led unsurprisingly to their high demand as co-brides. The safest bet for an ambitious young royal would be to marry both sisters and let the rest unfold. As one story says,

> It was declared by a brahman who saw them that they would have two sons, one of whom would be a *chakravartin* and the other a supreme Buddha. No sooner was this [prophesy] noised abroad, than all the 63,000 kings of Jambudvipa* sent to ask them in marriage; but all the preference was given to Suddhodana, king of Kapilavastu; and they became his principal queens.[31]

The commentator Buddhaghosa relates,

> When the Brahmins interpreted the characteristics of these two princesses . . . they declared they would give birth to a *chakravartin* king. Accordingly, the princesses . . . were raised to the rank of queens of Suddhodana. Maya gave birth to [the Bodhisattva] and [Prajapati] gave birth to Prince Nanda and Princess [Sundarinanda].[32]

Similarly, in his commentary on Mahaprajapati's verses in the *Therigatha*, Dhammapala says,

---

* Ancient name for India.

She was born in the lineage of Gotami, and that was her name. She was the younger sister of Maha-Maya. The experts in marks predicted, "The children dwelling in the womb[s] of these two will be wheel-turning monarchs."[33]

Less frequently, the sisters are named separately. The Kanjur mentions only Maya (the younger sister) holding promise as a future *chakravartin*'s mother, which is why she was Suddhodana's first choice. Mahaprajapati, on the other hand, has several such prophecies. A Sinhala source notes,

> On the day that the princess received her name, the diviners said that from the marks that they saw upon her body, they could tell that if after years she should have a son, he would be a *chakravartin*, or if she should have a daughter, she would be the queen of a *chakravartin*. It was on account of the good fortune that would befall her she was called Prajapati. . . .[34]

And from the *Abhinishkramanasutra*,

> Mahaprajapati was the youngest of the [eight] daughters, and when she was born, all the Brahman astrologers said, "This girl, if she has a son, will be the mother of a *chakravartin*." So gradually they grew up, and became marriageable. Then Suddhodana desired to have Maha-prajapati in marriage.[35]

Most confusing here is that the prognostications overall were not accurate. All traditions tell us Maya gave birth to the Buddha, not Maha-prajapati. This is odd because a false divination likely would not have been retained by later redactors formulating the literary records, or they might have tweaked it to align with known outcomes. Reading *chakravartin* as either "universal monarch" or "enlightened buddha" helps, but taken literally, Mahaprajapati gave birth to neither. The prophecies surrounding her birth appear to be literary canards.

Or are they? This type of conundrum—not at all uncommon in the ancient literature—challenges us to read the texts in new and different ways. Is it possible that *chakravartin* as "one who turns the wheel of dharma" is being used differently in this Buddhist context and is intended to include arhats as well as buddhas? In other words, those supreme exemplars on the spiritual path who achieve nirvana (rather than highest buddhahood) are also being heralded as *chakravartins*? Perhaps this is an example of early Buddhist editors adapting existing brahmanical conventions to fit a new and unique religious context. If so, the usage disrupts the traditional definition of *chakravartin* considerably by implying there can be more than one at a time and by losing the gendered notion that the *chakravartin* monarch must be male. However, it works in the context of Mahaprajapati's birth divinations, because according to the records, her daughter and son both took ordination and attained arhatship, making her, according to this scenario, the birth mother of not one but two *chakravartins*.

It's reasonable to argue that the divinations should simply be disregarded (also because they were likely concocted by narrators after the fact), but let's play with this refreshed view a bit longer. As the beloved leader and teacher of monastic women, Mahaprajapati was "mother" to myriad nun disciples to whom she frequently referred as her "daughters." At least five hundred of these nuns, we are told, attained arhatship. In this way she would be the "mother" of not one or two, but many *chakravartins*.

Stepping even further out on this limb, let's say the bodily marks the soothsayers saw on Mahaprajapati's body were the same as those on a male.* In this patriarchal culture where a girl's best future was to become a mother, they didn't get that Mahaprajapati *herself* was a *chakravartin*, destined to become the "wheel-turning" mother of Buddhism. In this way she was not simply the mother of countless wheel-turning arhats, but a universal monarch herself. Freeing ourselves of rigid conventional views opens up a new landscape where Mahaprajapati's birth divinations can be viewed as entirely accurate after all.

There are numerous possibilities, but a simple choice is also to return to a biological definition of motherhood. Just as Maya gave of her body to birth the Buddha, so Mahaprajapati gave of her body to nurse, nurture, and raise

---

* Okay, there is one mark that specifically describes the *chakravartin's* penis, where we learn that it is "well retracted" or "hidden." Isn't that an apt description of female genitalia as well? Metaphorically this detail is said to represent a guarding of modesty and chastity.

him. Neither was less or more the mother of the Buddha than the other. While the literature mostly parses the distinction between birth and foster mother, it can be argued that the soothsayers foresaw the sisters as equal co-mothers of a *chakravartin*, intentionally signaling reverence for both of them. While the texts rarely name Mahaprajapati as the Buddha's mother, we can see that she experienced herself that way, as reflected in these farewell words to her son at the end of her life:

> Women can easily obtain
> the name "King's Mother" or "Chief Queen."
> The name, "Mother of the Buddha"
> is the hardest [name] to obtain.
>
> O Hero, I've obtained that name!
> [I got] my wish because of you.[36]

Mother of the Buddha, mother to countless women arhats, wheel-turning monarch of Buddhism—Mahaprajapati was all of these. Reading her birth divinations in this way enhances our understanding of what may have been intended in the first textual records and how deeply she was remembered, revered, and loved in early Buddhist cultures.

## Co-Wives

The wedding of Maya and Suddhodana is beautifully described in several accounts from the Burmese and Thai traditions, while nowhere is there mention of a ceremony marking a union between Suddhodana and Mahaprajapati. Inconsistencies surrounding which sister was the older, younger, or preferred bride notwithstanding, the premise in this book will follow Pali tradition, with Mahaprajapati as Suddhodana's junior wife until Maya's death.

Where the sisters are mentioned together, the records describe them as equals:

> The great king Suddhodana holding a great festival at his coming of age, brought the two sisters home to his own palace.[37]

From the Sinhala tradition,

> On arriving at the proper age, [Prajapati] became, along with [Maya], the wife of Suddhodana; and the two queens lived together like two [goddesses] in one lotus flower.[38]

Further,

> These princesses were beautiful as the queens of the *deva-loka*; no intoxicating liquor ever touched their lips; even in play they never told an untruth; they would not take life, even to destroy insects; and they observed all the precepts.[39]

Mahaprajapati disappeared behind the veils of Suddhodana's harem once Maya became queen. The literature does not mention her again during this time, although we can imagine that the sisters remained close companions as they were uprooted together from their home in Devadaha and shared life in the women's quarters of the king's palace. Maya as queen would have been chief consort and head of the harem women. As her confidante with the rank of junior queen, Mahaprajapati likely would have been the equivalent of Maya's lady-in-waiting.

Sequestered in the "upper stories of the palace," the harem is described as a paragon of luxury and refinement, the ladies bedecked in silks and elaborate jewelry. It was also a festive place, resonating with rhythmic dance and the music of lutes, flutes, hand drums, kettledrums, bells, and cymbals.[40] While we don't know their names or how many harem women there were, it is worth reflecting that this all-female community would have bonded deeply during this time, centered around the two queens. Years later many of these same harem women would follow Mahaprajapati in renouncing palace life and taking ordination as nuns.

## 2

# Birth of the Buddha

*From women ... buddhas come into this world. ...*[1]

The Bodhisattva's conception garners a lot of attention in the traditional literature where the focus falls on Maya's dream where he entered her womb—without the participation of Suddhodana—in the form of a magnificent white, six-tusked elephant. Omitted from most legends are details about Maya herself during this time and a larger narrative context surrounding her experience of pregnancy and childbirth.* Two neglected areas, in particular, shed light on our investigation of her sister, the Buddha's co-mother, Mahaprajapati.

The backstory found in both Pali and Sanskrit sources is that the Bodhisattva put a great deal of thought into choosing his mother and birth family. To understand this, we must return to the Buddhist world of past-life stories where we learn that the Bodhisattva traveled countless lifetimes accumulating the supreme qualities of compassion and wisdom requisite for buddhahood before taking final rebirth in our era. While Maya enjoyed palace life as queen in Kapilavastu, her future son, the Bodhisattva, scanned the world from his perch in Tushita heaven, trying to decide where and under

---

* For extensive treatment of this topic, see Garling, *Stars at Dawn*, chap. 1.

what circumstances to take rebirth. In an almost comedic conversation with gods attending this dilemma, the Bodhisattva sought their counsel on five topics, including who his mother should be. As found in the *Nidanakatha*, he finally concluded,

> The mother of a Buddha is not lustful, or corrupt as to drink, but has fulfilled the Perfections for a hundred thousand ages, and from her last birth upwards has kept the five Precepts unbroken. Now this lady Maha Maya is such a one, she will be my mother.[2]

A similar passage appears in the *Mahavastu*:

> What woman is there who rejoices in moral restraint and in calm, who is of noble birth, of gentle speech, who is generous, radiant, and tender?
>
> What woman is there who is dignified, who has overcome ignorance, passion and malice, who is endowed with consummate beauty and is not base of conduct, and who possesses abundant merit?
>
> Who can bear me for ten months? Who has merit to win such honour? Who now shall be my mother? Whose womb shall I now enter?[3]

Maya, as we know, was chosen, although the clincher was one additional karmic requirement: a bodhisattva's mother had to be predestined to die seven days after giving birth. This was the alleged requirement and fate of all mothers of buddhas, one that Maya sadly fulfilled. After the four remaining topics were addressed (caste, *kshatriya*; family, Sakya; town, Kapilavastu; timing, ASAP), the Bodhisattva was ready to make his entrance into the world.

To some, this phantasmagoric detail in the Buddha's biography may appear rather silly. Yet weaving between layers of the ordinary and supernatural, we catch glimpses of values that were deemed important in those ancient times. It's curious that the "mother" detail in the selection process addresses bloodlines and literal biological birth without accounting for what was to happen to the exalted baby after the mother died in seven days. Who would care for the Bodhisattva then? What about his upbringing?

Wouldn't his first teacher, the mother who raised him, also need careful selection? These exceedingly important details for any child, but certainly for the Buddha-to-be, do not even come up.

While it's consistent that chroniclers of the Buddha's biography—presumably all male—were generally silent on matters to do with child-rearing and family, it's particularly glaring that Mahaprajapati, as the only mother the Buddha ever knew, is scarcely (usually never) mentioned in stories of his early life. In any case, it must be noted that in both the Pali and Sanskrit traditions, the Bodhisattva's own description of his ideal mother, including birthplace, caste, and family, could just as easily have been describing Mahaprajapati. Except for the premature death detail, she and her sister Maya *both* met all the criteria (returning us to their shared divinations). Thus, according to the Bodhisattva's own karmic intention, there was never really a viable second candidate for the mother who would succeed Maya, despite initial controversy surrounding the matter, as we shall see in the stories that follow. While Mahaprajapati's unique qualifications are nowhere acknowledged or validated in the records, they serve to remove the seeming arbitrariness of her becoming the infant Bodhisattva's adoptive mother, a role that she stepped into seamlessly and with love at his birth. What would Buddhism look like today had she not done that?

Another spot in the narratives where we can feel but not see Mahaprajapati's presence is during her sister's pregnancy, when Maya asks leave of her husband to live in celibacy and seclusion. Foreshadowing their lives together as nuns, the palace women all follow suit and join their queen in separating themselves from the men in the household, converting the harem into an all-female religious retreat with fasting, quiet, and contemplation. As described in the *Mahavastu*,

> Maya . . . took her thousand beloved principal maidens, went up to the fair mansion, and sat down surrounded by her entirely gracious attendants.
>
> On her couch that was the colour of a snow-white lotus, she whiled away her time in silence, contentedly calm and self-controlled.[4]

She set an example for the women by making spiritual vows during this time, saying,

> I wish from this night to undertake the eight special rules of self-discipline, to wit, not to kill anything that lives; not to defraud anyone; to have no sexual pleasures; not to lie; not to prevaricate; not to calumniate; to have no irreligious conversation; and, moreover, to pray that I may not covet, or be angry, or hold foolish doubts, so as to avoid all heretical teaching, and adopt all that is true and right. I now bind myself to observe these rules, and I desire to produce in myself a loving heart towards all living creatures.[5]

The *Lalitavistara* imputes added goodness to Maya by saying she invoked the king to "look upon all beings [benevolently and lovingly] as if upon an only child."[6]

Suddhodana magnanimously complies with Maya's requests, further commanding that the women's quarters be festooned with all manner of flowers, banners, and incense while protected by a brigade of palace guards. Perhaps it's simply because there were no consorts to be found, but Suddhodana follows Maya's example and spends his wife's time of seclusion in his own parallel retreat of celibacy and prayer.

Once again, we catch a glimpse of the women's community as much more nuanced than a stereotypical "brothel" or enclave of female servitude. A powerful sense of women's spirituality is introduced here, far earlier in the narratives than is normally represented. We can't know the dynamics of what was going on in the women's quarters during Maya's pregnancy, but her sister Mahaprajapati would have been there. So many questions arise. What was the nature of the relationship between the sisters? Did Mahaprajapati take the lead among the women while Maya was under their care? How did this group of women evolve their own relationships and practices, living communally as they did, undisturbed for many months? How did their spirituality take root such that it would give rise years later to their enthusiasm for the Buddha's teachings and their trust in Mahaprajapati as their spiritual preceptor and leader? While we can't know the answers, we can imagine that causes and conditions established at the time of this women's retreat of eight or more months during Maya's pregnancy would have flowed forward to influence events four decades later when Mahaprajapati and many of these women would form a separate spiritual community, first as laywomen and then as nuns. In a concluding note, while the accounts of the time of Maya's pregnancy usually emphasize the women's somber piety, other texts describe a festive time of music and dance when the women celebrated together and enjoyed each other's company.[7]

The notion of festivity continues at the conclusion of Maya's ten-month pregnancy when it is time for her to give birth. She informs her husband of her wish to proceed immediately to Lumbini's Grove, the sacred birthing site sanctioned only for women, located deep within the forest in the vicinity of Devadaha.[8] It was here, under the protection of the goddess Abhayadevi as embodied by a sacred *sal* tree,* that generations of women gathered to midwife and care for each other during times of childbirth. Maya's coterie of female attendants, including Mahaprajapati, accompanied her there in a grand procession.[9] It makes sense that women from Maya's Koliyan family, including her mother, would have joined them, participating in rituals and assisting with the birth. In the *Lalitavistara*, Maya says to her husband as her labor pains begin,

> I myself have carried a pure being within me for a long time now.
> The sala, that most wonderful of trees, is now in blossom;
> O Lord, it is therefore fitting for us to go to the pleasure grove!
>
> Spring, that excellent season, is a joyous time for women;
> The bees are humming and the cuckoos singing.
> Fresh and sweet, the fragrance of flowers drifts through the air,
> Please issue an order, and let us go there right away![10]

Delighted, the king swings into action. He commands his retinue,

> Arrange my horses, elephants, and chariots!
> Decorate the excellent garden at Lumbini![11]

The *Abhinishkramanasutra* tells us,

> Suddhodana Raja . . . immediately issued orders to have all the road between Kapilavastu and Devadaha made level and freed from all weeds, pebbles, filth, and obstacles of all kinds; and to have the ground swept and sprinkled with scented water, and all kinds of flowers to be

---

* *Shorea robusta.*

scattered along it . . . and moreover the queen Maya was ornamented with every kind of precious stone, and her person decorated with the choicest flowers and unguents . . . thus accompanied by music, dancing women and guards . . . she set forth on her journey.[12]

Reported variously in the texts, Maya rode out comfortably cushioned on the back of a gaily ornamented white elephant or ensconced regally inside a golden palanquin carried, according to one text, by scores of young women. The radiance and fecundity of the young mother-to-be* was mirrored in the natural exuberance of the sacred grove anticipating her arrival:

As soon as the cortege reached [Lumbini's Grove], five water lilies shot forth spontaneously from the stem and main branches of each tree, and innumerable birds of all kinds, by their melodious tunes, filled the air with the most ravishing music. Trees, similar to those growing in the seats of [gods], apparently sensible to the presence of the incarnated Buddha, seemed to share in the universal joy.[13]

While the Buddha's nativity is vividly described in most early biographical narratives, Maya's sister is not mentioned. Only the Burmese tradition, drawing from early Pali records, consistently reports that Mahaprajapati was present at the time of the birth. The text reads,

When [Maya] had entered [the grove] she descended from the palanquin and, accompanied by her younger sister and supported on each side by her attendants, proceeded to the propitious sal tree. When they arrived at the tree, the queen wished to take hold of a limb, which was wholly covered with flowers and, as a young rattan bends in the fire, it bent down to meet her hand. The queen, taking hold of the limb with one hand and of her sister with the other, was seized in labor, upon which the young maids in attendance made a screen [around her] and put the men on the outside.[14]

---

* This discussion does not follow Buddhaghosa's claim that Maya was forty when she gave birth, as no corroborating evidence was found in sources examined here.

Further,

> Maya, seated on her couch along with her sister Mahapajapati, desired her attendants to have it moved closer to a [sal] tree, which she pointed out. She then rose gently on her couch; her left hand clasped around the neck of her sister, who supported her in a standing position.[15]

Burmese art similarly places Mahaprajapati at the Buddha's birth. In a magnificent illustrated manuscript held in the British Library, she is depicted kneeling in front of Maya during the delivery. It must be noted that no gods are present in this portrayal; rather it is an all-female cast with four more women surrounding Maya, one of whom is poised to catch the baby.[16] An illuminated manuscript from the Wellcome Library in London displays similar details.[17]

A world away in Ladakh, we find a related image on a painted mural in the Sumstek Temple within the Alchi monastic complex north of Leh. Curiously arranged on the dhoti of a towering, four-meter-high Maitreya are more than fifty images depicting episodes in the Buddha's life. Only women are shown attending the Buddha's birth, with Mahaprajapati standing to Maya's left while she grasps the branch of the *sal* tree.[18]

To the west, visual narratives corroborating Mahaprajapati's presence at the nativity appear ubiquitously in early Buddhism's Gandharan art from present-day Afghanistan and Pakistan. The nativity scene is the most commonly depicted and is almost always portrayed as a triad with Maya in the center grasping the branch, a male god (Brahma or Indra) to her right catching the baby, and Mahaprajapati standing to Maya's left holding her about the waist. In some of the larger formations, there is another female attendant or two on Mahaprajapati's left holding a peacock feather, water vase, circular box, or mirror.[19] Identical triads appear in the sandstone sculptures of Mathura, datable from roughly the same period, or the first through seventh centuries C.E.[20]

We find in these samples what the literature mostly forgot: Mahaprajapati was remembered by early Buddhist populations as a loving presence and key participant at the Buddha's birth. Iconographic evidence elevates her role at this extraordinarily important event and arguably points to historical accuracy. So how and why is she absent from the early textual traditions? Diverse scholarly views could ring in on this, but here it is held that this is neither surprising nor particularly complicated. As discussed, the transition from oral to written records, or from early to later written records, typically entailed passing through the filter of male monastic editors whose androcentric focus saw women generally—and in this case, Mahaprajapati specifically—as largely irrelevant. That we know so little about a figure as central in importance to early Buddhism as Mahaprajapati suggests that she was a target of such early misogynistic editorial treatment.

It's fortunate indeed that we have early Buddhist art to serve as a counterpoint, if not a corrective, to literary narratives. Unlike written records generated more or less contemporaneously, artistic images—some literally chiseled in stone—could not be altered or redacted over time to suit Buddhism's evolving androcentrism. Further comparative investigation in the prodigious areas of early Buddhist art and literature is certainly warranted.

In any case, let's return Mahaprajapati to her rightful place at her sister's side during the birth of the Buddha. An iconic moment indeed, from which the entire story of early Buddhism can be told. The Buddha's first mother brought him into the world, while his second mother remained closely tied to him her entire life, raising him from infant to spiritual seeker bound for buddhahood, then proactively participating in his mission and legacy as an advocate for women and their rightful representation in his fourfold dharma community.

## Maya's Death: Two Stories

Missing from nativity accounts, both Pali and Sanskrit, is any emotional response to Maya's death. She was, after all, a beloved and generous queen to a large population in addition to being the Buddha's birth mother. Most narratives simply note the fact of her death, some adding a brief, if inadequate, explanation, such as she died of joy at having such a marvelous son,[21] or her body could never again be sullied by sex.[22] Understandably it was a tough call for the early bards and storytellers, since Maya's postpartum death was clearly linked to the Bodhisattva's birth. That she died as a consequence of childbirth is acknowledged in the *Abhinishkramanasutra*:

The prince royal now being seven days old, his mother the Queen Maya, being unable to regain her strength or recover the joy she experienced whilst the child dwelt in her womb, gradually succumbed to her weakness and died.[23]

How does one tell Maya's sad story without detracting from the Bodhisattva's joyous one? Perhaps the grief was too profound for the storytellers to relate. Most narratives simply switch gears at this point in the chronology and move on to stories of the precocious young prince growing up in Kapilavastu.[24]

However, two dramatic exceptions have emerged from outside the bounds of the Buddha's commonly known biographies. The stories that follow are spectacular for bringing alive the emotional experience of Maya's death, while also providing fresh evidence of the close bond between the two sisters. Taken together, they begin to fill a long-standing gap while also capturing some herstory of Buddhism's beginnings.

## KESINI'S GRIEF

The first story comes from the *Karmasataka* in the Tibetan canon, or Kanjur. Here we not only learn more about the two sisters, but we are introduced to an entirely new character—their servant girl Kesini. She is not named in Pali records, but according to this story Kesini clearly was on the front lines in Mahaprajapati and Maya's lives and at the dawn of Buddhism.

As related by the Buddha to his monks, her biography begins in typical fashion in a former life with her aspiration to awaken. However, quite significantly, in this story Kesini, Mahaprajapati, and Maya all aspire to awaken during the same episode. Further, their aspirations for the future include remaining in relationship with each other. The following summary is based on Jamspal and Fischer's translation of "The Story of Kesini."[25]

Many eons ago the blessed Buddha Vipassi was in the world. One day he visited the city of Bandhumati where two sisters offered him food. As she did so, the first sister (Maya in a past life) prayed,

> May I give birth to one as precious as this. May I please him. May I not displease him.

Hearing this, the second sister (Mahaprajapati in a past life) prayed,

> Wherever I am born, may it be as your sibling. May I rear one as precious as this.

Now a young servant girl who was their hairdresser (Kesini in a past life) was also present. Upon hearing the sisters' prayers, she fervently said a prayer of her own to Buddha Vipassi:

> Oh, but by this root of virtue, wherever these two are born, may I again look after their hair and serve them with great respect! May I please and not displease their precious children.

Kesini went on to ordain as a nun under the Buddha Kasyapa in a subsequent life. During this time, she observed him extolling the virtues of her preceptor, who is not named but presumably was Mahaprajapati in a former life. At the time of her death, Kesini prayed to ordain again as a nun under Gautama Buddha in order to continue her practice and attain arhatship. This time she added another aspiration:

> Just as the totally and completely awakened Buddha Kasyapa commended my preceptor for her superlative efforts, may the Buddha Sakyamuni, king of the Sakyas, also commend me for my superlative efforts.

Thus propelled by the karma of her aspirations and good deeds, in our era of Gautama Buddha, Kesini again became the hairdresser to Maya and Mahaprajapati, this time when they were young girls living in their father's household in Devadaha. She accompanied them to Kapilavastu at the time of their marriage to Suddhodana.

Now the story jumps to Maya's death, where Kesini's grief rocks the story to a degree not found elsewhere. Observing Maya's corpse, she became distraught:

> Young Kesini missed her so much that she clutched at strands of Mahamaya's hair and flung herself on the ground in grief, wailing and beating her chest. She was inconsolable.

Few words, but such explosive emotionality. Not Maya's husband, not her sister or family, not the Sakya people—it was a simple servant girl who is remembered for her profound grief over Maya's untimely death. Years later, Kesini's remaining aspiration bore fruit as she took ordination with the Buddha, Mahaprajapati as her preceptor, and was commended for her excellence. The Buddha said of her,

> [Kesini] has pleased me, not displeased me, gone forth in my very doctrine, cast away all afflictive emotions, and manifested arhatship, and I have now commended her for her superlative efforts.

Attending the two sisters as their servant over countless lifetimes was Kesini's means to the end of her true goal: arhatship. Along the way, her deep devotion and love for Maya and Mahaprajapati became part of her story, and part of their stories as well.

## MAYA GIVES HER SON TO HER SISTER

The following story comes from a living oral tradition in Cambodia. Here we must thank scholar Trent Walker, who spent years researching and learning Khmer dharma songs, which he has captured in audio and written form as the tradition becomes threatened with extinction.[26] While the provenance of any oral tradition cannot truly be known, these liturgical songs sung in Khmer and Pali have flowed through village life in Cambodia for generations. Walker describes their function as living dharma:

> Guiding people across the boundaries of birth and death, with their untraceable melodies and timeless phrases, Dharma songs resound the funeral drum of impermanence, suffering, and not-self.[27]

The heart-wrenching dharma song that follows maps these universal teachings to the Buddha's biography by bringing to life Maya's voice as she lay dying. In hauntingly beautiful verse, Maya comforts Mahaprajapati and, in a striking detail not found elsewhere, gives her newborn son into the care of her sister to raise as her own.

Little Sister Gotami!
Hold to these words of guidance
I ask you now to receive
Little Sister, forgive me.

Since giving birth to my son
Only seven days have passed
My life withers to nothing
As I pass on to the next world.

What can I do, when we are
Born only to be destroyed?
All humans and animals
Die and decay by nature.

Never lasting, never sure
Life is as the Pali phrase
ANICCAM DUKKHAM ANATTA
Little darling, you must know.

Now as for me, dear sister
Don't worry, for death is sure;
No more can I hold my son
The refuge of gods and men.

You who pity your sister,
You, lovely girl, that is why
I ask you to hug and hold
This motherless child of mine.

Nurse him and bathe his body
Attend to him day and night
Care for him like no other
Oh my golden girl, don't stop![28]

It would be hard to find a more moving, evocative passage in Buddhist literature.

Here it's worth a pause to reflect on the game-changing power of the moment described in this scene. We don't hear Mahaprajapati's voice and can't know her grief, but everything changed for her with Maya's death. No longer second fiddle living a life of potential anonymity in the harem, in one stroke of fate Mahaprajapati became mother of the Buddha and queen of the Sakyas. Her life was now on an unstoppable course, one that would play significantly in both her son's life and in the founding of his mission.

How differently the Buddha's birth story would feel to us today had his traditional biographical narratives captured tender, relational, believable moments such as we find in these two poignant nativity stories. The power of herstory returns us vividly to the subjective experience of the women present at that sacred event, reminding us that beyond miracles and male heroism, human love and suffering lie deeply embedded in Buddhism's beginnings.

# 3

# Mother and Queen

*Then [Prajapati Gautami], beholding the prince like an angel,*
*With beauty seldom seen on earth, seeing him thus born and now*
*his mother dead, loved and nourished him as her own child; and the*
*child regarded her as his mother.*[1]

The legends all stall after Maya's death. Where and how did she die? What happened next? What about a funeral? We don't find satisfactory answers in the literature. The narratives fall into silence or fragmented, murky contradictions at this point in the timeline where Maya simply vanishes after giving birth. With scant evidence to the contrary, the premise here is that she died in Lumbini's Grove, never to return home with her son to palace life in Kapilavastu.

Silence also surrounds her sister. How did Mahaprajapati's life pick up after she suddenly became mother to her newborn nephew? While she is not normally named in nativity scenes, we know from canonical references to her later life as a nun that, at the death of her sister, she gave her own infant to a wet nurse in order to breastfeed the Bodhisattva herself.[2]

Some texts mention an unnamed woman holding the newborn Bodhisattva following his birth.* For example, the baby is taken to the temple in the arms of a woman to receive the blessings of the Sakya clan deity.[3] He is held on a woman's lap in the return procession to Kapilavastu. Back at the palace, a woman seated next to the king holds the baby when soothsayers make their divinations. Scenes from these episodes can also be found in early Buddhist art, where the identity of the woman is unclear. It certainly was a time of confusion, or perhaps we're seeing a storyteller's reluctance to identify Mahaprajapati in her new role so soon after Maya's death. The assumption here is that Mahaprajapati would be the intended woman holding the Bodhisattva in the post-birth scenes, despite some identifications to the contrary (including some naming Maya[4]). Whether or not Mahaprajapati had been specifically deemed his adoptive mother so soon, it only makes sense that, as the baby's aunt, she would assume immediate responsibility for her deceased sister's child. He also needed to be nursed, and she was the one able to do so.

The Chinese *Buddhacarita* provides a uniquely detailed passage in which, immediately after Maya's death, Mahaprajapati appears in her new role not only as the Bodhisattva's mother but also as Suddhodana's queen. Here the king comes to fetch the baby from Lumbini's Grove. After making ritual offerings and waiting for auspicious signs, he returns to Kapilavastu in procession with his "queen" when his son is ten days old. With Maya dying at seven days, it is implicit that the queen here is Mahaprajapati and that Suddhodana is fulfilling his duty to retrieve his son while seeing to proper funerary rites for his wife. In the following passage, her invocation of "heavenly spirits" before departing Lumbini's Grove suggests Mahaprajapati's own ritual response to the death of her sister, as well as the birth of her nephew and new responsibilities as mother and queen. The text reads,

> They took the child back to [the king's] own palace . . . in a richly adorned chariot . . .
>
> [The baby had] ornaments of every kind and color round his neck; shining with beauty, exceedingly resplendent with unguents. The queen, embracing him in her arms, going around, worshipped the heavenly spirits.

* Variously "woman," "nurse," and "queen."

> Afterwards she remounted her precious chariot, surrounded by her waiting women; the king, with his ministers and people, and all the crowd of attendants, [led] the way. . . .[5]

This text goes on to name Mahaprajapati as the one who brings the baby to the seer, Asita, who reads his bodily marks in order to divine his future:

> And now the Bodhisattva having awoke from his sleep and arisen, Mahaprajapati, enfolding him in a white and silk-like robe, came with him to the place where the king was.[6]

As Asita makes his prognostication, his eyes fill with tears at the power of its import. Speaking with one voice, the king and queen are confused and concerned:

> On this the king and Mahaprajapati were moved at heart, and with reverence [folded palms] addressed [Asita] thus: "Is there then something unlucky? oh! tell us then its purport!"[7]

We see Mahaprajapati and Suddhodana clearly named here as the Bodhisattva's parents. They are stunned to hear that their marvelous baby is to become the Buddha for our era. Whatever does that bode for his future? What about theirs? A new chapter has just opened in Mahaprajapati's life.

### On Becoming Siddhartha's Mother

A handful of stories tell us about the Buddha's childhood, and a scant few of these mention that Mahaprajapati was his mother. The Pali tradition tells us that he was raised by multiple "nurses"—wet nurses and nannies—who were selected for their attractive bodies:

> [Suddhodana], with the tender solicitude of a vigilant father, procured for his beloved offspring nurses exempt from all corporeal defects, and remarkable for their beautiful and graceful appearance.[8]

While both traditions acknowledge that Mahaprajapati succeeded her sister as mother and queen, the ambivalence cast by the silence surrounding her during the years she would have spent raising the young Bodhisattva is striking. She was, after all, the only mother the Buddha ever knew. Surely stories about her mothering the little prince would have flowed beyond palace walls into the early oral traditions. From most literary evidence we have today, it would appear as if the Buddha-to-be grew up motherless, tended only by servants in his father's household.

We will explore some rare exceptions, found mostly in the Sanskrit tradition, where we catch glimpses of a profoundly loving relationship between mother and son. First, let's return to events immediately following Maya's death and several stories that focus on a formal selection of Mahaprajapati as the baby's foster mother. The first comes from the *Lalitavistara*, where she is named a woman in the harem but not the king's junior wife. The following is a summary.

Back in Kapilavastu, the first order of business for Suddhodana is to set up a household to care for his newborn son. Not the king's strong suit and also not entirely within his purview. Although he is deemed king of the Sakyas, important decisions fall to a council of elders, women and men, charged with upholding the values and best interests of the people. Deciding the fate of the little prince and heir to the throne is a charge they take very seriously. Suddhodana asks them,

> Now that this babe has lost his mother, who is there we may select to take her place, and act as a foster mother to the child?[9]

The elders all agree she should be "a skilled and kind person who could care for him in a loving and kind atmosphere."[10] After vetting more than five hundred eager volunteers—young Sakya women all deemed too young and foolish for the job—the elders unanimously choose Mahaprajapati. In announcing their decision, they note her relationship with both Maya and the king:

> The Prince's maternal aunt Mahaprajapati would be able to raise the Prince so that he is happy and well. She will also be able to please King Suddhodana.[11]

A similar scenario unfolds in the Chinese *Buddhacarita*, but here the exchange takes place on an entirely different level: the elders are aware they are choosing a mother for a bodhisattva, not an ordinary child:

"It is a difficult task to train aright and lead into obedience one possessed of such saintlike wisdom as the prince . . . for when he begins to grow up who then will be able to attend on him and direct him aright?" . . . Then they all agreed that Mahaprajapati alone was able to nourish (the child), and with loving heart to protect him from the heats and damp of his abode, and to feed him with [the breast] by which he might grow to maturity.

Mahaprajapati, the prince's maternal aunt, pure and faultless, she, they said, is the one to protect and cherish, and ever be near the person of the prince. Then Suddhodana-raja and the Sakya princes, being all agreed on this point, went together to the abode of Mahaprajapati and expressed their wishes on this point:

"The prince's mother being dead, we beg you, his maternal aunt, to take charge of him and bring him up, that he may grow up (to manhood)."

So Mahaprajapati undertook the office.[12]

Of exceptional importance in this passage is the reverence and respect shown Mahaprajapati, not just by the author of the text but by the Sakya elders, her husband, and his brothers. Her role as the future Buddha's mother is established at this early point in the narrative. Beyond her capacity simply to love and cherish Siddhartha, she is chosen for her ability to raise an exceptional child, as well as fulfill the sacred role of being a future buddha's mother.

Other Sanskrit texts note the depths of her motherly tenderness and loving kindness. From the Nepali *Buddhacarita*:

Then the queen's sister . . . undistinguished from the real mother in her affection or tenderness, brought up as her own son the young prince who was like the offspring of the gods.[13]

And the *Abhinishkramanasutra* says,

She . . . attended him without intermission . . . as the sun tends on the moon during the first portion of each month, till the moon arrives at its fullness. So the child gradually waxed and increased in strength; as the shoot of the Nyagrodha tree gradually increases in size, well-planted in the earth, till itself becomes a great tree, thus did the child day by day increase, and lacked nothing.[14]

Her abundant milk intimates their loving bond:

> The child causing his loving mother
> Always to abound in most nutritious milk,
> So that even supposing it were not sufficient (naturally),
> It became more than enough (thro his influence).[15]

A Korean verse reveals Mahaprajapati's love not just for her son but also—providentially—for the dharma:

> Seven days after giving birth,
>     his mother died and was born in Trayastrimsah.
> His aunt greatly loved the Way,
>     she brought him up without sparing any effort.[16]

Pali canonical sources only mention Mahaprajapati as the infant Buddha's mother after the fact, many years later when she is an elderly nun. In one example, Ananda says to the Buddha,

> Mahapajapati Gotami has been very helpful to the Blessed One, venerable sir. As his mother's sister, she was his nurse, his foster mother, the one who gave him milk. She suckled the Blessed One when his own mother died.[17]

## Motherhood Stories

The *Lalitavistara* relates a temple scene in which King Suddhodana presents the baby prince to the family deities.* Before departing the palace, Suddhodana asks Mahaprajapati to prepare the prince by dressing and ornamenting him in his finest attire. While she is doing so, a curious conversation takes place between the infant and his mother. In full Bodhisattva persona, Siddhartha speaks and is aware of the implications of all that is transpiring.

---

* Here a profusion of brahmanical gods, including Siva, Indra, Brahma, and others.

Smiling at his mother, he inquires about the upcoming festivities. Note that in this dialogue he calls Mahaprajapati "mother," while the narrator calls her "aunt."

> "Mother, where are you taking me?"
> She replied: "Son, I am taking you to the temple."
> The Prince then smiled, laughed, and spoke these verses to his maternal aunt:

> "When I was born, this trichiliocosm trembled.
> [The gods and demigods . . .]
> All bowed their heads to my feet and paid homage to me.

> "What other god is there who is superior to me,
> Who my mother takes me to worship today?
> I am superior to all the gods; I am the God of Gods.
> There is no other god like me, so how could anyone be superior?

> "Still, mother, I will allow worldly customs;
> When beings see my miraculous displays, they will be pleased.
> It will inspire them with great respect,
> And gods and humans will know that I am the God of Gods."[18]

Mahaprajapati tells the little prince she will be taking him to the temple, although her further participation is not noted in the story.

Additional festivities on behalf of the infant prince take place sometime later. Here citizens from across the kingdom converge on the sacred Vimala garden—named for the guardian goddess of that place—bringing lavish gifts of jewelry for the little Bodhisattva. Surrounded by multitudes of cheering crowds, he arrives with his mother in a lavish chariot:

> Then Mahaprajapati, with the child on her knee, rode in the precious chariot, and proceeded to the garden.[19]

Once inside she holds Siddhartha on her lap while reverent Sakyas pass by one at a time, paying their respects and offering gift after splendid gift.

While directly honoring the prince, they are also honoring his mother, the new queen.[20]

Next, we move forward in time to a springtime festival celebrating the first plowing of the fields. All Sakyas, including the king and his entire household, bring picnics and gather in the countryside to witness this joyous, annual event. Left alone under the shade of a rose-apple tree, young Siddhartha enters into meditation, achieving an initial level of realization that augurs his impending buddhahood. In most versions of this well-known story, a "nurse" or "nurses" are identified as his caretakers. Distracted by the festivities, they forget where they have left the prince, leading to panicked pandemonium later when he cannot be found. Only in the *Lalitavistara* is Mahaprajapati named in this story. Frantic with fear like any mother, she implores her husband to find their son:

> I have searched but did not find him;
> Your Majesty, please find out where the boy has gone.[21]

Of note, Mahaprajapati* is only identified in the verse portion of this story. In the prose that frames it, normally considered a later addition, she is absent and one of Suddhodana's ministers performs her role in conversation with the king.

Elsewhere, Mahaprajapati is remembered as mother of the prince in the *Ashokavadana*, or tales of King Asoka who reigned in India in the third century B.C.E. Here the king is visiting Buddhist pilgrimage sites and, upon arriving in Kapilavastu, is told,

> In this place, great king, [the Bodhisattva] was reared by Mahaprajapati; here he was taught how to write; and here he became master of the arts appropriate to his lineage such as riding an elephant, a horse, or a chariot, handling a bow, grasping a javelin, and using an elephant hook.[22]

An exquisitely beautiful description of the close bond between Mahaprajapati and her son is found in the thirteenth century Sinhala text

---

* Here called "maternal aunt."

*Pujavaliya*. Related in her own words at the end of her life, she lovingly reminisces with the Buddha about being his mother in their years together during his childhood:

> Oh my son! Earlier, when you were young, you played games fit for a child here and there outside the palace, surrounded by 80,000 princes, like a miniature full moon surrounded by stars. And I would look for you, and not finding you in the royal compound, I would search here and there. And when I found you, I would pick you up in my two hands, and placing you against my breast, I would protect you from the rain, wind, heat, and cattle. Taking you back inside the palace, I would lie down on sumptuous beds, and I would pacify you, putting you against my stomach, and make you fall asleep. I gave to you who are incomparable, the ordinary attention paid to a child that all mothers of the world give to all children.[23]

A more tender and telling testimonial to Mahaprajapati's love for her son would be hard to find in Buddhist literature.

While these brief snapshots are about all we have of Mahaprajapati mothering the young prince, more stories emerge once he is older and begins to show signs of struggle and a determination to leave home. These are discussed later in this chapter, where we find her vividly cast in all her early roles: mother, queen, and chief consort in the harem.

## Mahaprajapati's Birth Children

While Mahaprajapati's stories as a mother typically center on her adoptive role with Siddhartha, it is important to remember that as junior wife to the king, she also gave birth to two children: a daughter named Sundarinanda and a son called Nanda. Through their mother these two were the Buddha's first cousins, and through their father they were the Buddha's half-siblings. Their birth order is uncertain, although the Buddha is normally cited as the eldest. There is no mention anywhere of Mahaprajapati's pregnancies, although what's significant to the overall story is that she was lactating at the time of Maya's death, giving her own child over to a wet nurse in order to feed her nephew herself.[24] Which of her two children was given over to the wet nurse is unknown and largely unimportant. However, it should be noted that birth order carries great significance in past and present Asian cultures. Citing the Buddha as older than his siblings was likely not accurate as much as a narrator's tweak to reflect deference. It also may signify that Siddhartha, though younger in age, was born of the senior queen.[25]

Very little is known about Mahaprajapati's two children other than that they both ordained as monastics later in life, becoming their brother's disciples. Both eventually attained arhatship. Not surprisingly in this androcentric literature, there are more stories about Nanda than his sister, although both are similarly distinguished in the stories by their vanity, a narrative theme elaborated as a fundamental stumbling block to their respective abilities to spiritually awaken. Like their mother, Sundarinanda and Nanda have autobiographical records in the *Khuddaka Nikaya* of the Pali canon, which begin with their past-life encounters with the previous Buddha Padumuttara that inspire their passion for the dharma and their respective aspirations to awaken.

As Mahaprajapati took Maya's place as queen, the innermost royal family grew to five. While there are no stories of her mothering three children, the siblings would have grown up together in the women's quarters of their father's palace, surrounded by many other children and their mothers. Those stories are lost to us, but it's worth recapturing what we can about Sundarinanda and Nanda, the Buddha's half-sister and half-brother.

## SUNDARINANDA

*One hundred thousand eons ago, I was blessed to be born at the time of the Buddha Padumuttara, Great Victor, the Merciful and Compassionate One, Well-Wisher of all that breathe. Growing up in my wealthy father's household, I knew every luxury and happiness. At that time, I heard the Great Teacher giving a discourse on dharma, the ultimately sweet ambrosia that makes known the ultimate truth. As I watched, he conferred on a certain nun the accolade Foremost among Nuns Who Meditate. Hearing those words, my heart broke open with recognition and resolve. I invited the Awakened One to my home and offered him abundant requisites and alms with my own hands. My head at his feet, I invoked my aspiration one day to achieve that supreme position: Foremost among Nuns Who Meditate. "You will achieve that well-wished place," the Wise One told me then. Overjoyed, I spent countless lifetimes creating the causes for my present birth where this aspiration would be fulfilled.*[26]

Born into her father's harem by his junior wife, Sundarinanda was probably older than her brothers, Siddhartha and Nanda. Her name, meaning "Beautiful Joy," was confused in the records with other women named Nanda (Nanda, Abhirupananda, Rupananda, Janapadakalyani, and Janapadakalyani Nanda).[27] There is no way to untangle that skein here, but an obvious conflation appears with Janapadakalyani, who is variously identified as either Sundarinanda or her sister-in-law, wife of Nanda. Mahaprajapati's daughter is described in an early commentary:

> She was born in the Sakyan royal family. They named her Nanda. Afterwards, because of the perfection of her figure, she was known as Sundari-Nanda (Beautiful Nanda), the beauty of the district. She was like [Yasodhara] the auspicious lady of the Kapila clan. There was no need for a lamp in a room of twelve cubits. She illuminated it with the radiance of her body.[28]

While there appear to be no childhood stories of Sundarinanda, her name emerges at the time of upheaval later in Kapilavastu when Sakyas, both women and men, were rapidly leaving household life to take ordination as monastic followers of the Buddha. Probably in her forties by that time, Sundarinanda is said to have felt sad and bereft after the death of her father and the loss of both brothers, her nephew Rahula, her sister-in-law Yasodhara, and her mother Mahaprajapati to the religious life. Half-heartedly, Sundarinanda followed suit, not because she was religiously inclined, but because she missed her family and did not want to be left behind. She thought,

> My elder brother abandoned the kingship of a wheel-turning monarch and went forth. He has become a Buddha, the foremost individual in the world. His son, Prince Rahula, has also gone forth, and my brother, King Nanda. And my mother, Maha-Prajapati-

Gotami and my sister [in-law], Rahulamata, have gone forth. Now what shall I do in the house? I shall go forth.[29]

So she took ordination with her mother and became a nun. Sundarinanda relates in her own words how Mahaprajapati's gentle urging convinced her to take this difficult step:

My eldest brother's the Buddha,
the middle one's likewise a saint;
staying alone in the lay life,
I am exhorted by my mother:

"Child, you're born in the Sakyan clan,
following after the Buddha.
Why do you sit [there] in the house,
bereft of [all your] joy?

"Thought impure is youthful beauty,
under the power of old age;
even a life which is healthy,
ends in disease, ends in dying. . . .

"In no time at all, old age
is going to overpower [it].
Young one, choose the Teaching, O blameless one."

After hearing my mother's words,
I went forth into homelessness
in body, but not in my heart,
still enthralled by youth and beauty.[30]

True to her name, Sundarinanda was caught up in the vanity of her physical beauty and unable to progress in the meditation practices her mother gave her. Embarrassed and aware of her shortcomings, she avoided the Buddha, thinking, "The Teacher disparages and finds fault with beauty." When he gave a teaching, she would send another nun as proxy so she would not have to come in contact with him. However, the all-knowing Buddha saw through her scheme. Seeing that she was intoxicated by her own beauty, he declared,

> Let each one come and receive her exhortation for herself. None of the *Bhikkhunis* may send others.[31]

With no way to get out of it, Sundarinanda reluctantly went before her brother.

As with all his disciples, the Buddha directly saw not only the obstructions to Sundarinanda's spiritual growth but also the antidotes needed to help her overcome them. One size does not fit all. Clearly his teachings on such philosophical abstractions as the Four Noble Truths were not getting through to her. For his sister, he conjured an illusion of a magnificently beautiful woman—one far more resplendent and seductive than herself, Sundarinanda had to admit. However, right before her eyes, the female apparition began to morph into hideousness. A boil appeared on her forehead, oozing pus and blood. Her mouth dribbled with rotten smelling excretions; her breasts shriveled, and her limbs began to shake. Just as her brother intended, Sundarinanda became alarmed and overwhelmed with disgust. He said to her,

> Nanda, look at your own body,
> [also] a sick [and] putrid corpse.
> Through disgustingness cultivate
> [your] mind, well-composed and tranquil.

> Just as is this, so is that;
> Just as is that, so too is this:
> putrid [and] emitting a stench,
> causing delight [only] to fools.

> Considering that in this way,
> industrious by day and night,
> you will see with your own wisdom,
> having turned away in disgust.[32]

A tough lesson requiring a steep learning curve, but the Buddha's tactic did the trick.* Her vanity vanquished by this shocking experience, Sundarinanda found inner peace and soon attained arthatship. She said,

> My defilements are [now] burnt up;
> all [new] existence is destroyed.
> Like elephants with broken chains,
> I am living without constraint.
>
> Being in Best Buddha's presence
> was a very good thing for me.[33]

So purely and diligently did Sundarinanda practice the dharma after this encounter with the Buddha that she eventually earned the accolade Foremost among Nuns Who Meditate, fulfilling her lifetimes-long aspiration.[34] With both her mother and brother as guides, no longer attached to appearances and family, Sundarinanda attained nirvana, the highest state of tranquility and peace.

## NANDA

*In the foregone era of the Blessed One Padumuttara, I gave the great sage a golden-colored cloth. He then made this prophecy to me: "Due to giving this piece of cloth you will have the color of gold . . . [and] incited by your wholesome roots, you will be the younger brother of Gotama the Blessed One." He went on to foretell that in my lifetime as the Buddha's brother, I would be greedy for pleasure, plagued by the tentacles of lust. However, incited by him I would renounce the world, and through my past wholesomeness, I would attain nirvana.*[35]

---

* By seeing him exhort Sundarinanda to use her own wisdom to investigate the insubstantial, transient nature of her appearance, we gain a deep view into the Buddha's teaching method. He does not shame her or preach to her; rather he provides an opportunity for her to see her obstructions for herself and come to her own conclusions. Nowhere is this passage sexist, as some might argue; rather the Buddha's point is that all bodies are subject to decay and, in that regard, worthy objects of meditation. He gave similar meditations to both women and men.

We now turn to Mahaprajapati's son Nanda ("Joy"). Although he was Siddhartha's half-brother, the Pali records refer to him through his maternal line as a cousin (*matuchaputta*).[36] While he is usually cited as younger, it is also sometimes said that he was the infant given over to the wet nurse so his mother could nurse the Bodhisattva at the time of Maya's death, thus making him older. The *Mahavastu* claims Nanda and Siddhartha were co-natal, their births virtually simultaneous.[37]

A mostly insignificant figure, of all the characters in the Buddha's life Nanda is the one who oddly became the subject of a very early biography written in classical Sanskrit by the poet and dramatist Ashvaghosa. The narrative focuses on Nanda's spiritual evolution from hedonist to arhat, although we do learn a few scant details of his family life along the way. The following passages describe the joy Nanda brought his parents at the time of his birth:

> As kindling gives rise to fire, so the younger queen . . . gave birth to a son named Nanda, a bringer of constant joy to his family. He was long-armed and wide-chested, with the shoulders of a lion and the eyes of a bull—and he bore the epithet "handsome" due to his superlative looks. He was like the onset of springtime in his pleasing loveliness, like the rising of the new moon, or the god of love in human form.[38]

For Suddhodana, Nanda and Siddhartha together were his "two good sons," lauded for the glory they brought their father:

> The king brought up the two with much joy, just as great wealth in good hands fosters dharma and pleasure. In time his two sons grew up to do him credit, just as dharma and wealth bring profit to a gentleman with ambitious projects. Between his two good sons the king of the Shakyas stood resplendent like the middle country between the Himalayas and the Vindhya mountains.[39]

The poem skips over Nanda's childhood to land directly on the central conundrum: his youthful, lustful ways. Many other accounts describe his infatuation with his beautiful wife, Janapadakalyani, but none approach the colorful prosody of Ashvaghosa, who demonstrates the dramatist's flourish for vivid, erotic detail:

> Blind with passion, the couple took pleasure in each other, as though they were targets of [Cupid and his bride], as though they were a home to joy and rapture, as though they were a vessel for arousal and satiety. With eyes only for each other's eyes, they hung upon each other's words and rubbed off their cosmetics through caressing each other, so mutually absorbed was the couple. They were resplendent in their play like [two birds] standing in a mountain waterfall intent on love, as though wishing to outdo each other in beauty and splendor. The couple gave each other pleasure by exciting passion in each other, while in languid moments they teasingly inebriated each other by way of mutual entertainment.[40]

Early soft porn! The author's stated purpose was not to titillate but to reveal the extreme opposite of nirvana's sublime equipoise where the flames of sensual desire have been utterly and forever extinguished.[41] Clearly Nanda had his work cut out for him.

Turning to other sources, as youths in Kapilavastu the brothers Nanda and Siddhartha, along with their cousin Devadatta, often appear as rascal competitors up to mischief, demonstrating athletic prowess and pursuing the young ladies. In these stories, Devadatta and Nanda play opposites, the former wicked and the latter well-intentioned if inept. Siddhartha, of course, is perennially the hero. A well-known tale describes Devadatta coming across a magnificent white bull elephant that is being brought into the city as a mount for Siddhartha, who has just defeated him in competitions. Enraged with jealousy, Devadatta kills the elephant with a single smack of his hand, leaving it dead on the spot where it blocks the city gate so no one could pass. Along comes Nanda, who drags the elephant seven paces out of the way. As bystanders cheer Nanda's strength, Siddhartha outdoes both rivals by lifting the elephant with his toe and, "concerned it would fill the city with a horrible stench," hurling it out of the city over seven walls and seven moats,[42] all the while chastising Devadatta and praising Nanda. The sites of these escapades—where the elephant was killed and where it landed, leaving a deep indentation in the ground—became ancient pilgrimage sites noted by the seventh-century Chinese pilgrim Xuanzang.[43] Concern for the poor elephant notwithstanding, the pairing of evil Devadatta and dutiful Nanda is repeated in other stories concerning an archery contest and a wrestling match.

Besides establishing Siddhartha's superiority in every imaginable martial art, the athletic competitions are set up to impress and woo young women. The love story between the Bodhisattva and Yasodhara begins here and is bolstered by accompanying Jataka stories. An especially intriguing Jataka appears in the *Mahavastu*. It begins with the frame story of Yasodhara being courted by both Devadatta and Nanda, not as a maiden but as Siddhartha's wife after he had gone forth to pursue awakening. The argument from both suitors is that since her husband has left her to become a recluse, she should become their "chief queen." In the Jataka version, Yasodhara is a tigress who not only rejects but also insults both suitors (Nanda a bull, and Devadatta an elephant) in favor of her beloved Bodhisattva (a lion).[44]

To close the gap between Nanda's lust and his eventual arhatship, we must return to his marriage with the alluring Janapadakalyani. The story is told in many different ways, often with thinly veiled, bawdy humor. Clearly the storytellers had fun with this clumsy love story, although underlying the playfulness is a serious homily on overcoming life's transient pleasures as an essential step toward the goal of final liberation. To appeal to public audiences, the narrators employed absurdity—and a generous dollop of sexism—to deliver the message.

Nanda's story begins when his brother, Siddhartha (now the Buddha), returns home to Kapilavastu for the first time, six or seven years after his enlightenment.* Sanskrit versions abound with detailed accounts of the Gautama family members' responses upon seeing their beloved kinsman again after his long absence. A theme that runs through all these episodes is that the Buddha has returned not as the confused son, husband, father, prince, and brother the family once knew, but as an enlightened being whose sole purpose is to free all beings, including them, from the sufferings of ordinary life. Needless to say, the family encounters are awkward and, in Nanda's case, get off to a rough start, since the Buddha arrives on the very day Nanda is set to marry Janapadakalyani. While Ashvaghosa penned an

---

* The Sanskrit chronology is followed here. See Garling, *Stars at Dawn*, 203n16 for numerous sources.

entire text around this story, the summary that follows captures highlights, some of which are also taken from the *Abhinishkramanasutra*.

The Buddha stops by to take a meal as the marriage festivities are under way. Wishing his brother "good luck," he hands Nanda his alms bowl and departs. Out of politeness, Nanda does not call out to return the bowl but quickly follows after his brother, who leads him all the way back to his monastery. Distraught, with tears streaming down her face, Janapadakalyani cries out from a window that her new husband should return quickly. Once at the monastery the Buddha asks Nanda if he would like to ordain and, despite the infatuation he feels for his wife, Nanda agrees.

A big mistake, but too late. Nanda ordains as a monk but is miserable and deeply regrets what he has done:

> Nanda knew no gladness; he bore the signs ordained by the teacher on his body, but not in his heart, and was discomfited by conjectures about his wife . . . he lived in a monastery, but found no peace.[45]

His vanity as yet unbridled, Nanda takes to imitating the Buddha in manners of dress, and when this is disallowed, he garishly adorns himself with spangled robes, silk slippers, and painted eyes, carrying an umbrella (a symbol of royalty) in his left hand.[46] Pretty ridiculous. Once again the Buddha intervenes, but Nanda is only becoming more miserable and soon seeks to run away to return to the bedchamber of his adored wife. The Buddha comes across him hiding behind a tree and asks his brother what is wrong. Nanda replies,

> I was going back to my home for I cannot reconcile myself to give up the pleasures of my palace and the society of [Janapadakalyani], and I can find no comfort in the practice of [celibacy], I therefore desire to give up this attempt and to return home.[47]

With this, the story shifts, and the Buddha takes Nanda through the sky on a magical journey to the heavenly realms, resplendent with celestial dancing girls who are, Nanda must admit, far more beautiful than his wife. Believing that these heavenly maidens will be his reward upon attaining arhatship, the foolish Nanda returns to the monastery, roused to practice the dharma relentlessly in order to fulfill his goatish fantasies.

However, with the increasing realization of profound meditative states, Nanda soon sees the folly of his ways. No longer does he desire women, sex, or the life of a family man. Contented at last, he settles peacefully into monkhood and eventually attains arhatship. Of Nanda's transformation, the Buddha said,

> Even as rain breaks through an ill-thatched house,
> So lust breaks through an ill-trained mind.
>
> Even as rain breaks not through a well-thatched house,
> So lust breaks not through a well-trained mind.[48]

So, after innumerable lifetimes engaged in wholesome deeds and a final lifetime overcoming erotic distractions, Nanda attained his longed-for goal of nirvana. It is not without irony that the Buddha deemed his brother Foremost among Those Who Guard the Senses.[49]

## The Great Departure

We return now to Kapilavastu during the time of Siddhartha's marriage, when he too is experiencing youthful struggles, although they are of the opposite kind. Now a young husband with a wife and harem of his own, he is eager to give up erotic pleasures and has no interest in succeeding his father as king. Grief suffuses the palace as he acts out his inner turmoil in ways that make it clear he will soon be leaving home. The entire royal household—his mother, father, wife, friends, and harem—become engaged in this drama, as demonstrated by a profusion of heart-wrenching stories that emerge during the Bodhisattva's final chapter as a prince. From all sides, Siddhartha's loved ones are deeply distressed and step forward to reason with him and thwart his departure. No one is more ardently invested in keeping him home than his mother.

With abiding sadness, speaking for Mahaprajapati as well as for himself, Suddhodana says to his son,

> Pray do not [leave] my lotus-eyed and charmingly beautiful son. Great grief would I suffer if I were bereft of you. Your mother as well as I would go to unwelcome death. What sort of special bliss is

this then that for its sake you would leave me, your people and your kingdom? Live the way your father lived, my son and be content, as long as I live or as long as she, your mother, will live. For seeing you go away, of a surety I will die.[50]

So anxious is Mahaprajapati that she has nightmares about her son's departure. From the Sanskrit tradition, the dreams that follow have different nuances. In the first, from the *Abhinishkramanasutra*, we feel a sad sense of chaos and helplessness:

> On this night, also, the Queen Mother Gotami, called Prajapati, in her sleep had the following dream—she thought she saw a white ox-King in the midst of the city going on in a wistful way bellowing and crying, while no one in the place was able to get before it to stop it or hinder it.[51]

In the *Mahavastu* variant of the same dream, we feel her profound sadness together with a mother's unconditional love in the face of losing a son she equates with love itself. Here she appears to accept Siddhartha's decision to leave home, acknowledging that her obstinate son has made up his mind. Tenderly recounting her dream to him, she says,

> My boy, who art beautiful as a mass of gold, in my dream I saw a noble bull, white, with an exceeding lovely hump, with an extra horn, whose very motion spoke of love, and it was sleek of body.
> The bull bellowed most sweetly, and ran out of Kapilavastu, taking the path his heart was bent on. There is none that can beat his bellowing when he bellows—the noble bull that is like a heap of flowers.[52]

Mahaprajapti's dreams in the *Sanghabhedavastu* are more prophetic. Reflecting the Sanskrit tradition where Rahula was conceived the night of Siddhartha's Great Departure, she dreams the moon is eclipsed by Rahu,* the

---

* While the Pali tradition translates Rahula as "fetter," the Sanskrit tradition tells us Rahula was so named because of an eclipse that occurred on the night of his birth. (In Indian mythology, an eclipse occurs when the god Rahu swallows the sun or the moon.)

sun rises in the east, and a large crowd of smiling people bow down before her.[53] Perhaps these last details augur the brilliance of the dharma the Buddha would bring to the world and her joy as his esteemed mother. They may also be suggestive of the reverence with which she would be remembered in her future role as a leader of women and the first Buddhist nun.

Perhaps most surprising among these glimpses into Mahaprajapati's personal world during this time are two stories that recall her role as chief consort in the king's household and advisor to the ladies of Siddhartha's harem. Here we catch a peek into the hidden life within the private women's quarters. We know Siddhartha spent a lot of time there, but now we see vivid details from the other side of the diaphanous curtain. The following summary comes from the *Abhinishkramanasutra*.

Frantic that her son will soon leave, Mahaprajapati cajoles the consorts to intensify their seductive efforts to engage him. Perhaps more sex will do the trick and keep him at home. To bolster her argument, she points out that his satisfaction is their satisfaction; in other words, if he leaves home the women will not only have failed in their duties but will be bereft of sexual gratification themselves.

> Mahaprajapati Gotami within the palace assembled all the women of pleasure and upbraided them with their want of influence over the mind of the prince—"Let none of you," she said, "fail to provide amusement for him night and day; let there be no interval of darkness, and never be without wine and burning perfumes; let there be guards at every door to prevent ingress or egress. For, remember, if the prince escape, there will be no other pleasure within the palace."[54]

This scene is further dramatized in the *Lalitavistara*. Here Mahapraja-pati is not just enlisting the consorts' seductive skills but is also asking them to arm themselves with weapons lest he try to escape. These methods are intended only to thwart Siddhartha, of course, as no harm should ever come to their beloved prince. We hear the urgency in Mahaprajapati's voice as she directs the women to quickly prepare themselves for his arrival:

> Adorn yourselves with necklaces of jewels and pearls;
> Wear flower ornaments, half-moon ornaments, and chains.

Adorn yourselves with belts, rings, and earrings;
Take care to fasten your anklets well.

Should this benefactor of humans and gods, who acts like a
      proud elephant,
Try to escape in a hasty manner,
You should confront him in such a way
That no harm is done to him.

You girls with lances in your hands,
Who surround the bed of this pure being,
You must not slip into laziness,
But watch him with eyes like a butterfly.

In order to guard the Prince,
Adorn this palace with bejeweled lattices
And take up your flutes and play them to your fullest.
Protect the Stainless Being through the night!

Keep each other awake
And do not rest.
Otherwise he may certainly leave his home behind,
Abandoning the kingdom and all his subjects.

If he were to leave home,
Then the royal palace would become a place with no joy.
The continuity of the royal lineage, which has endured so long,
Would become interrupted.[55]

Thus Mahaprajapati deploys all her skills and wisdom as mother, queen, and chief consort. Besides her personal grief at the prospect of losing her son, it is her duty as queen to preserve and uphold the royal succession for the sake of her husband and the Sakya people. Parental persuasion has not been effective, so her final tactic is to enlist the seductive powers of the harem ladies. A Buddhist lesson is sewn into the fabric of this story, since desire and attachments—here misogynized as women—are the biggest obstacles to realization. Although the Bodhisattva seeks to escape desire and attachment, his family seeks to use them as lures.

Nothing works, of course, and the prince takes off in the night on horseback, guided by his trusted charioteer, Chandaka, to pursue the religious life. After traveling some distance, they say their good-byes. With sadness, Chandaka chides Siddhartha for causing grief to his parents, particularly his mother. He says,

> Gotami, too, who has nourished you so long, fed you with milk when a helpless child, such love as hers cannot easily be forgotten; it is impossible surely to turn the back on a benefactor;
>
> The highly gifted (virtuous) mother of a child, is ever respected by the most distinguished families; to inherit distinction and then to turn round is not the mark of a distinguished man.[56]

In the Sanskrit *Buddhacarita*, Chandaka's language is even stronger,

> You [should not] forget like an ingrate [the] kind treatment [of] the queen, your second mother, who exhausted herself in bringing you up.[57]

Meanwhile Suddhodana sends a posse of ministers to retrieve his son. Finally finding Siddhartha after traveling for several days, they invoke his mother's distress to incite him to return:

> Your loving mother who cherished you so kindly, with no regard for self, through years of care, as the cow deprived of her calf, weeps and laments, forgetting to eat or sleep;
>
> You surely ought to return to her at once, to protect her life from evil; as a solitary bird, away from its fellows, or as the lonely elephant, wandering in the jungle.[58]

Back at the palace everyone is distraught. Mahaprajapati is frantic, just as she was when the prince could not be found during the plowing festival:

> Mahaprajapati Gautami collapsed on the ground lamenting and said to King Suddhodana: "Your Majesty, get my son back quickly."[59]

Chandaka returns to Kapilavastu and delivers the prince's regal ornaments to the king and queen, but Mahaprajapati finds them so painful
to look at that she has them thrown into a pond.[60] Her grief is vividly
dramatized in the *Abhinishkramanasutra*:

> Like a cow bereaved of its calf, [she] uttered every kind of lamentable
> cry, unable to control herself she raised her hands and said, "My son!
> My son! Alas, my child!"[61]

Years later, while speaking to his monks, the Buddha acknowledged the
pain his departure brought his parents:

> While still young, a black-haired boy blessed with youth, in the
> first phase of my life, I shaved off my hair and beard—though my
> mother and father wished otherwise and grieved with tearful faces—
> and I put on the yellow robe and went forth from the house life into
> homelessness.[62]

Unlike the prince's wife, Yasodhara, whose angry lament focuses on her
personal loss, Mahaprajapati's anguish arises more from her motherly worry
over how her son, now a wandering mendicant, will survive in the forest.
Raised with every manner of luxury, how is he going to get by sleeping on
the hard ground and begging for food? It is incomprehensible to her that
the delicate boy she held, bathed, and nurtured for twenty-nine years would
choose rags and alms over the lavish privileges of his upbringing. Scandal
over his departure was one thing, but as his mother, Mahaprajapati is most
concerned for her son's health and safety. With "tear-strewn face," she
agonizes,

> Ought such a one live in a hermitage? . . .
> His feet are soft . . . Shall they tread on the hard ground of the jungle?
> His powerful body is accustomed to sitting or lying on the palace
>     roof . . . How will it fare in the forest in the heat, the cold, and
>     the rains?
> He is ennobled by race, goodness, strength, beauty, learning,
>     majesty and youth. . . . Is he to practise begging alms from
>     others?

> He has been sleeping on a spotless golden bed . . . How then shall he
> lie in accordance with his vows on the ground with only a piece
> of cloth . . . ?[63]

Thus stricken with thoughts of her son, Mahaprajapati lies weeping on the ground. The harem women, also consumed with grief, tenderly raise her up and wipe her tears.

We're told that Mahaprajapati went blind from weeping for her son. Just as Western traditions cite a "broken heart" as evidence of grief, so these stories employ the metaphor of blindness to capture this mother's sorrow. Her blindness also suggests that life as she knew it drew to a close and darkness set in when her son left home. It would not be until twelve years later that he would come back—as the Buddha—and her eyesight would return. Not only would she see her son again, but her life would enter its spectacular, concluding chapter. Illuminated by the dharma, with her son as her teacher, Mahaprajapati's own spiritual journey would commence, not alone but in the company and companionship of five hundred Sakya women.

### Mahaprajapati as Siddhartha's Birth Mother: Past-Life Stories

Often compared to Aesop's fables, Buddhism's Jataka tales draw us deeply into an alternative world that often expresses emotions and relationships between characters that are rarely found in the literature's "real-life" narratives. Framed as told by the Buddha himself to his monks, they are typically inserted as backstories to explain behaviors and outcomes that are karmically traceable to previous lifetimes. These tales conclude with the Buddha naming who's who among the characters, thereby linking the past to the present. This is the format in the following four Jatakas, which vividly illustrate a profound, loving intimacy between Mahaprajapati and her son. All four are exceptional because they portray Mahaprajapati as the Buddha's birth mother.

#### THE ELEPHANT AND HIS BLIND MOTHER

This Jataka is offered as an explanation for the grief and blindness Mahaprajapati experienced as a result of her son's absence, mentioned earlier. It concerns a young bull elephant (the Bodhisattva) caring for his elderly, blind mother (Mahaprajapati). Especially poignant in this story is the reversal of roles: just as his mother once tenderly cared for him as a helpless child, so now he is committed to caring for her when she is elderly and infirm. Of added interest here is that the character of the king (Nanda) supports the Bodhisattva's commitment to his mother. The following summary combines elements from several variants.[64]

The story opens in a lush, deep jungle on the slopes of the Himalayas, home to cave-dwelling hermits and an abundance of wildlife.

> [There was] a wood full of thousands of flowering and fruit-bearing trees. It had lotus pools and retreats and was the resort of a number of seers, being secluded and remote.[65]

Here dwelt a large herd of mighty, six-tusked elephants. Among them— the mightiest of all—was a young bull elephant, his head the color of cochineal, his body like a white lotus. From the time of his birth, this young elephant was piously devoted to his mother. When he grew up, he attended to her every need, providing for her food and drink before eating and drinking himself. He groomed and cleaned her with vines from the forest and washed her body with fresh water. In this way, he always kindly looked after his mother with filial love and the respect due to a teacher.

Whenever his mother was resting, the young elephant would roam about nearby with his elephant friends. One day a hunter spotted him and, dazzled by the magnificence of this beast, brought word to the king that he should acquire him for a mount:

> Your majesty . . . there is such a young elephant living in the forest yonder, such a beautiful and handsome one as would be suitable for your majesty.[66]

The king captured the young elephant himself and took him into the royal stable, showering him with favors, ornaments, and delicious food. But the young elephant took no interest, wasting away and weeping with worry now that he was separated from his mother. He vowed not to eat or drink until he could once again bring her food and drink, and care for her.

Now the king was righteous and kind, always intent on caring for others. He became quite concerned about his charge's dwindling spirit and kindly asked the young elephant why he was so unhappy. In human speech, the elephant replied,

> What I need is nothing that can be supplied to me in service or food. For my mother dwells in the forest yonder, and she is old, advanced in years, past her prime, blind and infirm. Ever since I grew to years of discretion, I do not remember myself eating before I gave food and drink to my mother. Though it be the death of me here, it is my resolve that I will not myself take food or drink again without giving my mother some.[67]

Astonished by this supreme expression of filial devotion, the king was also concerned. Not wishing to cause further suffering, he immediately released the young elephant to return to his mother, saying,

> Go and welcome, thou faithful elephant [King],
> Nourish and cherish thy [mother] as in duty bound.
> I would rather lose my life, and end it now,
> Than cause thee . . . the grief of separation.[68]

The young elephant headed straight back to the jungle. Meanwhile, his mother had become confused and distraught when he had not returned. Overwhelmed with grief, she went blind from weeping. Wandering alone and lost in the jungle, tired and hungry, she became tangled in vines and covered with filth:

> But meantime, his mother from grief at losing her son, had wept herself blind, and so had wandered away from that place where she had dwelt before, nor could she find her way back to the spot she had left.[69]

The young elephant looked everywhere for her when he returned but could not find her. Finally, climbing to the highest hilltop, he roared a tremendous roar that echoed through the hills and valleys. Knowing well her son's voice, his mother bellowed in response. Joyfully the two were reunited, and the devoted son resumed his diligent, loving care. Finding that his mother had gone blind, he filled his trunk with fresh water and gently rinsed her eyes. As the muck washed away, her sight returned even more clearly than before. Happily gazing on her son once again, she said,

> My son, where did you go, leaving me in my helplessness and blindness?[70]

As he explained the circumstances of his absence, his mother became very pleased and danced with joy. With gratitude rather than rancor toward the king, she expressed the wish that he and his family would rejoice in each other's company and always take care of each other just as she and her son were able to do once again.[71]

The Buddha later told this story to his monks to explain Mahaprajapati's grief when he went forth as a young man, concluding with words that expressed his love for her:

> I was that noble elephant . . . and my mother was the female elephant. So today as well am I her son, and Gotami is dearly beloved of me.[72]

## THE CULA-NANDIYA JATAKA

While Jatakas often serve to soothe and inform, they are also no strangers to violence and cruelty. The endings are by no means always happy, as we see in the following story where the Bodhisattva gives his life to save his mother. The theme of blindness recurs, where the primary characters Nandiya (the Bodhisattva) and Cula-nandiya (Ananda) are monkey brothers who take care of their blind mother (Mahaprajapati) and head up a herd of eighty thousand monkeys. The cruel hunter is the ever-wicked Devadatta.

On the slopes of the Himalayas, Nandiya and Cula-nandiya spent their days gathering sweet, wild fruit from the trees, which they sent via messengers to their blind mother who lived at some distance, confined to her lair. Unbeknownst to them, the messengers did not deliver the food but ate it themselves. Their mother was starving, swiftly becoming little more than skin and bones.

One day Nandiya visited her and was appalled by her condition. Overcome with remorse that he had not taken better care of her himself, he called out to Cula-nandiya,

Brother . . . you tend the herd and I will care for our mother.[73]

But his brother was of the same mind, and so the two of them left the herd and took their mother away to a forest of banyan trees where they cared for her together.

Now one day a hunter was returning home, having caught nothing at all to feed his family. Eying the banyan grove he decided to give his luck one more try. As he approached, he saw the blind mother monkey, weak with age, and decided she would be easy prey. However, as the hunter raised his bow, Nandiya spotted him and quickly said to his brother,

> [Cula-nandiya], my dear, this man wants to shoot our mother! I will save her life. When I am dead, do you take care of her.

And so Nandiya jumped out of the tree, saying,

> Don't shoot my mother! She is blind and weak for age. I will save her life; don't kill her, but kill me instead!

Without hesitating, the cruel hunter shot and killed Nandiya and then turned to shoot the mother monkey. At this Cula-nandiya reflected,

> Yon hunter wants to shoot my mother. Even if she only lives a day, she will have received the gift of life. I will give my life for hers.[74]

And so the scene repeats. Cula-nandiya too was killed, and then the hunter killed their mother anyway. Stringing all three monkeys on a pole, he triumphantly set out for home with his day's catch. However, karmic justice did not delay. At that very moment, the hunter's home was struck by lightning, killing his wife and two children. As the hunter wailed and wept with arms outstretched, the earth yawned open, swallowing him into the depths of hell in a sea of flames.

## CULLADHAMMAPALA JATAKA

The following story is so cruel it is painful to read. At the same time, it pulls us into the boundless depths of a mother's love where she would willingly give up her life for her child. We also see a timeless story of savage domestic abuse and a man cruelly commanding dominion over a woman. The setting is a royal palace where the little prince Dhammapala (the Bodhisattva) is seven months old, seated on the lap of his adoring mother, the queen Canda (Mahaprajapati). The evil King Mahapatapa (Devadatta) is her husband.[75]

Queen Canda's heart brimmed with joy as she delighted in the company of her infant son, bathing him in scented water, dressing him, and playing with him. So absorbed was she, "filled with a mother's love for her child," that she failed to notice that her husband had entered the room. He paused, staring at her, expecting her to stand in obeisance. Enraged that she did not notice him, he blamed their son for the perceived slight and vowed to have the baby murdered. As the king stormed off in a jealous rage, Canda held her son to her breast, weeping and trembling with fear.

Back on his throne, the king ordered the executioner to gather his tools of torture and fetch the child. When the queen resisted, the executioner struck her, grabbed her son out of her arms and took him before the king. "What is your pleasure, Sire?" the executioner asked. "Cut off Dhammapala's hands," the king responded.

Sobbing, the queen implored him,

> Great king, my boy is only a child, seven months old. He knows nothing. The fault is not his. If there be any fault, it is mine. Therefore bid my hands to be cut off.

But the king ignored her, and the boy's tiny hands were chopped off. Holding them tenderly, bleeding in her lap Canda lamented and wept.

Next the king ordered the baby's feet cut off. Again, Canda begged that her feet, not his, be taken. But the king gave a sign to the executioner and Dhammapala's tiny feet were cut off. Holding them in her blood-soaked lap, Canda again implored her husband,

> My lord, Mahapatapa, his hands and feet are cut off. A mother is bound to support her children. I will work for wages and support my son. Give him to me.

But next the king ordered the baby's head chopped off. Again, Canda begged that it be hers instead, crying out,

> Slay not the heir that from thy loins did spring. . . .
> Slay not the boy who owes his life to thee.

Not only was the baby beheaded, but the king had his body thrown into the air and chopped to bits:

> Then . . . catching it with the edge of his sword, [the executioner] encircled him with sword cuts, as it were with a garland, and scattered the bits on the dais [around the throne].

Gathering the bloody remains of her son's flesh onto her lap, Canda now directed her anguished words to her deceased child:

> Dhammapala . . . by right of birth [you were] the lord of the earth:
> Thy arms, once bathed in the oil of sandalwood, lie steeped in
>      blood.
> My fitful breath alas! is choked with sighs and broken cries.

Lamenting thus, utterly devastated, "her heart broke as a bamboo snaps, when the grove is on fire." Canda fell dead on the spot from grief. A fiery chasm opened in the earth swallowing the king and plunging him into the depths of hell.

Whew. Absolutely a hard read. Yet that is the narrative's purpose. Extricating ourselves from the dreadful details, we find a gifted storyteller pulling out all the stops to evince the fathomless mother's love that Mahaprajapati felt for her son.

## THE JATAKA OF NALINI

There are many different versions of this next ancient tale, which centers on a young ascetic's fall from innocence. This story is thought to be pre-Buddhist in origin, with possible antecedents in Mesopotamia.[76] As told in the *Mahavastu*, we find a curious blended family where the father, Kasyapa (Suddhodana), is a kindly, powerful seer living in a remote forest hermitage; the mother is a doe (Mahaprajapati); and their son is a human boy (the Bodhisattva) named Ekasringa. Although a doe, his mother suckles him, mentors him, and is closely bonded with her son in every way.

The story opens as Kasyapa took ill and passed urine mixed with semen in a stone pot. Along came the doe who mistakenly drank from the pot, thinking it held water. Ripe for conception, her lips smeared with semen, she licked her sexual orifice and conceived a child. Time passed, and she gave birth to a human boy.

Kasyapa noticed this and, puzzled, asked himself,

How is it that the doe, being a brute, has a human offspring?[77]

He reflected deeply and, with his superior insight, came to understand the method of the doe's conception, further realizing that he was the boy's father. The text reads,

> So carrying the infant in his cloak of antelope's hide he took him to his hermitage, the doe following behind him. The seer cut the child's umbilical cord with a knife, rubbed him with sesamum oil, and washed off the impurities of the womb with sweet water. He put the child to the doe's teat and she suckled him. He even put the doe's teat in the child's mouth.[78]

The doe would roam with her herd, returning to the hermitage to suckle her child and wash him with her tongue. As the boy grew older, he would grasp her teat for himself and roam with her in the forest, with the other young deer as his playmates. When Ekasringa came of age, he cared for both his parents, sweeping the hermitage, fetching water, and tending the fire. He never took food for himself until they had eaten first. With his father as his teacher, and "by constant application of vigilance, endeavor, effort and exertion," he too became an esteemed rishi, "chaste ... powerful and influential, known among devas and men."

In many ascetic traditions, including those of ancient India, chastity is the key to spiritual power. So far Ekasringa is totally innocent of sex and women, but this is about to change.

The scene turns to a nearby king who had many daughters and desperately wanted a son. Hearing of Ekasringa's great gifts, he determined that the young ascetic would make an ideal son-in-law. Loading carriages with an abundance of delicious, sweet foods and drink, he dispatched his daughter Nalini (Yasodhara) and her female attendants, along with a retinue of ministers, to the hermitage. With the clatter of their arrival, all the birds and deer fled in distress. Ekasringa was curious but clueless about what was going on. He had never seen a human female or garments other than antelope hide, and before his eyes were royal maids laughing and playing, resplendent in finery and jewels.

What happens next is pretty obvious. A Pali version was deemed so pornographic it went untranslated until recently.[79] This version is fairly tame, with the seduction sequence taking place over several visits. First, Nalini enticed the young sage with her gifts of sweet foods and drink, which utterly charmed him since all he had ever eaten were bitter roots and berries. Then she invited him to enter her "portable hut"—her horse-drawn carriage—but he refused, offended that it seemed to be yoked to deer. As she plied him with kisses and embraces, he began to notice that her female body was different from his. A narrative segue tells us that they had been husband and wife in many past lifetimes.

Soon Nalini left and Ekasringa returned to the hermitage, so preoccupied with the ravishing Nalini that he completely neglected his duties. His father queried him and quickly figured out what happened. Kasyapa warned his son to stay away from women, but meanwhile the king plotted his daughter's next visit, having her travel to the hermitage this time by boat. The romantic storyline mostly repeats, with the lovers' ardor all the more intense. Nalini then persuaded Ekasringa to return home with her where, unbeknownst to him, a priest married them in a traditional fire ceremony.

Their marriage still not consummated, the couple returned to the hermitage, where Ekasringa's doe mother spoke for the first time, asking him where he had been. Soon enough she too figured out what was going on and, further, that her son had just married a princess. Acknowledging their inviolable bond, both parents gave their blessing. The couple returned to her home and over time had thirty-two sons, with Ekasringa eventually succeeding his father-in-law as king. After many years, he anointed his eldest son as his successor, returned to forest life, and once again achieved the superior ascetic powers he had attained as a youth.

4

# Reunion of Mother and Son

Just as Mahaprajapati's life was upended when Maya died, it was about to happen all over again. Twelve years had passed since Siddhartha left home. For him, those years were momentous indeed: he became a fully enlightened buddha, began to teach the dharma, and garnered a vast following of monks and laypeople as his emerging ministry took root (the order of nuns had not yet been established). In contrast, his family back home in Kapilavastu languished in a cloud of sadness: Suddhodana was still without an heir; Yasodhara was in limbo as a wife without a husband; Rahula had never known his father; and Mahaprajapati bided her days in heartache waiting for her son to come home. While Siddhartha's family did not understand his reasons for leaving, they remembered his promise to return. Mahaprajapati would probably have been in her sixties when this finally took place.*

## The Buddha Returns to Kapilavastu

Word reaches Kapilavastu that their prodigal son has become a famous saint, teaching a new doctrine of truth called *dharma* throughout the regions of

---

* The texts are contradictory about her age throughout.

Magadha in India to the south and west of the Sakya kingdom. Suddho-dana hears the news with delight and anticipation. He misses his son very much and determines that if Siddhartha is spreading good will in distant lands, it is high time he come home to share some of that beneficence with his family. The king dispatches the family confidante, Kalodayin, to relay his wishes:

> Say respectfully to Siddhartha: You formerly promised to come back after enlightenment. Now I hope you will keep your former promise and come back at the right time to see me.[1]

After a rapid exchange of messages, his son—now the Buddha—makes the long trek home, accompanied by a retinue of more than five hundred monks. Joyfully anticipating his son's arrival, the king has his ministers prepare a large, well-appointed encampment outside of town called the Nigrodha (Banyan) Grove. He further instructs that the streets of Kapilavastu be lavishly festooned with banners and flowers to welcome their prince:

> The Buddha will come. You have to adorn the city and make it clean to the utmost degree, clean the streets, erect flags and banners all over the city, provide abundant flowers and perfumes and wait for consecrating him.[2]

Overjoyed to hear that her son has returned, Mahaprajapati rides out to the Nigrodha Grove in a chariot with her husband and Yasodhara to welcome him. Recall that she is blind. Although she cannot see the festivities, she is thrilled to hear the loud jubilation of the crowds. A throng of eager Sakyas has already gathered to see their prince, but some of them are skeptical. What's all the fuss about Siddhartha's alleged accomplishments? His uncles, the Sakya princes, in particular are arrogantly expecting that their nephew will pay them and the king obeisance by bowing down to them in the tradition of their caste and tribe.

Through his direct insight, the Buddha knows this to be the case. However, he also knows that everything has changed—for real. No longer is he a scion in the lineage of the Sakyas, but the successor in a long line of enlightened buddhas. Not only would it be untoward for him to bow to family members, but their heads would split open into seven pieces if he were to do so (this same conundrum arose earlier when the infant Bodhisattva was taken to the temple to pay homage to the clan goddess, Abhayadevi). Sizing up the predicament, out of compassion for his family, the Buddha preemptively rises into the air and performs miracles, manifesting the supernormal powers (*siddhis*) that naturally arise as a side effect of enlightenment. Not only does this prove his attainments to them once and for all, but surreptitiously, by rising above the Sakyas' heads, he does their prostrations for them.

As Mahaprajapati's chariot approaches, the Sakyas are shouting, "Bravo! Bravo!" over the miracle of water streaming in jets from the Buddha's body. Because she cannot see what is happening, she asks her daughter-in-law to explain:

What is the meaning of these thousand shouts of bravo?

Cupping her hands together, Yasodhara collects some of the blessed water and replies,

Here is the Exalted One standing in the air and performing various and diverse miracles. . . . But you cannot see them.
Come, I shall contrive that you see them.[3]

Yasodhara gently bathes Mahaprajapati's eyes with the sacred water, and lo, her blindness is "pierced through the virtue of the Buddha."[4] Her vision restored, Mahaprajapati and her son are reunited at last. Her joyful gaze clearly sees the radiance of the Buddha, who is still Siddhartha in this mother's heart. Bowing down at his feet, she reverently pays homage to him, then joins her husband sitting to one side, as parents and son catch up on news.

## Turning to the Dharma

Meeting with their son in the Nigrodha Grove was just the first step in the family becoming reacquainted. Quite understandably, no one knew what to make of Siddhartha's transformation. What exactly did becoming a buddha mean? How were family members to resume their former relationships with him? What was different, and what was the same? What did it mean to be the father, mother, wife, or son of a buddha? To address questions such as these, ancient storytellers skillfully spun anecdotes that clarified the family's "new normal," not just for what it meant to them but also what it meant to their Buddhist audiences.

In one such story, the king is aghast to hear that his son, the newly arrived Buddha, is passing from door to door in Kapilavastu begging for alms. Embarrassed and outraged, Suddhodana meets his son in the street and upbraids him for his unprincely conduct, an indignity both to the family and their proud line of Sakya ancestors. Why not just come home to the palace for dinner? In the conversation that follows, the Buddha gently explains that his behavior and allegiance no longer stem from family bloodlines but from his karmic ancestry and that of the enlightened buddhas. He is no longer beholden to the Sakya clan but to the Buddha clan. The king has more struggles ahead before he can accept that his relationship with his son is forever changed.

In a related story, we learn that Yasodhara desperately hopes for a reconciliation with her husband. She is still furious that he left and has been unhappily coping with life as an abandoned wife and single mother. When the Buddha accepts his father's invitation to dinner in the palace (bringing along his assembly of five hundred or so monks), she refuses to appear, saying that he must come to her private quarters instead. Out of kindness, he does so with two attendants in tow, even allowing her to embrace his feet, which normally would be forbidden. (These were necessary karmic steps, he had earlier explained to his monks, preparing Yasodhara and other harem women for eventual ordination.[5]) Despite Yasodhara's tears and anguish during their encounter, there is no turning back. He is not going to return as her beloved husband. Yasodhara's new normal is to give up any hope of saving her marriage and to face the future alone.

Only Mahaprajapati takes her son's return in stride. There are no rough spots for her, when all she has ever wanted is to see her cherished son again. Siddhartha or Buddha, he is simply her son. Rejoicing in his presence, her mother's love for him flows forward effortlessly and unconditionally as demonstrated over and over in the stories that follow.

After their first meeting in the Nigrodha Grove, Mahaprajapati too invites the Buddha and his monks to dinner. Here we catch a glimpse of harem life, as her invitation is for the monastics to take a meal in the women's quarters of the palace, the queen's personal domain as chief consort. She has been the matriarch of this all-female community since the time of Maya's death, more than forty years earlier. Many of these women would have been Siddhartha's former consorts too. No doubt they recalled the night of his Great Departure, their seductive efforts to keep him home, and the sorrow that followed in the palace and kingdom. We can only imagine their emotional responses to the prince's return, but we're told they followed Mahaprajapati's lead in welcoming him back. The following story is found in the *Mahavastu*.[6]

Unlike her husband and daughter-in-law, Mahaprajapati readily grasps the utter transformation that has taken place in her son. Bowing to his feet with humility and reverence, she says, "Let the Exalted One consent to eat tomorrow at my house." Overflowing with joy when he consents, Mahaprajapati sets about all manner of effusive preparations. Just as the king had Kapilavastu festooned in welcome, her house is swept top to bottom, draped with fine cloth, strewn with heaps of flowers, and made fragrant with the finest incense. A worthy seat is specially prepared for her son, with careful attention to seating arrangements according to rank for the attending monks.

The Buddha and his retinue arrive dressed in simple mendicant robes, holding their alms bowls. Even though Mahaprajapati is queen and always doted on by servants, she serves her guests piously and joyously with her own hands:

> And Mahaprajapati Gautami with her own hands regaled and served with plentiful solid and soft food first the Buddha and then the company of his monks.

What happens next is of special significance not just to Mahaprajapati's personal story but to the story of the founding of the nun's order. In detail not found elsewhere, we're told the Buddha gives his mother and her assembly of women their first dharma teaching:

> When the Exalted One had finished eating, washed his hands and put away his bowl, and the company of monks had done likewise, he gave Mahaprajapati Gautami and the women of the court a graduated discourse on dharma.

What exactly does that mean?

> Now this is what the graduated discourse of exalted Buddhas is, namely, a discourse on charity, a discourse on morality, a discourse on heaven, a discourse on merit and a discourse on the fruition of merit.

An arrow of insight pierces Mahaprajapati's heart. Instantly she understands the meaning of her son's words. So the Buddha continued:

> And then the Exalted One revealed to her the four [noble] truths of ill, the arising of ill, the cessation of ill, and the Way leading to the cessation of ill. And while she sat there on her seat, Mahaprajapati Gautami won a clear dharma-insight, pure and unsullied into things.

Mahaprajapati is struck with profound understanding and attains stream entry, or the first stage in the four levels of realization leading to arhatship from which there is no turning back.[7] In that moment, presiding as queen and surrounded by a close-knit community of women, her life turns inexorably to dharma.

Mahaprajapati was undoubtedly the first Sakya woman to become a laywoman, or *upasika*, in the burgeoning community of faithful that comprised early Buddhism. The texts don't comment on the reactions of the harem women after this first dharma teaching, but we know the experience transformed them too, since in stories that follow they also became *upasikas* and looked to their queen for leadership as the new faith took root and flourished among the Sakyas. Later still, many of them joined Mahaprajapati in taking the added step of ordaining as nuns.

With the Buddha's return, Mahaprajapati's star was rising again. No longer the mother of an errant prince who had disrupted the kingdom and disappointed his kin, now she was the mother of the Blessed One, the Buddha, the newly minted minister of dharma, who fulfilled his promise to return to his people with messages of truth that would free them from worldly suffering. In her twin roles as mother and queen, she was now the most intimate relation—female or male—to both a buddha and a king.[8] It is worth a pause to reflect on this turning point in her life. Momentous for her, of course, but we're also seeing further seeds of Buddhism planted as Mahaprajapati is the one who will eventually partner with her son to help bring his fourfold community to its completion.

As we shall see, Mahaprajapati eased into her new role with grace and dignity. She never faltered in the limelight, rather she expanded her personal power over time into assuming responsibility for hundreds, if not thousands, of women who trusted her for her compassionate guidance in bringing them to the dharma. Her role as the mother of the Buddha had only just begun, but it was one that Mahaprajapati would fill with selfless dedication, generosity, and wisdom until the end of her life.

## 5

# Empowerment of the Sakya Women

We now return to the streets of Kapilavastu where the Buddha's long-awaited arrival has rocked the Sakya people outside as well as inside the palace. Soon Mahaprajapati will face her first challenge as mother and wife to two powerful men.

A stunning but little-known story recorded in several sources in the Sanskrit tradition tells us that when the Buddha first returned home, only men were allowed into the Nigrodha Grove to attend his teachings. The prohibition had nothing to do with the Buddha, rather his father, the king, and the Sakya princes set up the rule: "Whenever Buddha-god . . . [teaches] . . . (a woman) is not to come."*1

Imagine how the women must have felt seeing their husbands, fathers, and sons bustling off in excited anticipation each day, passing through sentries to enter the Nigrodha Grove and returning later with reports of the marvelous dharma the Buddha was preaching. That's what this story describes. Being excluded affected the women deeply, and they were outspoken in their indignation:

---

* While "Buddha-god" appears here, the Buddha was a human being usually characterized as a saint or sage.

At this time the law of the land made a difference between men and women. The king, the ministers, and the [men] listened to the Law (dharma) preaching every day and were enlightened by the Law, many of them being rescued. The women felt grudge and resentment, (saying): "Although the Buddha and the Community (sangha) come back to his native country, yet only the men have the good fortune to see him and hear his preachings. We women alone are not favored by the Buddha."[2]

So their beloved prince had finally returned home bringing the gift of dharma, and they were not welcome? The women would not have it. There is much more to this story, so we'll begin by weaving together versions that appear primarily in the Kanjur and *Sanghabhedavastu*.

After only three teachings, the Sakya men, including Suddhodana, are all delighted by the Buddha's messages of truth, described as "sweet as pure honey."[3] Many men have already attained higher levels of realization, and some have even ordained as monks. A chief minister named Mahanaman is so pleased after a dharma teaching that he comes home from the Nigrodha Grove and enthusiastically raves about it to his wife:

> Ah, Buddha! Ah, the Dharma! Ah, the Sangha! How fruitful is the rising of the Dharma for us![4]

Oh, *really*? His wife emphatically points out to him that "us" refers to men but not to women. She says,

> The arising of the Lord Buddha in the world is for the sake of men, not women.[5]

Apparently clueless, Mahanaman objects and tells her that the Buddha's teachings are intended to benefit all beings and that she should go see for herself. He says,

> Say not so . . . his mercy extends to all creation. Go seek him and you will hear the truth from his mouth.[6]

But how can she when women are barred from the teachings? Out of love for his wife (perhaps also because the Buddha's egalitarian message has sunk in), Mahanaman now takes up the women's cause, but he hesitates over the propriety of going directly to the king over a personal matter concerning his wife. Instead he decides to take her concerns to Mahaprajapati.

In an interesting twist, Mahaprajapati agrees to help but does not act until Mahanaman's wife and a throng of wives from other Sakya households approach her with the request themselves. Anticipating some pushback, the women express their eagerness to hear the dharma and suggest a skillful compromise with the men. They say,

> Gautami, you know what? We have heard that in front of an assembly of several hundreds [of men], the Lord teaches sweet, sweet Dharma, sweet as pure honey. . . . So we too wish to listen to the Dharma in the presence of the Lord. Please inform the king of our matter so that the king would go before the Lord in the morning and we in the afternoon.[7]

Beyond the immediate interdict, they appear to be addressing a social awkwardness, if not prohibition, concerning women attending a public gathering in the presence of the king. Their skillful suggestion is that the men, including the king, attend the teachings in the mornings, while the women take their turn in the afternoons. Mahaprajapati responds,

> Sisters, it is excellent that you have given rise to this thought. Please wait a moment while I go see King Suddhodana.[8]

She delivers the women's request almost verbatim, urging her husband to heed their words. The king's acquiescence is described with startling specificity:

> As was the practice of King Suddhodana, when Mahaprajapati Gautami was giving orders he remained standing, with his body stiff as a rod, and the king did not sit down until Mahaprajapati had completed giving her orders.
>
> With his head bowed, he said, "Gautami, so shall it be."
>
> Following that, Mahaprajapati Gautami, accompanied by five hundred women, went to the Nigrodha Tree Park to hear the dharma directly from the Lord.[9]

Did we just catch a glimpse of who wore the pants in that royal marriage? Apparently so, but the key takeaway here is that Mahaprajapati exercised her influence as wife and queen to clear the way for the Sakya women to attend the Buddha's teachings.

It is important to note that the initiative to attend the teachings arose from within the population of Sakya women, not from the queen. While Mahanaman did his best to help, it was his wife who spotted the injustice and rallied the women to take their grievance to their queen as the one with due influence. Further, Mahaprajapati acted only after hearing their request directly (rather than from a husband), reflecting the depth with which she heeded the women's appeal and auguring her future prudence as a teacher. The women were the ones to concoct a ready-made solution that Mahaprajapati was only too happy to put before the king.

This is a much more nuanced portrayal of the relationship between Mahaprajapati and the community of Sakya women than we typically find, one that is significant in its departure from a hierarchical description of Mahaprajapati as the "leader" and Sakya women as her "followers." Perhaps it is more accurate to think of them here and henceforth as a collective of women, all with their own aspirations and agency, who turn to Mahaprajapati with affection and trust to be their voice in a patriarchal world that otherwise does not hear or represent them.

This important story is told somewhat differently in the Tocharian *Maitreyasamiti-Nataka*. While much content is sadly missing due to a badly damaged manuscript, we can bridge some of the gaps by bringing elements from the previous versions together with threads of common sense. Here the fierceness of the Sakya women's conviction shines through as they take a stand on their right to hear the Buddha's teachings. A summary follows.

The housewives of Kapilavastu take matters into their own hands from the outset when they are refused access to the Nigrodha Grove. Observing the "glory" their men attain after each of the Buddha's discourses, they respond with indignation and resentment:

> Having seen that, the Sakya women ... came to each other and complained: Why did the Buddha-god the teacher (preach) the Law only to men?[10]

They bring their grievances directly to their queen and urge her to speak to her husband on their behalf:

> The Sakya women got together, [and] paid respect to Mahaprajapati Gautami. [The] Buddha-god the teacher [has] arisen in the world. But now he does not preach the Law to us. . . .
>
> Make an effort so that we have a chance to listen to the good Law, (and to see) Buddha-god the teacher.[11]

Mahaprajapati immediately speaks to Suddhodana, who agrees to ease the ban and allow women to attend the Buddha's teachings.

However, the Buddha is already fully aware of the rising tension between the Sakya women and men. Skillfully accommodating the concerns of both sides, he suggests to his father that women and men attend his teachings on alternate days:

> The Buddha knew [the women's] thoughts and then told the king: "From now on, you order that men and women are allowed to hear my preaching every day in turn, one day for each group."[12]

The women are delighted with this outcome and arrive in droves to the Nigrodha Grove on their first appointed day. The men, however, are decidedly unhappy. The young Sakya men in particular bombard the women with insults as they come and go from the Buddha's discourse, denigrating them for what the men perceive as the inability of women to understand the dharma due to their sex. A war of words definitely follows, but it is not always clear from the text fragments which insults are directed at whom! It appears to be the men who accuse the women of being "(without) conscience, ungrateful and passionate, a stain on moral conduct."[13] They blame women for the same worldly sufferings the Buddha is preaching about.

As the fur flies, the women counter sharply, pointing out what to them could only be obvious (the text does not flow smoothly here, but the following lines provide the gist). Taking a powerfully feminist stance, they declare,

> "Women have carried Siddhartha in their womb, women have given birth to him, women have raised him. . . .

"Therefore do not send us back from hearing the Law because of words of the arrogant Sakyas!...

"We have come (to meet the Buddha-god the teacher). May he not put blame on us! Therefore let us go listen to the Law!"[14]

At one point the women meet with the Buddha and express their indignation. The text is badly damaged here, but he appears to extol the five virtues of women, which include the fact that women give birth to buddhas:

The Sakya women went to the Buddha-god the teacher. The Buddha-god the teacher (understood) the thought of women....

[The Buddha said:] "From women, Buddhas, Pratyekabuddhas, ... (have come into this world)."

Having heard that, and having become glad, the women say: "Shame on the denouncers ... we will hear the Law!" Thereupon the Buddha-god the teacher preached the Law in such a way to the Sakya women.[15]

Now the results of the Buddha's glorious dharma are reflected in the Sakya women as well. Thousands upon thousands benefit from his salvific teachings and begin to attain higher levels of realization. Having achieved their heartfelt goal to become *upasikas*, they return to their households as part of the growing sangha of laywomen in the new Buddhist faith.

The story is extraordinary for the women's forceful claim to legitimacy and equal rights based specifically on their sex. How dare men exclude women, the very bearers and nurturers of buddhas! Not only that, but the Sakya women were demonstrably equal to the men in their enthusiasm and capacity to learn the dharma. In a much broader context, this exceptional story relates an organized women's protest against misogyny and patriarchy that took place more than twenty-five hundred years ago. Could this have been the first such protest? And that was just the beginning for the Sakya women, as five years later they marched again to the Nigrodha Grove to request the Buddha's permission to ordain as nuns (to be discussed in a later chapter). Indeed, contemporary women can take heart from our fierce foremothers who struggled and overcame obstacles not dissimilar from ours today.[16]

What we learn from this "forgotten" story is how the Sakya women became *upasika*s first and did not plunge directly into monasticism without prior experience of the Buddha and the dharma. It only makes sense that they took this first step during the Buddha's first visit home and on his subsequent visit felt prepared to make the commitment to ordain as nuns. As I. B. Horner said,

> There can be little doubt that there was a following of women lay-disciples during the first five years of the ministry, else it is hardly conceivable that Mahaprajapati should have been accompanied, as it is recorded, by so large a concourse, so ardent in aspiration.[17]

This story of the rigor of the Sakya housewives provides an essential missing piece in the puzzle of early Buddhist history. It goes back further than before, telling us that women were dharma enthusiasts and advocates before the question of ordination arose, that women as householders first laid claim to equal rights with men in learning the dharma and becoming lay practitioners. Regrettably, we see that from the very outset, gynophobic mores and social structures sought to undercut and denigrate them. The Buddha always welcomed women, but the men—in this story, laymen—not so much. By confronting misogynist challenges, these brave women laid the groundwork for the Buddha fulfilling half—emphasis on *half*—of his intended fourfold assembly. Only forgotten if we continue to neglect it, this remarkable story of an early Buddhist women's march for religious freedom needs to be remembered, revalued, and reinserted into today's living Buddhist narratives.

One further thought should be added here: Perhaps the Buddha was also prescient in firmly providing for the Sakya women's early dharma education. It would only be a few more years before their husbands abandoned them to become monks and the king died without an heir, leaving the Sakya population vulnerable and in a state of collapse without the patriarchal norms to support it. Confronted with the unstable, changing nature of their circumstances, dharma was one constant the women could rely on. Having each other and their sangha of *upasika*s was another. No longer could they turn to their prince, Siddhartha, as their new king, but the Sakya women could and did turn to the Buddha for refuge of a different kind.

# 6

# Mahaprajapati Makes a
# Robe for Her Son

*My son! Gotama Lord Buddha! I was your mother in previous lives,
and in this birth, even though you were not born from my womb, I did
everything a mother does with the greatest love. Because of this, I am
your mother, and you are my child.[1]*

We come now to one of the most, if not *the* most important story in
Mahaprajapati's life. Whether or not one agrees with that assertion, it is a
story with implications that exceed women's issues introduced thus far and
one that deservedly should be known across Buddhist traditions. While
very little evidence of Mahaprajapati exists at all in the literature, it is particularly surprising that this story—we'll call it *The Robe Story*—has gone
underreported, appearing only as disconnected fragments here and there
or, more prevalently in most canonical accounts, as an interrupted narrative
that is fused with an altogether unrelated ending.[2] This last assertion is
arguable, of course, but it's the premise underlying the rest of this discussion.

Faxian and Xuanzang, the early Chinese pilgrims who chronicled their
journeys to Buddhist sites across India in the fifth and seventh centuries
respectively, learned *The Robe Story* from local priests and villagers via oral
traditions that flourished during that time. The narrative takes place over an

extended temporal period and across far-flung areas: Kapilavastu, Vaishali, Benares, and Rajagriha. At each of these sites, one or both of the pilgrims noted the applicable episode from the narrative and the associated holy pilgrimage spot, often marked by a stupa. Indeed, we see that in the early centuries of Buddhism, *The Robe Story* was widely known and deeply revered.

With the pilgrims' outlines as a guide and sometimes benchmark, together with corroborating textual and iconographic evidence captured from a variety of Buddhist traditions, the following reconstruction attempts to bring back a complete narrative of *The Robe Story*, not just because it centers largely on Mahaprajapati but because it introduces (or reintroduces) complex themes of the feminine and the sacred feminine that have been lost in contemporary Buddhism yet are more relevant today than ever before. Implicit in this methodology is an invitation for further scholarly investigation, particularly the translation of new, related materials. For now, *The Robe Story* is too important to leave abandoned in pieces, as if on the floor of an ancient editing room. What follows is a first rough cut meant to bring it back to life for contemporary Buddhist audiences and offer it with all its nuances to the growing portfolio of Buddhism's remembered women's stories.

On the face of it, this story is quite simple and centers on Mahaprajapati making a very finely embroidered, golden-colored robe for her son. She did this while he was away on his twelve-year religious quest and she reigned as queen of the Sakyas. While timelines are always debatable, *The Robe Story* is normally located within the cluster of stories already related to the Buddha's eventful first return home, because Mahaprajapati offers him the robe as a gift in the Nigrodha Grove during that visit. Following the *Maitreyasamiti-Nataka*, it would have taken place after the Sakya housewives and Maha-prajapati rallied to secure access to his public teachings as related in chapter 5, since that host of women was present to witness the offering.

Among all the variations of *The Robe Story*, two details remain constant: Mahaprajapati entreats her son to accept a fine robe that she has made herself, and the Buddha directs her to give it to the sangha. In most cases Mahaprajapati and the robe (sometimes described as two cloths) are mentioned only briefly, serving more as an introduction or frame story for a broader narrative. Perhaps the best-known version in this format is "The Exposition of Offerings," or *Dakkhinavibhanga Sutta*, that appears in the *Majjhima Nikaya* of the Pali canon. It is told this way:

Thus I have heard. On one occasion the Blessed One was living in the Sakyan country at Kapilavatthu in Nigrodha's Park.

Then Mahaprajapati Gotami took a new pair of cloths and went to the Blessed One. After paying homage to him, she sat down at one side and said to the Blessed One: "Venerable sir, this new pair of cloths has been spun by me, woven by me, especially for the Blessed One. Venerable sir, let the Blessed One accept it from me out of compassion."

When this was said, the Blessed One told her: "Give it to the Sangha, Gotami. When you give it to the Sangha, the offering will be made both to me and to the Sangha."

A second time and a third time she said to the Blessed One, "Venerable sir, . . . accept it from me out of compassion."

A second time and a third time the Blessed One told her, "Give it to the Sangha, Gotami. When you give it to the Sangha, the offering will be made both to me and to the Sangha."[3]

This simple dialogue serves as a departure point for what turns into the Buddha's detailed homily about the fourteen kinds of personal offerings, classified according to what degree of merit one might expect in each case in return. His point is that his mother (as an example) would achieve much more merit or karmic benefit to herself were she to give the robe to the sangha rather than to the Buddha alone. He is turning her attention away from what would be a personal gift to one that benefits his legacy. The sutra concludes without further comment from Mahaprajapati or an indication of what finally transpired with the robe. Her appearance in this story, even the robe itself, serves chiefly to frame the Buddha's discourse and is largely insignificant. Analayo has suggested that this canonical version in the *Dakkhinavibhanga Sutta* is the fusion of two originally distinct stories:

> The account of the attempted offer of a robe to the Buddha and the description of the recipients of gifts might have been originally two separate textual pieces. During the course of oral transmission these two parts could then have been combined to form a single account.[4]

An intertexual reading across multiple sources reveals that this account of Mahaprajapati's robe offering in the Pali canon is not the full story but rather the tip of an iceberg in a much larger, more significant tale. What happens both before and after this episode is reported in various ways but on the whole exposes elements of a hidden story centered on Mahaprajapati that arguably rivals in importance even her critical role in spearheading monastic ordination for women. What could this be?

Let's begin by examining the backstory, which is entirely missing in the canonical version. Why did Mahaprajapati make this robe in the first place? It certainly meant a lot to her since she implored the Buddha three times to accept it. Stepping back, what was the larger context for this episode, and why did the Buddha tell her to give the robe to the sangha? It turns out these details are of critical importance, as is the eventual outcome with the robe. As usual, we'll proceed by looking at a variety of sources.

### A Mother's Grief

To put *The Robe Story* back together, we need to circle back to some already familiar narrative details. Recall the story where Mahaprajapati was reunited with her son after eagerly traveling out to the Nigrodha Grove with her husband and Yasodhara to greet him. Afterward she invited him to dinner in the women's quarters of the palace, where she lovingly served him a meal with her own hands. Significantly, she attained stream entry at that time, while the Buddha gave her and the palace women their first dharma teaching, as related in detail in the *Mahavastu*. Further, it was during this visit that Mahaprajapati was enlisted to represent the voices of the Sakya women who rose up in protest after they were denied access to the Buddha's teachings. In all these stories she is portrayed as queen of the Sakyas as well as the Buddha's mother. In other words, these events took place before she ordained as a nun.

But to locate *The Robe Story* within this context, we need to back up even further, to the years in Kapilavastu while the Buddha was gone. We know from accounts of his Great Departure that both his parents were extremely distraught when he left home. His mother is described as collapsing from grief:

> Mahaprajapati Gautami, hearing that the prince had not returned, fell fainting on the ground, her limbs entirely deprived of strength, even as some mad tornado wind crushes the golden-colored plantain tree. . . .

Thus, thinking of her son, her heart was full of sorrow, disconsolate she lay upon the earth.

The [harem] women raised her up and dried the tears from off her face.[5]

As we've seen, stories thus far have characterized Mahaprajapati's heartache as so intense that she went blind from weeping. Clearly her mother's grief was a theme that captured the imaginations of storytellers and their audiences. The oral traditions would have been rife with dramatizations of this sort of powerful emotional content in relating the Buddha's heroic, albeit very human, saga and the impact it had on his family.

With equal power, *The Robe Story* portrays an entirely different side of Mahaprajapati's grief during this time. In these accounts, her eyesight must have been very good because we are told that she transmuted her sorrow by weaving a magnificent golden cloth for Siddhartha while he was away, laboring over every detail of its creation with complete focus so that one day she would have a worthy gift to give her son to welcome him home.

Robes were considered among the highest, most significant possible gifts in early Buddhist stories, conveying deep reverence for the recipient while producing vast amounts of merit for the giver. As an example, a story from the *Mahavastu* tells us when Siddhartha emerged from six years of near-starvation after fruitlessly practicing austerities, a poor washerwoman named Gava gave him a simple hempen robe to replace his filthy rags. Overjoyed to help him, she was also aware she would be reaping the merit of an improved rebirth. Sure enough, she soon died and was reborn in the heavenly realms. It was Gava's humble robe the Bodhisattva was wearing a short time later when he attained enlightenment under the Bodhi tree.[6]

Reminiscent of Penelope in the *Odyssey*, though faithful as a mother rather than a wife, Mahaprajapati's consuming motivation for weaving the robe was love for her son and longing for his return. Story fragments craft the enormity of her purpose through the ordinariness of detail. Her hands, the touching, the tactile sensations described in the following passages evoke the sense of a mother's intimacy with her child and remind us of Mahaprajapati's earlier worries about whether his fragile body, accustomed to the luxuries of princely life, would survive in the harsh wilderness. The Pali *Milindapanha* claims she fashioned the robe specially to shield him in the rainy season and that she herself "had carded and pressed and beaten and cut and woven the cloth."[7] Vivid details such as these address the minutia of the making of the robe in much the same way as the minutia of mothering a child, and they evoke the notion that she was consumed with thoughts of her son. Weaving and weavers generally were considered very low caste, thus it was all the more exceptional that the queen would choose to make her son's robe herself rather than assigning this specialized task to artisans.

Once again, we turn to the Tocharian *Maitreyasamiti-Nataka*, where exceptional elements of *The Robe Story* are introduced. The translator has enhanced the text fragments with a parallel, more coherent version of the material translated from the Chinese *Damamukanidana Sutra*. The following account weaves these two together.

The story opens as Queen Mahaprajapati joyously anticipates the return of her son to Kapilavastu. She has been told that he will soon be arriving in the Nigrodha Grove with his entourage of monks. She has dispatched her servant girl Pattini to scout for their arrival and bring back news. Mahaprajapati has not seen her son since he left home many years earlier and is eager to welcome him with her gift of a beautifully embroidered, golden robe she has made for him:

> At this time Buddha's aunt (stepmother) Mahaprajapati Gautami, (because) Buddha had become a monk, spun and wove with her own hands and prepared beforehand a piece of gold-covered cloth. She thought in her mind and waited eagerly for the Buddha.[8]

The town of Kapilavastu is jostling with crowds of women and men impatiently awaiting the return of their prince, whom they hear has now become an enlightened buddha—exciting news indeed. In conversation with a laywoman named Muktika, the servant girl Pattini explains her mission:

> I come here to ask about the coming of the Buddha-god the teacher, when he (is about to come). With great efforts on the part of the Sakya queen Mahaprajapati Gautami, (a cloth) has come into existence. Therefore she keeps asking when the Buddha-god teacher is about to arrive.[9]

Muktika asks why the queen, the "noblest among women," would make such a cloth when weaving is a lowly skill. Pattini responds that weaving the robe was not a task the queen would allocate to her servants because she wanted to do it herself out of love for her son:

> Not for want of means, nor of female servants, . . . out of joy and love for the Buddha-god the teacher has she made the jewel of a cloth.[10]

Pattini explains how diligently Mahaprajapati labored to prepare the robe:

> She herself with her own (hands), . . . made [the seeds] grow with boiled milk, she herself gathered them; she herself did the carding, and she herself indeed . . . wove the excellent cotton sheet.[11]

The servant girl goes on to relate how in a past life Mahaprajapati achieved the merit to become a future Buddha's foster mother by piously offering perfume, flowers, and delicious food and drink to the previous Buddha Vipasyin. Continuing this flow of merit she has now made this special robe for her son "with great effort": gathering and sowing the cotton seeds herself; nourishing them with milk; hoeing the weeds; picking and cleaning the cotton balls; carding, spinning, and weaving the excellent golden cloth, all with her own hands. Here we see the metaphor likening her labors to the delicate multitasking of raising a child expanded to include her tending a garden that is nourished with milk.

So the Buddha's mother sublimated her grief and longing for her son by arduously fashioning a magnificent cotton robe she could present to him upon his return.* Indeed, the finished golden robe is magnificent:

> Shining, this jewel of a cotton cloth. . . . Like an accumulation of lightening, . . . a piece of clothing having exceeded human dresses in refinements, it is worthy of the gods . . . it may go well with the tender and gold-colored skin of the Buddha-god, the teacher.[12]

---

*Cotton may seem commonplace today, but it was held as the most precious of fibers at that time for its softness, beauty, and breathability in intense heat.

A pause is in order here to note a similitude between Mahaprajapati's project making the robe and that of other women tied to the Bodhisattva during his absence. The scholar John S. Strong has described a parallel between Siddhartha's activities after his Great Departure and those of his wife, Yasodhara: while he practiced austerities in the wilderness, she did so in the palace; when he became emaciated, so did she; when he began to eat again, so did she; and so forth. The climax for both came when Yasodhara gave birth to Rahula at the same moment the Bodhisattva attained enlightenment, six years after his departure from home.[13] In similar fashion, the cowherd Sujata followed a parallel program while the Bodhisattva practiced austerities. For the six years he was starving, she made daily food offerings to itinerant beggars with fervent prayers that her food might similarly nourish and sustain him. Her twin purpose was that the Bodhisattva would succeed in attaining awakening so that she could become his disciple and attain awakening herself.[14]

Following this theme, Mahaprajapati's parallel activity during her son's long absence was to create a magnificent robe for him. While he was away struggling to attain supreme enlightenment, she bided the days laboring to perfect a cloth that would be a worthy expression of both her mother's love and his extraordinary accomplishment. Just as he dropped the pretenses of his royal caste by assuming the practices of an ascetic, so she did the same by working with her hands tilling and weeding the soil, spinning the fibers, weaving the cloth, and so forth. His impulse was love for humanity; hers was love for her son. The years he spent refining his mind she spent refining a magnificent golden cloth. The momentous result of his awakening has no worthy material symbol, but perhaps Mahaprajapati's glorious golden robe, "like an accumulation of lightening . . . worthy of the gods"[15] and made with a mother's love, comes closest.

## A Mother's Gift

The highly anticipated moment has finally arrived. Mahaprajapati will soon be giving the robe to her son. Let's join the women assembling in the Nigrodha Grove to witness this marvelous event. The location, marked by a stupa, is precisely noted in Xuanzang's records:

Not far from [the Nigrodha monastery] was a [stupa] on the spot where the Buddha, sitting under a large tree facing east, accepted a gold-embroidered monk's robe from his aunt and foster mother.[16]

Faxian further claimed that the tree, a banyan, was still in existence at the time of his visit, that the robe had been a *sanghati* (monk's robe) of fine muslin, and that the queen had made it herself. According to Faxian, "out of kindness to her," the Buddha accepted the robe and gave it to the sangha.[17]

In this scene, the *Maitreyasamiti-Nataka* variant expresses far more emotion than we found in the *Dakkhinavibhanga Sutta*. Mahaprajapati says,

Since you the Buddha left the home and became a monk, I missed you very often. Therefore I spun and wove [this robe] with my own hands, waited intensively for you, the Buddha. I hope sincerely you will take pity on me and receive it from me![18]

The Buddha responds,

I know that you, my mother, wish with single-hearted devotion to present it to me. But the benevolent love cannot get much merit. If you present it to the Community you can get much more rewards. I know this matter and therefore can advise you thus.[19]

There is a lot of commentary past and present on why the Buddha made the response he did.[20] One way of looking at it not previously discussed is that refusing the robe as a personal gift is another example of the new normal he demonstrated to loved ones and witnesses upon arriving home. As an awakened Buddha, his relational awareness now extended beyond traditional family ties, not just to all beings but also to karmic consequences past and future. Just as he had countered his father's insistence that he forego unprincely behavior and his wife's expectation that he return to their marriage, so here the Buddha is gently but firmly showing Mahaprajapati that their personal mother-son relationship has forever shifted. It's not that he loves her less or is not grateful for her gift or all that she has done as his mother. It's that that is not the point. Everything has changed. The Buddha is imparting his enlightened worldview through his actions as well as his words. His love is now great love extending equally to all beings, no longer a personal love with attachments to his own or others' worldly happiness.

The Buddha's heartfelt aspiration for Mahaprajapati flowed from his insight that she would benefit more in the long run—in other words, achieve greater karmic merit—by giving the robe to the sangha rather than himself. In this way, the sangha too would benefit, not just her alone. His interaction with her, as with all his disciples, was a form of teaching. In this case, he gently uncovered her powerful attachment to their former mother-son relationship, which had to be relinquished in order for her to advance spiritually.

But this is too high a bar for Mahaprajapati to accept. The Buddha's larger intent is lost on her, at least in this moment. In her mind her son has rejected her gift. Passionately she entreats him three times to accept it, and, as we saw in the *Dakkhinavibhanga Sutta*, three times he refuses:

> Then [Gautami] queen having taken hold with both hands of the golden-colored cotton cloth ... [says] ... the new gold-colored jewel of a cotton cloth spun by myself. For the Buddha-god, the teacher ... Therefore he may take it, the renowned compassionate teacher, (out of) love for us. ][21]

Again, he tells her to give it to the sangha, and again she says,

> I have prepared this cotton cloth. Why is the Buddha-god, the teacher not prepared to accept it from me? Oh venerable one! I have just spun myself (this) excellent, gold-colored cotton cloth ... out of observance of proper behavior, you should accept (it) from me, you should put it on because of me, having recognized the love of a mother.[22]

We can feel the passion, the pain in her words. For years her expectations have hinged on this moment, and now she is devastated. A third time she says,

> (I have) just (made) this gold-colored cloth ...
>     ... (accept it) from me, oh venerable one, fulfill my wish, put it on on my behalf! Show me compassion! [23]

Several phrases are telling here. Her call for "observance of proper behavior" speaks to her expectation that her son should accede to her request out of filial respect. Not that she was displaying arrogance, but as his mother and the queen that would be what she was accustomed to. However, the norm is not what is unfolding here. Proffering the robe with both hands, twice she pleads that he "put it on" right on the spot, so anxious is she to realize her dream of seeing her son wear the precious cloth she has so lovingly made. Finally, she asks him to recognize "the love of a mother" as the force that has driven the creation of her gift all along and her passionate plea that he accept it. But to no avail. In all ways Mahaprajapati is disappointed with the Buddha's response. Forever her son, it's a bitter pill for her to swallow that he is no longer recognizable as her beloved Siddhartha.

With tears in her eyes, Mahaprajapati turns to Ananda for help. His intercession on her behalf is a trope that appears elsewhere in the literature, most familiarly in the ordination sequence, which will be discussed later. One thing it does here and elsewhere is throw off the timeline, since Ananda (arguably) would have been too young to appear in these scenes.*[24] It is also out of place because the ensuing conversation prefigures Mahaprajapati's dharma accomplishments when in the rest of the story she is newly encountering the Buddha and his teachings. That discussion aside, Ananda's appearance sets up an interesting dialogue where the Buddha highlights the contrast between two types of love: a mother's nurturing love born of worldly concerns and the ultimate, nurturing love born of dharma. The Buddha skillfully uses a real-time analogy that captures Mahaprajapati's attention and his purpose in bringing her to a new understanding. With his palms together, Ananda beseeches the Buddha (again, all we have here are fragments):

> [Ananda:] Of great importance, oh venerable one, to you, is Gautami. . . . with the milk of her breast she has nursed you and brought you up. Therefore for the love of your mother [accept her gift]. . . .

> [Buddha:] Indeed, in the very same way, Ananda, is Gautami of great importance to me. . . . (as I was wretched), with the milk of her breast did she nurse this my body. I also, oh Ananda, am of great importance beyond any doubt . . . for [Gautami]. . . .

---

* Evidence in Sanskrit sources suggests Ananda is closer to Rahula in age, the Kanjur even stating they were co-natal (Rockhill, *Life of the Buddha*, 32).

...I nursed her [dharma] body...I dressed her with [dharma] garments. She adorned me with ornaments of the world....She washed me with waters of the world; but I washed her with the noble eightfold [path]....I removed the stain of the eighty-eight [mental afflictions], and in the same way I freed her from the continuity [of samsara]. She (decorated) me (with flowers) of the world...

...I decorated and adorned her with flowers [of the dharma]. There are no two sides of it, Ananda. Of the advantage of the [dharma]....[25]

Using ordinary examples of a mother caring for her child, he shifts the focus point by point to the supreme benefit of dharma. While this passage concludes with the notion that the gift of dharma eclipses all worldly gifts, it introduces a sense of parity or complementarity by suggesting that a mother's unconditional love is the highest expression of love in the conventional or samsaric realm, while dharma in its vastness is the expression of great or ultimate love. Similar conversations come up again later between the Buddha and Mahaprajapati, where their mother-son bond can be understood as a Buddhist metaphor for the highest truths.

A parallel version of Ananda's plea appears in the *Dakkhinavibangha Sutta* and repeats the theme of Mahaprajapati being the mother who adopted and nursed the Buddha at birth:

Venerable sir, let the Blessed One accept the new pair of cloths from Mahapajapati Gotami. Mahapajapati Gotami has been very helpful to the Blessed One, venerable sir. As his mother's sister she was his nurse, his foster mother, the one who gave him milk. She suckled the Blessed One when his own mother died.[26]

Significantly, however, in a Chinese version Mahaprajapati speaks for herself and Ananda does not appear at all:

I suckled and raised you, O World-Honored One. I have made this garment myself. And so I offer it to you, O Buddha. I hoped that you, O Tathagata, would accept it from me. Why did you say just now to give it to your sangha?[27]

While the Buddha telling her to give the robe to the sangha is consistent in all variants, what happens next is not. We've already seen the most common outcome, where the Buddha goes on to deliver a detailed sermon on the merit inherent in different types of offerings. A different and seemingly anomalous episode appears in the *Mahisasaka Vinaya*, where Mahaprajapati's offering is fused with her request on behalf of herself and five hundred Sakya women to take ordination. Here Mahaprajapati takes the robe she has made (here it is in two pieces), goes to the Nigrodha Grove followed by the five hundred women, and presents it to her son with the words, "O Lord, I have spun this robe myself for you. Please accept it." As before, the Buddha instructs her to give the robe to the sangha to obtain greater merit. Their conversation goes back and forth until her third plea, when he finally accepts one cloth for himself and gives the other to the sangha. Mahaprajapati now requests permission for herself and the five hundred women to go forth.[28] We do not hear the Buddha's response.

Thus far we have learned the backstory of Mahaprajapati making the robe, but there's little else to support the earlier claim that this is an exceptionally important story. So what happens next? To learn more, we must follow the journey of the robe after the Buddha's repeated directive that Mahaprajapati give it to the sangha. For that matter, how exactly does one give a single (or double) cloth to an entire assembly of monks? What ended up happening to this magnificent golden robe?

## On Giving the Robe to the Sangha

We return to the Nigrodha Grove where the Buddha has just refused Mahaprajapati's gift and instructed her to offer it to the sangha. A Thai version of our story tells us that this makes her extremely unhappy, and she begins to weep. Going about the Nigrodha monastery, she offers the robe in turn to the senior-most monks Sariputra and Maudgalyayana and then to other accomplished elders. But none of them will accept it since none of them feel worthy of such an exceptional gift. Out of options, she finally offers her fine cloth to the lowliest monk of all, a novice named Ajita who quietly and humbly accepts it. Sorrowful and beset with tears, Mahaprajapati reflects that her store of merit must be very low that a novice monk rather than the Buddha would be a worthy recipient of her cherished gift.

Seeing her weeping, the Buddha calls upon Ananda to fetch his alms bowl. Addressing the assembly of monks, he says, "Disciples, do not carry this alms bowl of the Tathagata; let this young Ajita carry it." With that he throws the bowl into the air where it almost disappears into the clouds. With their Teacher's permission, one by one the great elders use their superior powers to float into the sky to try to retrieve it. All of them return empty-handed. The Tathagata then instructs Ajita to retrieve the bowl. Knowing that he lacks the ability to fly, Ajita instead makes a heartfelt declaration:

> If I am leading the holy life as a novice in order to attain the Enlight-enment that can destroy the Four Deadly Floods . . . then may the alms bowl of the Tathagatha descend into my hands.[29]

The alms bowl not only descends into his hands, but it speaks to the assembly, saying,

> I did not come into the hands of the *mahasavakas*, but I come to the novice monk, because he will become not a *savaka*, nor a *paccekabuddha*, but a *sammasambuddha*.*[30]

Delighted by this miracle and good news, Mahaprajapati now bows reverentially to Ajita.

The story continues as Ajita humbly reflects that he should not keep the robe. He offers it to the Buddha by hanging a canopy over the ceiling of the Buddha's residence with one of the magnificent golden cloths and curtains with the other. Smiling at the young monk, the Buddha clearly approves. Speaking to Ananda, he announces that the novice Ajita will become a "lion among the [conquerors]," a buddha by the name of Maitreya in this very era.†[31]

A similar version appears in the Sinhala *Saddhammavavada-sangrahaya* but without the miracle of the talking bowl. Instead, Mahaprajapati is so moved by the Buddha's discourse on merit that she gives Ajita the beautiful robe on the spot, which he hangs above the Buddha as already described.[32]

---

* The bowl is announcing that Ajita will surpass all others in his spiritual accomplishments, becoming not an arhat but an enlightened buddha.
† While in these stories Ajita and Maitreya are the same person, not all traditions agree on this.

In the Pali *Samantabhaddhika*, we find a version of *The Robe Story* in which the Buddha accepts one of Mahaprajapati's cloths and tells her to offer the second to the sangha. None of the elder disciples dare come forward. Eventually, reflecting that the Buddha wants his mother to achieve merit, Ajita out of compassion bravely stands up in the assembly "like a king of the lions" and accepts the robe. The room buzzes with surprise and disapproval. Who does this novice upstart think he is? Reading the situation and wishing to dispel all doubt, the Buddha declares to the assembly,

> Do not say this [monk] is an ordinary [monk]. He is a Bodhisatta who will be the coming Buddha Metteyya.*[33]

Assorted parallel accounts describe similar scenes where Mahaprajapati's magnificent robe winds up being given to the monk Ajita/Maitreya rather than to her son.[34]

This is indeed an astonishing turn of events for Mahaprajapati and her robe offering. Nothing could be more marvelous or auspicious than her robe being given to the future buddha. Is this the outcome her son had in mind when he repeatedly directed her to give it to the sangha? In her confusion, she heard his words as rejection when in fact they reflected the Buddha's perfect insight into the magnitude of her gift. Yes, he saw that she would reap tremendous personal merit giving it to him and/or the sangha. Even more he recognized that only her robe, fashioned by her hand in each detail from the depths of a mother's love, held the merit worthy of the future buddha, Maitreya, the Buddha of Loving-Kindness. How could an ordinary robe, however exquisitely beautiful, created on the ordinary loom of an unnamed artisan come close?

It is said that the final stage of a bodhisattva's career (*anivartana-carya*) is irreversible and that he must be publicly anointed by the current buddha in order to proceed on his karmic path to buddhahood. Similarly, it is every buddha's obligation to formally identify and anoint his (or her) successor before passing into *parinirvana*.[35] The *Mahavastu* says,

> Exalted Buddhas do not pass away until they have anointed an heir to the throne.[36]

---

* Maitreya.

Elsewhere in that text the Buddha says,

> I must anoint the heir to the throne. For he, when I have passed away, will become a Buddha in the world. As I am now, so this Bodhisattva, Ajita, will become a Buddha in the world. His name will be Ajita of the Maitreya family.[37]

The esteemed scholar Padmanabh Jaini has noted that these requisites for anointing the future buddha are not met in any canonical text: there are no meetings between the Buddha and the future buddha, and there is no public investiture of the future buddha.[38] Yet such encounters are found in the previously mentioned extracanonical sources, where we see what amounts to the investiture of the future Buddha Maitreya with Mahaprajapati's robe. J. C. Wright has said,

> Maitreya's consecration as Gotama's ultimate successor . . . his admission to the pantheon, so to speak, . . . bearing in mind the symbolism of Queen Gautami's wondrous cloak, rejected by Gotama in favour of Maitreya, nothing more apposite than "Maitreya's investiture" comes to mind as a rendering.[39]

What does it mean that canonical texts appear to have redacted this story? Without context they include the singular detail of Mahaprajapati offering her handmade cloth to the Buddha, but neither the robe nor the episode is assigned any special value. The plot line is dropped, and we hear nothing further about her gift or its significance.

This is a huge lost story. And at such a cost—how differently Mahaprajapati would be remembered if *The Robe Story* had come down through the millennia as central (where it belongs) to Buddhism's narrative. How deeply energizing that same narrative would be today, holding memories of a mother's love—the Buddha's mother's love—not as something static in the past but as a continuing force flowing into a future marked by the promise of the Buddha of Loving Kindness. This is much more than one woman's story; it is a story of the sacred feminine that belonged to an earlier era and brings as much relevance today as it did then.

We return to more stories that provide evidence of Mahaprajapati's role in Maitreya's investiture. In a question-and-answer format, the *Samanta-*

*bhaddika* includes a passage, "Lineage of the Future," that names Ajita-Maitreya as the next buddha as follows:

> [Q] By whom was [the "Lineage of the Future"] pronounced?
> [A] By the all-knowing Buddha.
> [Q] Where?
> [A] At the city of Kapilavastu.
> [Q] When was it pronounced?
> [A] At the end (of the pronouncement) of the "Lineage of the Buddhas." . . .
> [Q] About whom was it pronounced?
> [A] This was pronounced about the Elder Ajita who accepted one length of cloth out of the two brought to the Buddha by Mahapajapati Gotami.[40]

A variant of the investiture episode that appears in the *Purvaparanta-kasutra* takes us to Benares,* where the Buddha presents Maitreya with Mahaprajapati's robe in her absence. Xuanzang noted a stupa that marked this spot.[41] Here Maitreya appears as a monk in the assembly, listening to a discourse where the Buddha prophesies that his successor, Buddha Maitreya, will appear in the world when humans have attained a lifespan of eighty thousand years. Venerable Maitreya stands up and publicly expresses the wish to be that buddha, and the Buddha accedes to his request. What follows is a summary from Lamotte:

> The Buddha then asks Ananda to give him the tunic of golden thread (offered to the community by Mahaprajapati Gautami). Ananda obeys. The Buddha takes the tunic and gives it to Maitreya: "Here Maitreya, take from the hands of the Tathagata this tunic of golden thread which was given to the Buddha, the Dharma and the Community. Why? Because the Tathagatas, who are free of attachment and perfectly enlightened, are the protectors of the world; they seek to ensure benefit, welfare, security and joy." Maitreya accepts the tunic.[42]

---

* Likely referring to Sarnath, or Deer Park.

Xuanzang also reports the following story: While on Vulture Peak in Rajagriha, the Buddha is said to have prophesied the coming of a brahman called Maitreya, "whose body shall be the color of pure gold, bright and glistening and pure." The Buddha continued,

> Leaving home, [Maitreya] will become a perfect Buddha, and preach the threefold law for the benefit of all creatures. Those who shall be saved are those who live, in whom the roots of merit have been planted through my bequeathed law.[43]

With this, the monk Maitreya stood up in the assembly and declared that he would like to become that future buddha. "Be it so!" said the Buddha.[44]

From these and other accounts, we see that the Buddha's prediction concerning his successor took place at different sites on more than one occasion, whether the monk Ajita/Maitreya was present or not.[45] What is constant is that in each case the investiture episode is characterized by Mahaprajapati's excellent golden robe being given to the future buddha.

The stories thus far suggest that Ajita/Maitreya, in his humility before the Buddha, was reluctant to accept the robe and tried to offer it back. This makes sense in the context of a disciple—bodhisattva or not—receiving an extraordinary gift in the presence of the Buddha, especially when the gift was made by the Buddha's own mother. We also have to remember that while the robe offering represented Maitreya's investiture, he did not at that moment become the next buddha. That would have been absurd and impossible as there can only be one buddha at a time, and the Buddha was sitting right in front of him. Given the challenges of bridging the continuity between eons, the Buddha (and the storytellers) orchestrated a public declaration and quasi-investiture that would be remembered during the current era as a preliminary step.

It was the Buddha's responsibility to further, if not complete, the karmic conditions for Maitreya's return as his successor. The public orchestration of Mahaprajapati's robe offering to Ajita/Maitreya—skillfully couched in the Buddha's instruction to make it a gift to the "sangha"—was a critical means to that end. With an eye on appearances, now and in the future, the Buddha created a tangible, or in Lamotte's words, "lively and dramatic," moment that engaged his purpose without ambiguity before witnesses.

Why would the Buddha do it this way? Perhaps one answer can be found in the *Milindapanha*, where the king asks the sage Nagasena, "Why would the Tathagata deem the sangha a more worthy recipient of Mahaprajapati's robe than himself?" Reading "Ajita/Maitreya" for "son," Nagasena's response takes on new meaning:

> Just as a father, O king, while he is yet alive, exalts in the midst of the assembly of ministers . . . the virtues which his son really possesses, thinking: "If established here [my son] will be honoured of the people in times to come . . . when I am gone, [he will] be highly thought of."[46]

According to Jaini, Maitreya as the Buddha's designated successor appears in all Buddhist traditions.[47] Like father to son, like king to an heir, in accordance with his lineage and legacy, the Buddha's job was to pass the torch to Maitreya to ensure the continuity of the dharma into the future. Jan Nattier has described this process:

> [Maitreya] . . . resembles his predecessors in virtually every respect . . . [his] primary function is to guarantee the continuity of the Buddhist tradition by preaching the same Dharma as those who have gone before.[48]

It is not without irony that the Buddha was concerned with ensuring his heir and successor when that had been his own father Suddhodana's preoccupation decades earlier. Karmic conditions had been at cross-purposes for the king back then, as his obstinate son Siddhartha opted out of royal life. Now steward of a different kingdom, the Buddha was taking every precaution to ensure that all sentient beings would be cared for in perpetuity through the longevity and flourishing of the sacred dharma.

## Guardian of the Robe

What happens next? Ancient storytellers would never let such a good story end here. More to the point, the Buddha's words and actions are never offhand or disingenuous. How do we connect the dots between the past and the present—or for that matter, the future? What happens to the robe? What if the Buddha's prophesy, Maitreya's preliminary investiture, and everything else is forgotten? After all, the future buddha won't be arriving for quite some time.

Leaving nothing to chance, the stories—now fewer and more fragmented—directly address these concerns and continue to follow the journey of Mahaprajapati's robe (we'll continue to call it her robe even though it has changed hands). The immediate chain of custody gets fuzzy after Ajita/Maitreya accepts it and then offers it back to the Buddha, but we'll see that the Buddha kept it for the remainder of his life. We'll also learn where the robe is now. As it turns out—and this only makes sense—the final stage in Maitreya's investiture can't take place until he returns. At that time in the far-flung future, the robe will be presented to him again. His acceptance will complete the investiture process begun by Gautama Buddha and mark the beginning of the Maitreya Buddha era.

To pick up *The Robe Story*, we now fast-forward to events at the end of the Buddha's life. His *parinirvana* is soon approaching, and he has already designated a senior disciple, Mahakasyapa, as guardian of the new religion after his passing. In a meeting with Mahakasyapa, the Buddha names three specific elements of his legacy that he is handing over: his canon of teachings, his fourfold assembly, and Mahaprajapati's magnificent robe to be presented to the future Maitreya. According to Xuanzang, these were the Buddha's words:

> For vast kalpas I have devoted myself zealously to austerities seeking to obtain the highest religion for all creatures; my aspirations have been realized; as I now wish to pass away, I commit to you all my canon to preserve and preach in its entirety; my gold-embroidered monk's robe, the gift of my aunt, keep to hand over to Maitreya when he comes to be Buddha; those who will be adherents of the religion I am leaving, monks and nuns, male and female lay-believers, are all to be saved first, and released from renewed existence.[49]

Needless to say, tending to the Buddha's entire scriptural canon and his vast fourfold assembly was a daunting assignment. To boot, the Buddha entrusted Mahakasyapa with the guardianship of Mahaprajapati's robe with instructions to deliver it to Buddha Maitreya as his proxy in the distant future. *What*? How was Mahakasyapa supposed to manage that?

A brief sidebar is in order here to say a bit more about Mahakasyapa and his unique relationship with the Buddha. Inclined toward austerity since childhood, he renounced his home and family to embark on a life of pious discipline as a wandering mendicant. One day he met the Buddha along the road and, immediately recognizing him as his teacher, requested and was granted ordination on the spot. Auspicious signs heralded to the Buddha that Mahakasyapa was a disciple of unmatched asceticism and virtue. Now traveling together, they stopped to rest under the canopy of a great tree, where Mahakasyapa took his own fine robe and folded it as a seat for his new teacher. The Buddha sat down and, touching the robe, praised its softness. There was some back and forth as Mahakasyapa offered his robe to the Buddha, and the Buddha inquired, "Then will you wear my worn-out hempen rag robes?"[50] Nothing would please Mahakasyapa more. So the exchange of robes took place, Mahakasyapa now donning the Buddha's decrepit robe.* The earth quaked in recognition of Mahakasyapa's unequalled status because no ordinary being would be fit to wear the Buddha's personal robe. In his commentary on the *Mangala Sutta*, Buddhaghosa gives an account of the First Council in which the Buddha's gift of his own robes to Mahakassapa (Mahakasyapa) is understood as being on the model of an investiture of a "crown prince," thus making Mahakassapa the Buddha's successor as leader of the sangha.[51] While less formal than the meeting with Ajita/Maitreya, here again we find an investiture taking place symbolized by the transference of a robe. In this case it is quite a humble robe in contrast to Mahaprajapati's dazzling golden cloth.

But back to Mahakasyapa's challenge. To complete Maitreya's investiture program some eons hence, he must personally deliver Mahaprajapati's robe. Leave it to the imagination of the storytellers (if not Mahakasyapa's own ingenuity) to figure out how to do this. Not a problem as it turned out.

Shortly after the First Council, Mahakasyapa makes the decision to enter nirvana. As an arhat, he has the wherewithal to do this, but there is

---

* This shabby cloth had been cast off in a cemetery by the slave girl Punna. Covered with insects when the Buddha retrieved it, the earth quaked in wonder when he put it on (DPPN, Mahakassapa, Bodhi, *Samyutta Nikaya*, 1:806).

still that last, nagging matter of delivering Mahaprajapati's robe to Maitreya. Deferring nirvana for the time being, he sets his sights on his teacher's instruction and, after transferring the Buddha's legacy to Ananda, heads off alone into the harsh, craggy mountains surrounding Rajagriha. Forcing his way through dense jungle full of prowling lions, tigers, and wolves, he performs miracles that cleave towering boulders, finally reaching the summit of the highest peak, known as Kukutapadagiri, or Cock's Foot Mountain.[52] Here Mahakasyapa sits down cross-legged and enters a deep state of meditation, draped in (some sources say holding) the wondrous golden robe. As he makes an ardent vow, the mountain miraculously splits open and seals Mahakasyapa inside. And there Mahakasyapa sits to this day, patiently waiting for Maitreya.

Visiting this region in the seventh century, Xuanzang reported that a stupa marked the spot at the top of the mountain where Mahakasyapa withdrew for his long hibernation. The pilgrim described the rough landscape thus:

> The sides of this mountain are high and rugged, the valleys and gorges are impenetrable. Tumultuous torrents rush down its sides, thick forests envelope the valleys, whilst tangled shrubs grow along its cavernous heights. Soaring upwards into the air are three sharp peaks; their tops are surrounded by the vapors of heaven, and their shapes lost in the clouds. Behind these hills the venerable Maha-Kasyapa dwells wrapped in a condition of *Nirvana.*\*[53]

Residents in the region were reportedly so awed and intimidated by the miracle in the mountain that they were afraid even to utter Mahakasyapa's name, referring to him instead as Gurupada, or Venerable Teacher. According to Faxian, the site became a sacred pilgrimage spot, and soil from nearby waters where Mahakasyapa washed his hands became widely known for its healing powers.[54] On quiet nights a soft glow could be seen from a

---

\* Beal points out that the term "nirvana" cannot be literally correct since that is an irreversible state, and Mahakasyapa is still waiting for Maitreya (*Buddhist Records*, 142n15). *Samadhi*, or deep meditation, is used in this discussion.

distance emanating from the mountaintop, but those ascending the mountain would see nothing at all.[55]

When Maitreya finally returns, he will encounter a vast population of doubters, despite having achieved the enlightened state of buddhahood. Due to the faults of pride and arrogance, the doubters will not be able to perceive his unique enlightened state or be receptive to his incomparable, sacred teachings. Always skillful, Gautama Buddha of our era must have anticipated this hurdle in devising his master plan, because Maitreya's next move will be to lead the doubters up the mountain to introduce them to Mahakasyapa. As they arrive, the mountain will split open at the snap of Maitreya's fingers, and voilà, there will be Gautama Buddha's disciple and proxy with the investiture robe.

Just what this future audience will see varies in the narratives. Some texts say the doubters will see Mahakasyapa's mummified body; others say his skeleton.[56] Still others say that he rests intact in *samadhi* and just needs his feet rubbed to reanimate.[57] The *Abhinishkramansutra* reports that his body did not disintegrate, and it was wearing only a robe. In the *Divyavadana*, no robe is mentioned, but Mahakasyapa is plucked from the mountain as a tiny skeleton that Maitreya lifts with two fingers.[58]

Only Faxian and Xuanzang have steadily followed this complicated narrative from the Nigrodha Grove to Cock's Foot Mountain. In this final episode, they relate in detail that Mahakasyapa will be found intact, resting peacefully in a state of *samadhi* inside the mountain, ready and waiting to deliver to Maitreya the beautiful golden robe Mahaprajapati made for her son.[59]

Other versions get iffy about the robe. It may be absent or its provenance unreported. In some texts the robe is said to be the Buddha's poor rag robe (*pamsukula*) that he exchanged with Mahakasyapa,[60] rather than the beautifully embroidered golden cloth made by Mahaprajapati. While this protracted tale may lend itself to confusion and missing story elements, the reported finale is generally a muddled anticlimax that excludes any mention of Mahaprajapati and her critical role in the overall narrative.

Let's begin putting the story back together by looking at the two possible investiture robes. Which one is intended for Maitreya? Well, which one makes the most sense? Is the narrator saying the Buddha intended that a poor rag robe be delivered as his investiture statement to Maitreya at the defining moment when dharma is to be reestablished in the future? What are we supposed to read into that? It doesn't make sense that the symbol of the future buddha's legitimacy, especially playing out before an audience of skeptics, would be a shabby old robe, however precious or sacred that robe might be to a devout follower. Disbelievers would only see threadbare tatters. How would that fuel the needed epiphany that Maitreya, indeed Gautama Buddha, had in mind to bring doubters to the dharma?

The Buddha was more prescient and skillful than that. He attended to the details necessary for introducing Maitreya into a future era with utmost care and intention. While of course there is no inherent difference between a poor rag robe and a golden one, he understood the power of appearances to unenlightened folk. Besides embodying untold merit, his mother's glorious, handmade cloth—together with the miracle of its delivery by Mahakasyapa—would convey an irrefutable endorsement from Gautama Buddha across the eons to his successor. The entire spectacle would capture the awe and admiration of a future dharma audience, thereby easing their resistance to the new Maitreya Buddha and his sacred teachings.

The differences between the two key characters here are distinct: Mahakasyapa acted out of obligation, while Mahaprajapati acted out of love. His karmic action will be complete with the delivery of the robe, while hers will carry on. It was her impulse, her mother's love, her exquisite handmade cloth that created the conditions for this outcome. Little did she know when she made the exquisite robe out of grief for her son that her pure intention born of love would not cease but would flow into the future to mark the future investiture of Maitreya, the Buddha of Loving Kindness. Her actions, together with the Buddha's compassionate insight in redirecting her gift to a simple monk-cum-bodhisattva, have ensured that seeds of the sacred feminine will not just arise in the future but will give birth to the next buddha era.

*The Robe Story* tells us that the Buddha did not and could not have accomplished laying the groundwork for his future dispensation alone. Others participated, of course, but Mahaprajapati was the one who quite literally planted the seeds that set the karmic conditions in motion. There is lots of room for discussion about why and how she was mostly erased from her own story, but the bottom line is that *The Robe Story* needs to be reassembled and the spotlight returned to Mahaprajapati and her incomparable, if unwitting, role in one of Buddhism's most important stories.

## Investiture of Maitreya Buddha

Today *The Robe Story* lies hidden, much like Mahaprajapati's golden robe still lies hidden somewhere in Cock's Foot Mountain. As the power of her intention endures, echoes from the past call to us to imagine the next chapter in this story. After all, the future hasn't happened yet. We're still living in the Gautama Buddha era, and Maitreya's arrival seems a long way off. The storytellers who have already announced what will happen when Mahakasyapa wakes up really don't know any more than we do. Let's venture writing the next scene, when Mahakasyapa finally meets Maitreya and fulfills his duty of delivering Mahaprajapati's magnificent robe. What will this moment look like?

Traveling to the future, we are back at the summit of Cock's Foot Mountain, and Maitreya has just snapped his fingers. As multitudes of disbelievers look on, the rock miraculously splits open with a thunderous roar. Deep inside rests the small figure of Mahakasyapa in a state of *samadhi*. He is draped in Mahaprajapati's luminous golden cloth, its radiance more brilliant than a thousand suns. Awestruck and blinded by the burst of light, the crowds murmur and step back. Maitreya turns and smiles at them, silently raising the palm of his right hand in a gesture of reassurance. Calling out to his audience, he declares,

> Kind people! The great Gautama Tathagata, the perfectly and fully enlightened Buddha, is the same as his disciple Mahakasyapa who you see before you. From Gautama's hands, he brings a magnificent golden cloth made with love by Gautama's own mother, Mahaprajapati Gautami, sanctifying me as his successor and your teacher.
>
> Long ago in Vaishali, in the presence of Gautama Buddha and me as a novice monk, all of you made the aspiration to awaken. "So be it!" the Blessed Teacher said, and promised that you would become the disciples of the future Buddha Maitreya. Women and men! That time has now come. The dharma and the fourfold assembly will be reestablished in the world. All of you are welcome.

As sunlight illuminates his cave, Mahakasyapa slowly gets to his feet and rubs his eyes. The crowd gasps. Some bow down. Drawing the beautiful golden robe from his shoulders, Mahakasyapa steps forward. His eyes meet Maitreya's with friendly recognition, appreciating that this long-awaited moment has finally come to pass. Falling to one knee, his head bowed at Maitreya's feet, Mahakasyapa offers Mahaprajapati's incomparable golden robe with his raised right hand and says,

> Never before has there been a monk who, like me, has known two Buddhas and who experiences as much happiness as I am now at being able to impart the words of the Buddha.[61]

Now the entire crowd is bowed low, their pride vanquished, their hearts illuminated with peace.

Just as Gautama had instructed him to do, in the presence of Maitreya and the gathered crowd of women and men, Mahakasyapa recites the long lineage of buddhas from Dipankara Buddha through the twenty-six buddhas of different epochs to his beloved teacher, Gautama Buddha. In conclusion, as Gautama's proxy speaking Gautama's words, Mahakasyapa names his successor, Maitreya, as his equal.[62] Like thunder, stillness claps across the mountainside. Even songbirds fall silent, and leaves pause their rustling. Maitreya Buddha accepts the robe from Mahakasyapa's hands and carefully dons it, gold now dazzling upon gold as light fills space in all directions.

With the parting words, "May you too release many beings," Mahakasyapa rises into the sky, performs a few miracles (in case there are lingering skeptics), and disappears into space. Mission complete, he enters the state of nirvana he has so patiently deferred.

Maitreya Buddha turns to the assembled crowd and gestures to a nearby shade tree. Here they will gather round as he delivers his first sermon. Like his predecessor, he will begin by skillfully illuminating the suffering of samsara, its cause, and the path to bring about its cessation. Dharma has returned for the benefit of all beings.

# 7

# The Fall of Kapilavastu and Rise of the Sakya Women

We return from the future to find Mahaprajapati is still queen in Kapilavastu. As we have seen, the Buddha's first visit home after his enlightenment was quite eventful. His family and the Sakya people were stirred from a state of sadness and loss to one of exhilaration and excitement. All reports tell us that citizens of every household and caste welcomed their returning prince and his teachings of the dharma. Social change was afoot as women gained equal access to his public discourses and established a community of practicing laywomen. Mahaprajapati assumed an unparalleled role as mother of the Buddha, now having the ear of the kingdom's two most powerful men.

While the timeline is uncertain, the Buddha returned to his hometown at least one more time, probably about five years later.[1] This time everything had changed again. Like a rudderless ship, the Sakya kingdom was in an unprecedented state of social and political crisis. Who could help them? Their beloved prince-cum-Buddha was far away in India, spreading the wisdom of his new faith and ministering to a growing population of monks and lay disciples. While the following two stories are framed separately, both are said to have prompted the Buddha's return for what was likely his last visit home.

## A Family Dispute

The first story, well known throughout the literature, concerns a dispute over water rights between the Buddha's relatives, the Koliyans from both his mothers' side and the Sakyas from his father's side. Recall that despite the separate naming, these two clans were both Sakya and are normally referred to as such. They can be thought of as cousins from different branches of the same original tribe. The boundary between the clan territories was the Rohini River, which both sides used to irrigate their crops.

At the time of this story, there is a terrible drought. The river dries to a trickle, and none of the farmers on either side of the river have enough water to produce their annual rice harvest. Both sides assert a claim of exclusive rights and begin to siphon off what little water remains. Tensions rise, and soon abusive insults fly back and forth across the river. The dispute spreads like wildfire, as do brawls and fist fights between the men.[2] Before long Koliyan and Sakya armies "as vast as the sea" are squared off on either side of the river armed and ready for war.[3] A Sinhala version adds that the women of both clans gather to entreat their menfolk to desist from fighting. But the women are ignored.[4]

Meanwhile, far away, the Buddha spends his early morning hour in a deep state of concentration, surveying the state of the world and perceiving all that is taking place. From Sravasti, he arranges his seat to face his native home and directly discerns the enmity rapidly unfolding between his family members. A devoted disciple, the monk Kalodayin can feel the profound compassion emanating from his beloved teacher sitting motionless in meditation. Himself a Sakya and a childhood friend from Kapilavastu, Kalodayin gently urges the Buddha to return to their homeland, saying,

> Let the Koliyans and the Sakyans behold thy face as stars behold Rohini.*[5]

A blinding light instantly blazes over the Rohini River. No longer can the armies see each other, just a dazzling display of the Buddha sitting cross-legged in the sky between them. Awed and ashamed, both sides throw down their weapons, knowing that it would be wrong to fight in the presence

---

* Here we have a pun, as Rohini was also the name of an auspicious constellation.

of "the jewel of their race."[6] The Buddha descends and takes his seat on a magnificent throne set in the sand along the riverbank where he receives his kinsmen, and they pay reverent homage to him.

What follows in some variants is a somewhat humorous passage, although a sad reflection on the nature of conflict in our world. The Buddha asks the respective generals, Sakya princes from both clans, the reason for their quarrel. They say they aren't sure but will ask their commanders. In turn, the commanders don't know the answer, so they ask their lieutenants. The lieutenants don't know either but ask their soldiers, and so on, until finally the question comes down to the farmers who explain the water problem to the Buddha. Chiding his people for valuing water over priceless human lives, the Buddha preaches the *Attadanda Sutta* discourse ("One Who Has Taken Up the Rod") and cites several Jataka tales that relate by way of analogy the folly of conflict.[7] Both of the armies sit with their wives along the banks of the river listening to the Buddha's words with rapt attention.

The warriors are very grateful to the Buddha for saving them from pointless bloodshed. Reflecting that in another time they would have shown obeisance to him as Siddhartha their king, they decide now out of gratitude to confer similar allegiance to the Buddha by ordaining as his monk disciples. Five hundred men, two hundred and fifty each from the Koliyan and Sakya sides, give up their lives as householders on the spot and become monastic followers of the new dharma.

What seemed like a good idea at the time shortly backfires, as their wives become furious and send their husbands angry messages telling them to come home. When that doesn't work, the women turn in desperation to their queen, Mahaprajapati, for guidance. What should they do? What can she do? Seemingly overnight, Sakya families were coming apart and the well-being of their beloved homeland lay teetering in the balance. On both sides of the river, entire households and towns became devoid of husbands, fathers, and sons. The extraordinary exodus of men left the women in an unprecedented state of vulnerability and confusion. Without protection, education, or skills to parlay into livelihood, they faced a bleak if not scary future.

What also must have been difficult for the Sakya women was that they too felt deep love and loyalty to the Buddha and the dharma, their passions on display earlier when they protested en masse for equal rights to attend his discourses. In the afterglow of the Buddha's first visit home, the entire community, women and men alike, had settled back into their households as lay practitioners. Now, just five years later, that harmonious way of life was in ruins as the men abandoned their families to become monks. What choices were there for the Sakya women? Their comfortable lives as *upasikas* wouldn't work anymore.

And it all began with a foolish argument over water rights.

## The Death of Suddhodana

However, an even bigger change was lurking. Tied closely to the story of the water dispute is the death of Suddhodana, husband to Mahaprajapati, father to the Buddha, and last patriarch of the Sakyas.* Losing scores of men was one thing, but losing the king was the final blow. A benevolent and conscientious ruler during his seventy-year (or so) reign, Suddhodana had always been a steady, guiding presence, the glue that kept the Sakya people and kingdom together. With the patriarchal social structure already crumbling, the king was the last ballast against its full collapse. But he was ninety-seven years old. The specter of death was lingering at his doorstep. What follows is drawn mostly from the Burmese tradition, originally from the Pali.[8]

Far off in Vaishali, deep in meditation, the Buddha's early morning scan of the state of the world reveals that his father is on his deathbed and extremely sad. Knowing that the end is near, Suddhodana pines to see his beloved son one last time. Without hesitation, the Buddha summons several close disciples and through the power of their *siddhis*, they fly through the air and find themselves quickly at the bedside of the king. As they form a loving, healing circle around him, the Buddha lays his hand on his father's head, saying,

> By the virtue of the merits I have acquired during countless existences, by the power of the fruits gathered during forty-nine days round the tree Bodhi, let this head be forthwith relieved of all pain.[9]

---

*In some texts, his death comes first. As always, the chronology is ambiguous.

And so, the king's head is instantly relieved of pain. Holding the king's right hand, his son Nanda voices a similar prayer, as do Ananda, Sariputra, and Maudgalyana. Soon the king is entirely free of pain, although still very weak.

He has just seven more days to live, his son informs him. The Buddha stays attentively by his father's side, giving him discourses on the transient nature of life and helping him prepare for death. Bolstered by the teachings, in the glow of his son's presence, Suddhodana now becomes peaceful and happy, fully prepared for the transition that lies ahead. Though he has never ordained as a monk, he achieves arhatship during this time.[10] On his last day, the king sits up on his couch and cheerfully gives a discourse on death to his wife, consoling her through her tears that she should embrace life's inherent ephemeral nature rather than grieve his passing.

But losing a loved one, especially a lifelong partner, strikes at the core of one's being. When the king breathes his last, Mahaprajapati is distraught with grief, wailing and beating her chest. Her son comforts her and gives her further teachings to assuage her sadness. He repeats these kind acts for the sorrowing royal household and the Sakya people following the king's funeral and cremation.[11]

Despite Suddhodana's oft-reported worries about his heir since the time of Siddhartha's birth, there appears to have been no clear successor when he died. Key candidates Rahula, Nanda, and even Ananda were out of the running since they had already become monks. From the Sinhala tradition, we learn that Yasodhara briefly became sole regent as queen but had no ambition for it and chose to go forth herself.[12] Whether it was suggested that Mahaprajapati assume this role or if she considered it, we do not know.

But now Mahaprajapati was a widow. Her future was just as uncertain as that of all the Sakya women who lost their husbands and primary male relations to monasticism. Also bereft were the women of her household—female servants, concubines, and relatives living in the women's quarters of the palace—over which she had prevailed for decades as queen and chief consort. Their ties to their patriarch now dissolved, the harem women too faced an uncertain future without protection or precedent for asserting personal agency. They were free, yes; but now what?

It was a time of darkness and confusion in Kapilavastu, but one point of light shone through: the women had each other. Each of them had her own unique story, but shared circumstances drew them together. Was it for protection? Comfort? Advice? Financial support? Companionship? All of the above? Or is this just what women do, seeking deeper connection and relationship, choosing to ride the waves of trauma and uncertainty together rather than alone?

It also must be remembered that the Sakyas by reputation were a fierce and resilient tribal group, closely knit for generations. The women had loyalty and persistence woven into their core. Their tenacity was clearly on display five years earlier when they came together in solidarity to demand equal access to the Buddha's public teachings. At that time, they asked Mahaprajapati to take the lead. Now again the Sakya women turned to her, more than ever the most powerful woman in the land. Suddhodana was gone, but Mahaprajapati was still their queen and—more importantly—still the mother of the Buddha.

8

# Ordination of Mahaprajapati and the Five Hundred Women

We now come to the story of the foundation of the order of Buddhist monastic women with Mahaprajapati as its star protagonist. Indeed, this is often the only story told about Mahaprajapati in today's Buddhism, her life as a sister, queen, and mother never acknowledged or long since expunged from the records. While highlighting Mahaprajapati's leadership role, however, the women's ordination story as traditionally told is beset with so much contradiction and weighted with so much misogyny that it does little to advance the true tale of an awe-inspiring leader of an equally awe-inspiring collective of five hundred indomitable women. It must not be forgotten that together, through extreme adversity, they completed the Buddha's original purpose of establishing a fourfold sangha.

In the ordination story, Mahaprajapati is identified as the Sakya queen and the Buddha's mother (although the texts typically describe her as his foster mother or aunt), who requests monastic ordination of the Buddha on behalf of herself and a large company of women, usually said to number five hundred. It's consistent across the canonical and extracanonical literature that her first request is made in the Nigrodha Grove outside of Kapilavastu, at which time the Buddha demurs, and the rest of the story—now varying widely—takes up from there. The premise adopted in this chapter (and mostly shared in the literature) is that Mahaprajapati's request was made shortly after King Suddhodana's death while the Buddha was still home attending to his father's obsequies and took place during the same visit as the two stories related in chapter 7. Using the timeline that the king's death occurred five years after the Buddha's first visit home (which took place twelve years after the Great Departure), Mahaprajapati probably would have been in her late sixties when she requested ordination.*

Before beginning a discussion of the different women's ordination accounts, it must be noted that this is a topic of tremendous importance in the Buddhist world today. A number of distinguished scholars—particularly monastics such as the venerables Bhikkhu Analayo, Damcho Diana Finnegan, Bhikkhuni Tathaloka, Bhikkhuni Dhammadinna, and Gelongma Karma Lekshe Tsomo, among others—have contributed brilliantly and extensively on the subject of the ordination of women at the dawn of Buddhism and beyond.† With deep appreciation for the work that has already been done, this author feels ill equipped to add more. The following discussion is mostly an overview of narrative content from a dozen or so ordination accounts with an eye for exceptional details or discrepancies worth noting. With tremendous gratitude to Venerable Analayo and Venerable Dhammadinna, for their dozen or so translations of variants of the women's ordination story from Pali, Sanskrit, Tibetan, and Chinese sources, this discussion will additionally consider several noncanonical accounts from the Sinhala and Burmese traditions.

## From Upasikas to Bhikkhunis

We return to our story where the Sakya women have just seen their husbands cross over from lay to monastic life. Steadfast as *upasikas* for the past five years and now "widows," their future as lay housewives in Kapilavastu was no longer viable. Only one option appeared possible if not obvious to them and that was to follow their husbands in taking ordination. As stated in a Sinhala text,

---

* It can't be overstated how convoluted the chronology is intertextually. Pali texts say she was eighty. The reader is urged not to be overly concerned with such matters, as the "facts" will never be known.
† See the bibliography for their important works.

The wives of the 500 princes, when they heard that their husbands had become [monks], thought it would be better for them also to become recluses, than to remain at home in widowhood.*[1]

But this posed an obstacle of a different sort: there was no precedent for ordaining women in the Buddha's ministry.[†] The women's goal to become monastics represented much more than a radical shift in their own lives. It would drastically challenge the status quo in the newly emerging religion because to date women had only participated as lay disciples.

Of course, the Sakya women could not have known what we know now: that the Buddha declared his intention of establishing a fourfold assembly shortly after his enlightenment, thus making a women's monastic order not only inevitable but essential to his lifelong mission. Unfortunately, the Buddha only shared that plan with Mara. If it had been public knowledge, how much easier the women's path to ordination might have been! It certainly might have helped keep misogynist attitudes at bay in the men who would obstruct their path. In contrast, the monastic and lay orders formed easily for men, while women met with obstacles almost every step of the way.

When the Sakya women led by Mahaprajapati originally went before the Buddha in the Nigrodha Grove to call out the injustice of being excluded from his teachings, at least there was already a precedent for *upasikas*, beginning with the first laywoman disciple Sujata, who converted shortly after the Buddha's awakening.[2] As we saw in the *Maitreyasamiti-Nataka*, after pleading their case, the Sakya women found the Buddha to be immediately amenable to their concerns. In no way did he share the misogyny of the Sakya patriarchs; to the contrary, he took immediate concrete steps to ensure that women had equal access to his teachings.[3]

That was during his first visit; now the Buddha was back tending to family matters with the water dispute and death of his father. Sakya women had been roused to the dharma all over again by his powerful sermon on the banks of the Rohini River, their joy followed in short order by devastation as their husbands abandoned them. With the determination that had driven them previously to the dharma as *upasikas*, the women now vowed to

---

* This text uses "prince" and "princess" to refer to the Sakya people.
† There appears to have been precedent for female monasticism in Jainism.

become *bhikkhunis*. Would an appeal taken directly to the Buddha work for them again? For five years they had practiced as devout lay disciples, which surely would qualify them in his eyes to take the further step of ordination. No one could deny their passion for the dharma, which was in plain view from the beginning. Horner describes the fiery resolve of the Sakya women:

> There can be little doubt that there was a following of women lay-disciples during the first ... years of the ministry, else it is hardly conceivable that Mahaprajapati should have been accompanied, as it is recorded, by so large a concourse, so ardent in aspiration.[4]

But the women had to act fast because the rainy season in Kapilavastu was ending. Together with his retinue of monks (which now included their husbands), the Buddha would soon be leaving Kapilavastu to resume his itinerant teaching ministry across northeastern India. It was carpe diem, or not at all. Such an opportunity would not arise for the women again.

That hundreds of Sakya women had just lost their husbands to monasticism provides a context that has mostly been lost in traditional accounts of the first women's ordination. Knowing their circumstances as we do here adds immensely to our understanding of the urgency of their resolve. As before, their best move was to turn to their trusted queen, Mahaprajapati, also now a widow, who saw no future for herself in Kapilavastu, especially since her younger son, Nanda, and grandson, Rahula, had also left home to become monks.[5] Sharing similar circumstances, the Sakya women and their queen collectively reached a decision to seek ordination:

> Now Mahaprajapati Gotami, [the king's] widow ... formed in her heart the wish to abandon the world. And when also the five hundred Sakya ladies had listened to the Teacher delivering the [*Attadandasutta*] sermon on the bank of the Rohini river, they all with one consent agreed to go to Mahaprajapati and say, "We all would enter the order under the Teacher," and making her their leader they resolved to go.[6]

What we are seeing in these early stories is that the five hundred women who went forth with Mahaprajapati were remembered as intelligent and articulate in their resolve and aspiration. Contemporary accounts tend to spotlight Mahaprajapati's leadership role while overlooking the shared vision and voice of the multitude of women in her company. A Burmese account makes clear that the women were all of one mind:

> The wives of the [five hundred Sakya and Koliyan] princes who had recently renounced the world, desired also to follow the example set before them by their husbands. They went to the queen's apartments and communicated to her their design, entreating her to help them in obtaining the object of their wishes. [Mahaprajapati] not only promised them her support, but expressed the determination to join their company.[7]

So for the second time, Mahaprajapati led a company of Sakya women to the Nigrodha Grove to seek a concession from the Buddha. It is important to note just how she did this. As the queen and the Buddha's mother, it would not have been difficult to meet with her son privately or make some other personal arrangement to see him. Rather than leveraging her position in this way, she appeared before him with the entire assembly present, advocating for women generally, not just for herself. She took their plight to heart as much if not more than her own. As Finnegan says,

> Despite [her] intimate family ties, . . . Mahaprajapati Gautami never presents her petition for ordination as a personal request. Indeed, she frames her appeal in the broadest terms possible, grounding it in an implicit argument about equal gender opportunity.[8]

Even more, Mahaprajapati's willingness to appeal on behalf of all the women reflected her humility, as well as the mutual affection and respect that she and the Sakya women shared for one another. Regardless of her peerless status as queen and mother of the Buddha, nowhere in the stories do we find her imperious or holding herself to a different standard than the other women. When Mahaprajapati went to the Buddha to request ordination, it was a public event with all five hundred women accompanying her, and when she spoke to her son, it was with one voice that spoke for them all.

*Requesting Ordination in the Nigrodha Grove*

Suffice it to say that the Sakya women's second meeting with the Buddha did not go as smoothly as the first. Accounts vary, but the bottom line is that it appears the Buddha did not immediately accede to Mahaprajapati's request for women to join the monastic order. We'll never know just what was asked and what was answered, but those are the details that lie at the crux of the debate and confusion around the inception of female monasticism in Buddhism. Let's hunt for some highlights and outliers in the various ordination accounts.

The *Mulasarvastivada Vinaya* variant of the ordination story opens with a beautiful episode that describes the women's joy in hearing the dharma. Here they arrive together in the Nigrodha Grove, and rather than bringing their request to the Buddha straightaway, they pay proper homage by touching his feet and then sit to one side for a teaching. We're told the Buddha "taught them the sublime Dharma in various ways, instructing, benefitting and delighting them"; thus inspired by the teaching, "her mind deeply filled with joy on hearing the Dharma," Mahaprajapati steps forward, palms together, and makes her request to ordain on behalf of herself and all the women.[9]

The women's devotion shines through in this prelude to the ordination sequence. Their love of the dharma is a constant we have already seen in previous stories. Was this frame episode known but dropped from other ordination versions? We can't know, but it's worth remembering now—as a positive, female-affirming detail drawn from the past that might well be added to contemporary accounts of the women's ordination story.

Just how Mahaprajapati's words are characterized in the different variants further suggests new ways to tell the story. In the more perfunctory accounts of the ordination request—for example in the *Haimavata*, which is similar to the Pali canon account—she simply asks permission for women to go forth: "Blessed One, can we women obtain [permission] to go forth in the Buddha's teaching?"[10] However, in the *Mahasamghika-Lokottaravada Vinaya*, her request is far more heartfelt, reflecting not only her devotion but also a deep understanding of the dharma. She says,

> Blessed One, it is difficult to come across the arising of a Buddha, and it is difficult to come across the teaching of the true Dharma. Now the Blessed One, being a Tathagata, an arhat, a Fully Awakened One, has

appeared in the world and he teaches the Dharma that leads to peace and to final Nirvana, which is declared by the Well-Gone One, and which leads to the attainment of the deathless and the realization of Nirvana.

Blessed One, it would be good if women could obtain the going forth and the higher ordination, the state of being a nun, in the teaching and discipline declared by the Tathagata.[11]

While earlier we saw that the women's decision to seek ordination was triggered by losing their husbands and way of life, from this and other passages, we see that their motivation was also deeply religious. Their time spent as *upasikas* had brought them to a profound appreciation of dharma's benefits. We know that Mahaprajapati had already attained the level of stream entry, and some texts tell us other Sakya women had as well. As expressed through Mahaprajapati's words, the women recognized the preciousness of the opportunity before them, the unique karmic intersection of time, place, and rebirth, where not only was a buddha born in the world, but he was teaching dharma to others, and they had the freedom and opportunity to benefit from those ideal conditions. With all the passion and devotion they could summon, they wanted to make the most of this once-in-many-lifetimes, soteriological opportunity, which meant forsaking the world as they knew it, ordaining as nuns, and turning their lives wholeheartedly to the dharma. Carpe diem, indeed.

Verses from the nuns' poems in the *Therigatha* underscore this notion that most first-generation Buddhist women welcomed the religious life, not missing their husbands or the drudgery of domesticity. As the nun Mutta said,

> I am quite free, well-free from three crooked things,
> mortar, pestle, and husband with his own crooked thing.
> I am freed from birth and death,
> what leads to rebirth has been rooted out.[12]

In the *Mulasarvastivada Vinaya* and similarly in the *Madhyama-agama*, Mahaprajapati's request to ordain is more hypothetical as she asks the Buddha an entirely different question:

> Blessed One, if women go forth, receive the higher ordination, become nuns in the Buddha's teaching, and firmly cultivate the holy life (*brahmacarya*), will they attain the fourth fruit of recluseship?[13]

What she is asking is if women, having gone forth as nuns, can attain the goal of arhatship or eventual nirvana. That goal was unambiguously achievable by men, and here she is checking to be sure that this same potential is available to women. In one form or another, the question comes up in all the ordination sequences, but generally as a question that Ananda, not Mahaprajapati, poses to the Buddha. It is significant to find this exception where Mahaprajapati is portrayed as having the personal agency and depth of knowledge to pose a question of soteriological consequence to the Buddha directly.[14] As a representative of the five hundred women, it can be presumed that her congregation had been mulling this question and Mahaprajapati was asking on behalf of them all: Can women achieve the same goal of arhatship as men? Certainly that would have been a key discussion point among the women as they debated the pros and cons of ordination. Would they have decided differently had the Buddha said no? In all the ordination stories, the Buddha's answer to this question is unequivocally yes: women can equally attain the goal of arhatship.

Farther along in both the *Mulasarvastivada Vinaya* and *Madhyama-agama* accounts, we find the Buddha extolling Mahaprajapati's dharma accomplishments and depth of understanding. Recall that she is still a laywoman when he describes her thus, one who shares and reflects the achievements of her female congregants:

> Because of me, Mahaprajapati has taken refuge in the Buddha; taken refuge in the Dharma; and taken refuge in the community of monks; she is free from doubt in regard to the three jewels and in regard to dukkha, its arising, its cessation and the path [to its cessation]; she is accomplished in faith, maintains the moral precepts, broadly develops her learning, is accomplished in generosity, and has attained wisdom; she abstains from killing ... abstains from taking what is not given ... abstains from sexual misconduct ... abstains from false speech ... and abstains from alcoholic beverages.[15]

He further identifies her as a "stream enterer," confirming what we learned earlier—that she attained this initial step toward arhatship after hearing her first dharma teaching years before as queen in Kapilavastu:

In regard to the nature of the four truths, she will never again have doubt or perplexity, she has attained the fruit of stream-entry and will eradicate dukha on realizing freedom from [future] births.[16]

So what was the Buddha's response to the women's request for ordination? The more conservative versions, again the *Haimavata* and Pali canon, lean toward a flat no ("I do not wish to permit women to go forth"[17]). However, there is a lot of variation across the texts, particularly where the Buddha does not refuse Mahaprajapati at all but suggests alternatives or what could be seen as a compromise. For example, in the Kanjur he urges her to continue practicing as a laywoman, implying that that path would bring her equal benefit:

Gautami, wear the pure white dress of laywomen; seek to attain perfection; be pure, chaste and live virtuously, and you will find a lasting reward, blessings, and happiness.[18]

In several versions the sticking point for the Buddha appears to be the issue of monastic homelessness, not the granting of ordination per se. Here he suggests that women live and practice *as if* they were nuns with shaved heads and monastic robes in celibacy in the privacy and safety of their homes. According to the *Madhyama-agama*, he says,

Wait, wait, Gautami, do not have this thought that women leave the home out of faith and become homeless to train in the path in this right teaching and discipline. Gautami, you shave off your hair like this, put on monastic robes, and for your whole life practice the holy life (*brahmacarya*) in purity.[19]

In the *Mahisasaka Vinaya*, he further asserts that this arrangement has precedent because buddhas of the past did not allow the ordination of women, recommending instead they practice at home. The Buddha is quoted as saying,

Buddhas of ancient times all did not permit women to go forth. Women who had personally taken refuge in a Buddha, stayed at home, shaved their heads, wore monastic robes (*kasaya*), and energetically practicing with effort they obtained the fruits of the path. With future Buddhas it will also be like this. I now permit you to undertake this practice.[20]

Regarding the Buddha making alternative suggestions to women going forth as nuns, Analayo says,

> For the Buddha to tell Mahaprajapati that she can live a semi-monastic life at home quite possibly constitutes an early piece of the narrative that was lost in some versions. This is significant because it changes the picture of the Buddha's refusal considerably. Once he proposes such an alternative, the issue at stake is not stopping women from becoming nuns in principle. Instead, his refusal would be just an expression of concern that, at a time when the Buddhist order was still in its beginnings, lack of proper dwelling places and other living conditions of a homeless life might be too much for the Sakyan ladies.[21]

Consistent with this assessment, a passage from the Sinhala tradition characterizes the Buddha's response to Mahaprajapati's request as hesitation—not refusal, the chief reason being timing. Here we see he planned to ordain women eventually (noting there *was* precedent among past buddhas), just as we know it was part of his game plan after his enlightenment when he dedicated his ministry to establishing the fourfold community of lay and monastic women and men. But was ordaining nuns at the time of Mahaprajapati's request too much, too soon? There were a number of serious concerns for the Buddha to consider.

> It was clearly perceived by the sage that if these females were admitted to the profession, they would derive therefrom immense advantages; and he also saw that it was the practice of former buddhas to admit them; but he reflected that if they were admitted, it would perplex the minds of those who had not yet entered into the paths, and cause others to speak against his institutions. He, therefore, thought it would not be right to accede to their request at once, and said, "Women seek not to enter my immaculate Order."[22]

Without the full context, this last remark could be construed as very negative and final, similar to the more conservative ordination accounts where the Buddha appears to make a flat refusal. Is this the type of editing that went on as monastic men served as gatekeepers to the women's ordination narratives (and women's stories generally)?

However, leave in the contextualization of the Buddha's refusal here and we learn a lot about his thinking and what he was up against as he founded his ministry. It wasn't that he was a misogynist, but that misogyny and patriarchy abounded in the world around him. A big challenge was integrating his vision of a fourfold community with the prevailing patriarchal social norms without creating a backlash that would undermine his lifetime purpose, which included equally benefiting women by including them in his ministry. Another challenge would be how to convince lay donors to support a community of monastic women who would need the same requisites of clothing, shelter, food, and medicines as the monastic men. Further, the Buddha could not responsibly take on a new order of itinerant mendicants if he could not also ensure their safety. He would have been well aware of the dangers and hardships of the homeless life. Did the Sakya women, accustomed to a life of luxury, really know what they were asking to get themselves into?[23] The Pali canon records an abundance of stories of rape and violence against women during this time. On this, Horner said,

> Crimes of violence are mentioned so often in some parts of the *Vinaya* that an impression is created of a land infested by thieves and brutal men constantly on the lookout for the violation or molestation of unprotected women.[24]

One of the more seemingly misogynistic refusals of Mahaprajapati's request appears in the *Dharmaguptaka Vinaya*, where the Buddha is said to have responded to her directly that ordaining women would result in the dharma not lasting long in the world.[25] Once again there is no context given for this statement. If he said anything of the sort, it was likely a reference to men's behavior causing the dharma's demise, not women's. Already it was a big job for the Buddha to "quell the passions" of his newly recruited monks. A Sinhala text tells us that, as he had with Nanda, the Buddha even whisked the five hundred Sakya husbands off on a quick airborne trip to the Himalayas to give them a firsthand teaching on the downside of lust.[26] The monastic texts are full of stories of the sexual misconduct of libidinous monks, with far fewer such stories about nuns. Celibacy was a hard sell for the men. What headaches were in store if the monastic order included both women and men? Recall the Buddha was still in Kapilavastu when the women first requested ordination. He had just ordained their husbands, and almost straightaway the wives asked to follow suit. Obviously, married couples ordaining simultaneously must have looked like trouble. How was it going to work? The Buddha apparently felt more time was needed to sort things out. The Sakya women, on the other hand, were not willing to wait.

### Who Were the First Buddhist Women?

Before continuing with the nuns' ordination story, let's pause to examine more closely the women who turned to Mahaprajapati for leadership. Individual women normally aren't named in these stories; for example, the harem is always just "the harem" or "consort wives," even though these women were reported to number in the thousands. The women following Mahaprajapati to the Nigrodha Grove are typically designated simply "the five hundred," although we are told that half of those women were Koliyan wives and half of them Sakya wives from Kapilavastu. But the numbers are not exact, and we know there were other women too, mostly from the royal household as evidenced by clues within these passages and from other sources, primarily the *Therigatha*. Rather than leaving these first Buddhist women unnamed or anonymous as women in history often are, let's take a look and see if we can bring any of them to life with names and maybe even an added detail or two.

A stunning contribution to this inquiry appears in the *Mahasamghika-Lokottaravada Vinaya*, where Mahaprajapati is described as approaching the Buddha with two women named Chanda and Dasachanda, together with the five hundred women. These two women are further identified as the foster mother and mother of Chandaka, respectively.* This small detail provides a marvelous window back into Mahaprajapati's palace life as queen

---

* It's unclear how or why Chandaka would have both a mother and a foster mother. As *dasa* means "servant," perhaps Dasachanda had been Chandaka's wet nurse.

and chief consort in Suddhodana's harem. It also gives us clues about the nature of relationships among this cohort of women.

Recall that Chandaka was Siddhartha's charioteer (sometimes identified as his groom), who assisted the prince in fleeing Kapilavastu on the night of his Great Departure. So revered was Chandaka in ancient Buddhist lore that he, like Yasodhara and others, was described as co-natal with the Buddha, born at the same moment and destined to live his life closely tied to his master.[27] Chandaka and Siddhartha grew up together as playmates in Suddhodana's harem, and later in life Chandaka became a monk and the Buddha's devoted disciple. Further, implicit though not stated in the texts is that Chandaka and the Buddha were likely half-brothers, Chandaka's mother being a concubine in Suddhodana's harem.[28] Here we finally have her name: Dasachanda. We never knew Chandaka had a foster mother, but now we know her name too—Chanda.

Women who were concubines in their youth became servants in their later years. Here we see that Dasachanda and Chanda, who would have been attendants to Queen Mahaprajapati in her court, were now close at her side as she asked her son to allow women to ordain. So close were they, in fact, that they were remembered individually. Clearly the relationship between the women did not end with the dissolution of palace life, and why would it? The one thing these women had as their lives fell apart was each other. If prior hierarchal caste or class relationships among the women had not already shifted toward mutual support and friendship, they did so now. That said, rapid social change did not necessarily mean a wholesale change in roles. It's touching to see here that it would be Chandaka's mother(s) who would be Mahaprajapati's closest, trusted companions, mirroring the lifelong relationship of their sons. These three women, having known each other at least since they were young mothers together, would likely have been about the same age.

Imagine the memories and emotions churning for Dasachanda and Chanda as they stood before the Buddha, placing their fate in his hands: a man they had known since his infancy; a child they had certainly held, nurtured, and perhaps even disciplined in the women's quarters of his father's palace; a boy they had seen grow up and bring untold heartache to his family, particularly his mother, with his decision to leave home. Now as the Buddha, he offered a refuge they never could have imagined back then.

While this is the only account found here in which Dasachanda and Chanda are named, the *Madhyama-agama* variant and a Chinese counterpart may be parallel since they note that Mahaprajapati was accompanied by "some elderly Sakyan women" in addition to the five hundred.[29]

One woman who may have gone forth with Mahaprajapati was the Buddha's wife, Yasodhara. We know she ordained at some point, and the texts are mixed as to whether it was right away when the Buddha returned home or sometime later. The Burmese legend and Tibetan *Mulasarvastivada Vinaya* both claim she was among the five hundred women who ordained with Mahaprajapati.[30] Horner speculates that Yasodhara's ordination may have preceded Mahaprajapati's and that she may have gone forth followed by a company of women from her own court prior to Suddhodana's death and her mother-in-law's ordination.[31] However, there does not appear to be evidence to support this theory in the *vinaya* narratives. Perhaps what Horner was referencing are reports that Yasodhara begged her husband on a number of occasions to let her accompany him on his religious mission, even asking for ordination, although it was not granted.

We first saw this on the night of Siddhartha's Great Departure, when Yasodhara had nightmares about his leaving and said, "O, my lord, where e'er thou goest, there let me go too." Thinking she was referencing nirvana, he consoled her, promising, "So be it; wherever I go, there mayest thou go also."[32] Yasodhara actually just wanted to stay with her husband and didn't mean nirvana at all, although this passage foretells her future as his disciple. Later, as noted earlier, while he was away practicing austerities, she demonstrated her devotion and willingness to give up royal privilege by living an equally ascetic life in the palace. When her husband, now the Buddha, finally did come back, she was still furious that he had left her and looked for ways to restore their marriage.[33] Nothing worked, and some sources tell us that as a last resort she requested ordination (likely not so much for religious reasons). A Sinhala text reports that the Buddha refused her request because "[he] saw that the right of entrance to the order of the female priesthood belonged first, to the queen-mother, Prajapati."[34] At this time Suddhodana said to his daughter-in-law,

> By and by you also will become an ascetic; but it will be better to delay now, as people would say you have renounced the world on account of your sorrow.[35]

This Sinhala text goes on to say that Yasodhara waited until Suddhodana died, renounced the queenship she had inherited, and left Kapilavastu leading one thousand Sakya women to join company with Mahaprajapati, who was already in Vaishali. There Yasodhara and her entourage received novice ordination from Mahaprajapati and shortly afterward received full ordination from the Buddha.[36]

In a twist, the Sanskrit tradition holds that Siddhartha had several wives in his vast harem (sixty thousand we are told) and that they all ended up becoming nuns. Yasodhara is normally named as his chief wife or consort, while his junior wives variously appear as Gopa (Gopika), Mrgadja (Mrigi), and Utpalavarna.[37] Gopa and Yasodhara appear conflated in some sources; for example, in the *Lalitavistara*, Gopa is named as his principal wife. The Nepali *Buddhacarita* names Gopika and Mahaprajapati as coleaders of the nuns.[38] The *Theri-apadana* in the Pali canon claims that Yasodhara was the leader of eighteen thousand nuns.[39]

Several women already mentioned would have ordained with Mahaprajapati, including her daughter, Sundarinanda, who we learned was very reluctant to become a nun, as well as her childhood servant Kesini, who had accompanied Mahaprajapati and Maya on the occasion of their marriage to Suddhodana.

Another trusted servant to go forth with Mahaprajapati was her childhood nurse Vaddhesi,* although we are told that she found monastic life a struggle. Her verse in the *Therigatha* offers a glimpse of the ambivalence some women must have felt who experienced monasticism as a lifestyle change that was thrust upon them by changing circumstances rather than being a studied decision they had reached of their own accord:

> With no peace in my heart, dripping with sexual desire,
> I entered the monastery, wailing, my arms outstretched.[40]

In contrast, the Sakya nun Uttara, previously a royal concubine, appears to have made peace with worldly desires:

> Self-controlled with the body,
> with speech, and with the mind,

---

* Dhammapala calls her "a certain Theri."

having pulled out craving down to the root,
I have become cool, free.[41]

A complete list obviously cannot be known, but at least ten more nuns are named in the *Therigatha* as Sakya palace women who went forth with Mahaprajapati: Tissa, Dhira, Vira, Mitta, Bhadra, Upasama, Sumana, Uttara, Visakha,* and Sangha, the first six being former concubines of the Bodhisattva.[42] Their voices still resonate in *Therigatha* poems, described thus by Foley:

> [The] lines are often not so much sentences as rosaries of words, each word to the ancient Buddhist being fraught with pregnant and precious import.[43]

## The Journey to Vaishali

Returning to our story, we find Mahaprajapati and her company of five hundred women very disappointed that they had not received permission to ordain before the Buddha left Kapilavastu. First bereft when their husbands left them, now they faced separation from their Teacher and the teachings they had counted on to bring them refuge and a hopeful future.

Their determination to be included in the Buddha's assembly unabated, the Sakya women now cut off their hair, dressed in monastic robes, and set off following the Buddha and his company of monks. The accounts variously report their emotional state as sorrowful or charged with religious fervor. The following is from the *Haimavata Vinaya*:

> Gautami and the five hundred women, their mind affected by sorrow and grief at not being themselves in the ranks of the Buddha's teaching, each shaved their heads, put on monastic robes and left, following after the Buddha.[44]

---

*Not to be confused with the well-known laywoman Visakha from Sravasti; see Garling, *Stars at Dawn*, 243–54.

From a Burmese text:

> As a token of the sincerity and earnestness of their resolution all the
> ladies, without the least hesitation, cut their beautiful black hair, put
> on a dress in accordance with their pious intentions, and resolutely
> set out on foot in the direction of Vaishali.[45]

The hardship of walking barefoot for hundreds of kilometers to Vaishali
is dramatically recounted in several sources. Although accustomed to luxury,
these Sakya women chose to demonstrate the sincerity of their commitment
by forgoing any conveyance or assistance on their journey. After all, the
Buddha and his monk disciples had just left Kapilavastu on foot, so why
should they proceed any differently? The Sinhala tradition says,

> The queen-mother thought that it would not be right for them to go
> in chariots, as it would be contrary to the institutions of the recluse;
> they must travel in some manner that would be attended with fatigue;
> and they, therefore, set out for Vaishali on foot. . . . In consequence of
> their extreme tenderness, their feet were soon covered with blisters.[46]

The text continues that townsfolk along the way offered assistance:

> The people of those parts, who had previously heard of their beauty,
> no sooner knew that they were on their way, than they came from
> all directions to look after them. Some prepared food and requested
> they would do them the favour to partake of it; whilst others brought
> vehicles and litters, and entreated that they would make use of them;
> but [the women] resolutely refused to take advantage of these kinds
> of offers of assistance.[47]

A more patriarchal variation of this account appears in the *Manorathapurani*, where Buddhaghosa writes that Sakya and Koliyan kings (we
don't know who these would be) provided golden palanquins for the five
hundred women, who turned them down. Next the kings provided sentries
to guard the front and rear of their procession while sending along cartloads
of provisions. According to Buddhaghosa, the guards were further ordered

to cook for the women along the way. A curious story in which we can't help but recognize the kings' kind intentions.

However, the *Mahasamghika-Lokotarravada Vinaya* reports that the women did use chariots for their journey. This passage is also exceptional because we hear Mahaprajapati pitching a plan B directly to the women:

> Honourable Ones, what if we cut our hair on our own, put on monastic robes and, in chariots with chassis made of straps, closely follow the journeys of the Blessed One in the regions of Kosala?* If the Blessed One gives us permission, we will go forth; if he does not permit it, we can still live the holy life (*brahmacarya*) like this in the presence of the Blessed One.[48]

She points out that even if the Buddha denied their request, they could still live a religious life in celibacy in the presence of the Blessed One and continue to take joy in the teachings.[49] Not that she had the details worked out (including his permission), but this alternative must have felt appealing, or at least preferable to a bleak future in Kapilavastu. Come what may, by making this journey the women would all remain close to each other and their loved ones. We can feel Mahaprajapati's mixed yearnings here too. As both his mother and his disciple, she had a heartfelt wish to remain close to her son, the Buddha.

That the women cut their hair and donned the garb of monastics to follow the Buddha could be construed as an act of defiance. However, as we saw in some of the variants already mentioned, they were doing exactly what the Buddha himself had suggested they do as an alternative to going forth. As Analayo points out, if the women sincerely wanted to ordain, it seems unlikely that they would openly defy their Teacher. Further, Mahaprajapati as a stream enterer, by definition, had unshakeable faith in the Buddha, making it even more unlikely, if not impossible, that she would deliberately disobey him, especially publicly.[50] To do so would also undermine the trust and confidence that her company of women had placed in her. According to Analayo, what makes more sense is that the Buddha offering the women an alternative rather than a flat refusal is a narrative detail—a significant one—that has been altered or lost in some ordination accounts. He says,

---

* This and several other accounts report that the women followed the Buddha to Sravasti rather than Vaishali.

The Buddha's granting to Mahaprajapati Gautami and her followers the option of shaving their hair and donning robes seems to underlie even those versions that do not explicitly report such a permission, but which nevertheless show that Mahaprajapati Gautami and her followers acted accordingly.... It seems reasonable to assume that such a permission by the Buddha, explicitly or implicitly, would have been part of an early version of the foundation history.[51]

Rather than defiance, the women's actions demonstrated the sincerity of their intentions and their willingness to assume the harsh conditions that monastic life demanded. The Buddha certainly would have noted this resolve in further considering their request. Analayo points out that nowhere in the narratives is there reproach or censure of Mahaprajapati and the women for preemptively shaving their heads and wearing monastic robes. Had their actions been deemed in any way inappropriate, they surely would have received a rebuke from the Buddha, also perhaps Ananda.[52]

In fact, the women appearing *as if* nuns were following the Buddha's proposal, no doubt hoping that this would just be an interim step before he granted them actual ordination. Some accounts even say that Mahaprajapati and the five hundred women left Kapilavastu at the same time the Buddha did, trailing behind him and his monks, sitting for his teachings along the way, "always staying overnight wherever the Blessed One stayed overnight."[53] More commonly we hear that the women met up with the Buddha in Vaishali after their long journey—exhausted, filthy, and hungry, but more resolute than ever to commit themselves to the monastic life and the dharma.

## Ordination of the Sakya Women

Arriving in Vaishali, the Sakya women's goal was to petition the Buddha once again to ordain as nuns. Failing that, at least they were where they wanted to be—back in the company of their beloved Teacher and, for many of them, their husbands, fathers, brothers, and sons, who were now monks in the Buddha's assembly. Mahaprajapati repeated her request to the Buddha multiple times, her words in Kapilavastu echoed in Vaishali. But now Ananda, the Buddha's close disciple, is introduced into the narratives as an intermediary and advocate on behalf of Mahaprajapati and her entourage, similar to his appearance earlier in *The Robe Story*.

Often depicted as sensitive and emotional, Ananda is overcome with anxious worry when he first sees the women arrive in Vaishali:

> When Ananda saw them, with bleeding feet, covered with dust, and half dead, his breast was full of sorrow, and his eyes filled with tears, and he said, "Why have you come? For what reason have you endured these hardships? Have the Sakyas been driven from their city by their enemy? Why does the mother of Buddha remain in such a place?"[54]

In several versions Ananda directs his questions not just to Mahaprajapati but to all the Sakya women, and they respond in unison. An example appears in the *Mahisasaka Vinaya*, where they say,

> Venerable sir, the Blessed One does not permit women to go forth and receive the higher ordination. For this reason we are personally grieving. We wish you to report this on our behalf, so that our aspiration will be obtained.[55]

Ananda plays a pivotal role in bringing their dreams to reality, but before going further, we need to pause again. Who is Ananda? Almost nothing is known about him prior to his discipleship, which is strange for a figure of such stature in early Buddhist history. Traditionalists might argue that he ranks second in importance only to the Buddha himself, while in this volume, we'll give him a close third behind Mahaprajapati, whose extraordinary contributions to the foundation of Buddhism, too long overlooked, are unsurpassed. But Ananda's great gift was parlaying decades of intimate proximity to the Buddha—his teachings, thoughts, and actions—into a complete and detailed remembered account of his ministry. This tremendous sum of knowledge was held orally for several hundred years and eventually written down, forming the scriptural basis for the sutra portion of Buddhist canonical literature.

Of added importance here is that beyond his role as devoted disciple and later attendant, Ananda was a member of the Buddha's Sakya family. It is traditionally reported that he was a first cousin, perhaps the son of one of Suddhodana's brothers, possibly Amritodana. But curiously there are almost no records citing this early period of Ananda's life. This author's thesis, argued previously in *Stars at Dawn*, is that Ananda may have been the Buddha's biological son from his junior wife Mrigi when, as Prince Siddhartha, he had a vast harem.[56] While controversial and impossible to prove, this detail—if accurate—would suggest tremendous emotional depth in our current narrative, particularly because Mahaprajapati would be Ananda's grandmother.

When Ananda greeted the bedraggled Sakya women arriving from Kapilavastu, he was looking out over a sea of faces, many of which he would have recognized from home. Foremost he would have seen Mahaprajapati, the beloved queen and family matriarch. No wonder he was emotional and teary. The circumstances had completely shifted from earlier years, but as we've seen all along, Sakya family ties didn't disappear with the transformation of Prince Siddhartha to the Buddha, or his introduction of monasticism as an alternative to household life. They just became more complicated as everyone adjusted to a new normal.

Several accounts relate that when Mahaprajapati and her entourage first arrived, they sat in on a public teaching that once again instructed, benefited, and delighted them.[57] Still travel-worn, Mahaprajapati approached the Buddha afterward and repeated her previous request for women to ordain. He repeated his previous answer. She became discouraged and wept, which is when Ananda appeared and offered to act as go-between to take the women's petition to the Buddha himself.[58] It's significant that in these accounts Mahaprajapati initially had direct access to her son upon arriving in Vaishali and was not dependent on Ananda.

The *vinaya* literature repeatedly describes Mahaprajapati as dirty and weeping when she arrives in Vaishali. Analayo suggests this "negative portrayal" was intentional and meant to imply that she was weak and otherwise unworthy of the monastic life.[59] He kindly does not point a finger, but this treatment certainly would suggest the handiwork of sexist monk editors whose mission seems to have been to undermine, if not denigrate, Mahaprajapati's tremendous contribution and that of the five hundred women to early Buddhism.

Rather than disparaging Mahaprajapati's physical appearance, highlighting the women's arduous journey as an expression of their commitment to personal freedom and the dharma would have been a worthy narrative topic. Anyone traveling such a distance barefoot on dusty roads for days would be dirty (didn't the men just make the same journey?). And why *not* tears? The women were exhausted, had just lost their families, journeyed far from home and all that was familiar, and still their futures hung in the balance. If only we could hear their version of this grueling trek. Can we imagine it now? There are many inspiring ways the literature could have woven the first Buddhist women's pilgrimage into the fabric of early narratives, linking stories of their valorous struggle anecdotally to dharma teachings and soteriological purpose. Truly this was a missed opportunity, one that exposes the stark silence of women's voices that continues to echo from Buddhism's earliest foundations.

Returning to our story, a lot of back and forth concerning the women's request for ordination now begins between Mahaprajapati (standing outside the monastery, presumably weeping) and Ananda and the Buddha who are inside talking it over. Nothing new emerges as we hear once again that granting women ordination would shorten the duration of the dharma (with lengthy analogies), as well as the Buddha's positive assurances that women and men have equal potential to realize the fruits of the path, or arhatship. In the *Mahasamghika-Lokottaravada Vinaya*, we find rich elaboration on this last detail when Ananda reminds the Buddha of the precedent of a fourfold community. Their exchange goes as follows:

[Ananda]:
Blessed One, how many assemblies did former Tathagatas, arhats, Fully Awakened Ones have?

[Buddha]:
Former Tathagatas, arhats, Fully Awakened Ones had four assemblies, namely monks, nuns, laymen, and laywomen.

[Ananda]:
Blessed One, can women who dwell alone, diligent, energetic, and secluded, realise these four fruits of recluseship, namely the fruit of stream-entry, the fruit of once-return, the fruit of non-return, and the supreme fruit of arhatship? . . .

[Buddha]:
Ananda, women who dwell alone, diligent, energetic, and secluded, realise these four fruits of recluseship, namely the fruit of stream-entry . . . *up to* . . . the supreme fruit of arhatship.

[Ananda]:

> Blessed One, since former Tathagatas, arhats, Fully Awakened Ones had four assemblies, namely monks, nuns, laymen, and laywomen and [since] women who dwell alone, diligent, energetic, and secluded, realise these four fruits of recluseship, namely the fruit of stream-entry ... *up to* ... the supreme fruit of arhatship [therefore] it would be good if women could attain the going forth and the higher ordination, the state of being a nun, in the teaching and discipline declared by the Tathagata.[60]

Bravo, Ananda, for presenting a reasoned, philogynist argument in support of ordaining women, even citing precedent. However, as Analayo points out, the Buddha (being the Buddha) would not have needed reminding that women had the same potential as men,[61] or that there was the precedent of the fourfold assembly, or for that matter, that he himself had made a commitment to forming a fourfold assembly shortly after his enlightenment. The Buddha would have known exactly what was going on and had his own unique handle on how this important karmic event was meant to play out. We can't know what that was, but one way or another, we can be glad that it did. A Sinhala passage reflects his omniscience on this matter as he speaks to Ananda:

> Are the Buddhas born in the world only for the benefit of men? Assuredly it is also for the benefit of females as well. When I delivered the *Tirokudha-sutra*, many women entered the paths, as did also many goddesses when I delivered the *Abhidhamma* in Trayastrimsa. Have not Visakha and many other upasikas entered the paths? The entrance is open for women as well as men.[62]

A breakthrough in the debate finally comes when Ananda takes the personal tack of reminding the Buddha that Mahaprajapati is his mother. Would playing the family card make a difference? His determination perhaps inspired by hers, Ananda makes the argument that it was Mahaprajapati who took the Buddha to her breast when his birth mother, Maya, died and raised him from infancy. For this reason, if no other, shouldn't the Buddha grant her ordination request? In the *Mahisasaka Vinaya*, Ananda says,

Shortly after the Buddha was born, when his mother passed away, Gautami raised the Blessed One with [her] milk until he grew up. As she has done him a great kindness like this, why not requite her for it?[63]

And in the Burmese tradition it is said,

Ananda respectfully reminded Buddha of all the favors he had received from Mahaprajapati who had nursed and brought him up with the utmost care and tenderness, from the day his mother died, when he was but seven days old.[64]

As in *The Robe Story*, the Buddha acknowledges his mother's gifts to him, while countering that any perceived debt has been more than repaid through his gift of the dharma to her. The *Mahasamghika-Lokottaravada Vinaya* conveys a feeling of parity between the twin gifts by describing them both as "difficult" (*duskara-carika*), a word choice unique to this variant:

[Ananda]:
Mahaprajapati Gautami has done for the Blessed One what is difficult, she was his nurse and foster mother, the giver of milk when his mother passed away, and the Blessed One is one who acknowledges and is grateful.

[Buddha]:
Ananda, Mahaprajapati Gautami has done for the Blessed One what is difficult, she was his nurse and foster mother, the giver of milk when his mother passed away, and the Tathagata is one who acknowledges and is grateful.
     Ananda, yet the Tathagata has also done for Mahaprajapati Gautami what is difficult . . . because of the Tathagata Mahaprajapati Gautami has taken refuge in the Buddha, has taken refuge in the Dharma, and has taken refuge in the community. . . . [and so forth for many passages describing the limitless gifts of dharma].[65]

Mahaprajapati undertook the difficult task of raising a child and nurtured him with mother's milk; her son undertook the difficult task of pursuing life's deeper truths and nurtured her with dharma's wisdom. Mother's milk as a metaphor for the dharma. This beautiful passage communicates a mutual tribute where we see again the purity and purport of a mother's unconditional love held up as the closest worldly counterpart to the *buddhadharma*.

The conversation about his mother tips the scales, and the Buddha concedes that women should be allowed to enter the monastic order. The Burmese text explains, "[The] Buddha's scruples were overcome by the persuasive language of the faithful Ananda,"[66] while the Sinhala text says,

> When [Ananda] had concluded [enumerating the benefits that the Buddha received from Mahaprajapati in his childhood] the great teacher saw that the time had now come in which it would be proper to admit the [Sakya women] to the [monastic order].[67]

Great news that the Buddha agreed to ordain women, but now comes a glitch in the story. All accounts report that the Buddha's concession came with a big caveat, one where he stipulated eight "heavy" rules (*gurudharmas*), or restrictions, that applied only to nuns. These the Buddha allegedly spelled out to Ananda as non-negotiable conditions for women's ordination. Still in place today and the subject of much controversy, these eight female-focused rules are highly misogynistic as they function to subjugate women within the monastic orders. Was that the Buddha's intention? Did he really stipulate these additional rules in the first place? Evidence found in this author's investigation of early narratives finds their sexist nature completely out of character for the Buddha and supports many contemporary views that they are of doubtful authenticity, at least in their present form. As Analayo has said,

> It seems... safe to conclude that the elements in the canonical accounts that express a negative attitude toward nuns seem to stem from a later textual layer. These stand in direct contrast to the numerous canonical texts that present the Buddha's attitude toward the order of nuns in a positive light, indicating that he wanted an order of nuns, whose existence should be reckoned as one of the prerequisites for the duration of his teachings.[68]

The eight heavy rules are subject to intense scholarly scrutiny as Buddhist monastic women today still struggle to claim equal status and voice alongside monastic men. Many theories about the rules have arisen. One suggested here is that the Buddha indeed stipulated eight new rules, but they are not the same rules that were eventually recorded in the *vinaya* texts we see today. In other words, rather than later male monastics altogether inventing a list of eight, is it possible that a list originated with the Buddha whose items later became switched out or altered? How and when could this sort of redaction even have taken place? Logically very early and in India, sometime before the dispersal of *vinaya* material into the different, emerging Buddhist schools. Unlikely perhaps, but let's imagine such a scenario.

Recalling (and trusting) the Buddha's hesitancy in ordaining women, perhaps the original eight rules flowed from his concern about their welfare and were in fact female-friendly, protective even, as he sought ways to ensure women's safety as they transitioned from the protections of patriarchal society to homeless life. After all, the Buddha had a huge responsibility to get it right. Not wanting anyone to come to harm, the future and reputation of his ministry also was at stake. As elaborated by Analayo,

> The Buddha's refusal to grant women the going forth could have originally been an expression of apprehensions that conditions were not yet ripe for this move ... it could have reflected concerns regarding how to accommodate women living the holy life in celibacy as homeless wanderers at this early stage in the development of Buddhist monasticism, when safe dwelling places for Buddhist monastics were still scarce and public recognition not yet widespread.[69]

It has been noted that the Buddha generally formulated new rules in response to offenses or specific occasions as they arose, not preemptively as would be the case here.[70] As an example, a later *vinaya* rule stated that nuns could not dwell in forests.[71] The intention was not to treat women less fairly (yes, monks could dwell in forests), but to ensure their safety because it had been brought to the Buddha's attention that nuns dwelling in forests had been raped. His impulse to protect newly ordained women would appear especially plausible when we consider that among them was his own elderly mother, with many elderly women also in her company. Concern for the safety and well-being of the first female monastics would be totally in character with the Buddha we see attentively seeing to the welfare of his disciples throughout the four-and-a-half decades of his ministry.

We can't know what immediate concerns arose when the women arrived in Vaishali, but, as Analayo suggests, the Buddha's eight injunctions may have been aimed at ensuring a smooth transition and cooperation between the two orders.[72] He says,

> Mahaprajapati and her followers have left the lay life behind. They have thereby entered the sphere of the monastic jurisdiction of the Buddha. In reply to their following him...the Buddha now regulates how things should proceed in order that they become fully part of the monastic community.[73]

One matter that may have appeared as a priority, for example, was maintaining celibacy and proper, separate accommodations within the expanding community, especially as many of the newly ordained monastics were married couples. The Buddha had practical matters like these to address in order to ensure the stability and longevity of his dispensation. He needed to preserve the integrity of his newly forming monastic institutions, which, among other things, meant avoiding scandal, particularly since the lay population, including donors, looked to monastics as role models.

There are many different ways this critical period in Buddhist history can be imagined. Perhaps after the Buddha's death, his monks—who we already know were not happy about the entrance of women into the monastic order—or their successors swapped out the contents of an original eight rules to suit their own agendas. Just a few self-serving tweaks would secure their superior, controlling status going forward, while, at the same time, preserving the original frame of eight rules created on the occasion of women's ordination. As Analayo has said,

> The eight *gurudharmas* appear to result from a textual development whose final outcomes are different from what might well have been their starting point.[74]

A seemingly minor but significant discrepancy across the various ordination stories surrounds some vagueness about whether Ananda brought the terms of ordination—the eight heavy rules—solely to Mahaprajapati for her acceptance or to Mahaprajapati together with the five hundred women. As it is usually told he negotiated directly with Mahaprajapati, whose acceptance, while not always stated, implied acceptance on behalf of all the women, despite their not being present.

However, several accounts that follow make it clear that Ananda negotiated with the group as a whole with Mahaprajapati as the spokesperson. As he ferried back and forth with updates from the Buddha, all the Sakya women (not just Mahaprajapati) eagerly waited outside the monastery to hear the news. This latter rendering is significant and more consistent with the pattern we've seen since Kapilavastu where the five hundred women first joined forces and asked Mahaprajapati to represent them. From this, it follows that they would have collectively considered the Buddha's offer in Vaishali and responded with one voice.

In these variants it is further said that the women's collective acceptance of the eight heavy rules constituted their collective ordination. From these accounts, then, Mahaprajapati would not have been the first Buddhist nun per se, as much as she and the five hundred women simultaneously became the first Buddhist nuns. The Sinhala legend says,

> The eight ordinances were repeated by Ananda to Prajapati and the other [women], and when they heard the conditions upon which they could be admitted to [the Order], they were greatly delighted, and at once promised that all the ordinances should be strictly observed. They were admitted to [the Order] in the presence of [monks]; and when they received full ordination, Prajapati was appointed by the Buddha to be the chief of female recluses and to instruct her relatives in the necessary discipline.[75]

In similar passages, both the *Dharmaguptaka* and *Haimavata Vinayas* tell us that the women's collective acceptance of the eight rules constituted their ordination. The latter states,

> Ananda went outside and asked the female disciples: "The Buddha has declared eight principles to be respected. Are you able to receive them respectfully?"
>
> On having heard these words, the women were filled with joy and delight. They requested Ananda to return and tell the Blessed One: "Today we have received the Blessed One's gift of the teaching and we shall receive it respectfully."

Ananda reported these words to the Blessed One. The Blessed One said, "Thus they have already obtained the higher ordination."[76]

In the Burmese legend, Mahaprajapati spoke on behalf of all the women when she accepted the eight rules. Using the plural "we" rather than "I," she likened their joy at the prospect of ordination to a bride's anticipation of her wedding day:

> On hearing the good news, Prajapati, in the name of her companions, spoke to Ananda: "Venerable Ananda, we all rejoice that the favor so often asked for has been at last granted unto us. As a young maid, who has bathed, and washed her hair, is anxiously desirous to put on her fine ornaments, as she receives with delight the beautiful and fragrant nosegays that are offered to her, so we are longing for the eight precepts and wish for admittance into the assembly."

And further,

> They all promised to observe the rules of the [order] to the end of their lives.[77]

It is worth noting that in the last three samples, the women accepted the eight rules with "joy" and "delight," even "longing," yet the rules themselves are not listed. Perhaps the women were just eager. Or, could it be they were responding to a different, more affirmative list of eight rules—rules that were later altered that we have never seen?

Perhaps the most beautiful description of the women's entrance into the order is found in the *Mulasarvastivada Vinaya*, where we feel their deep sense of faith as expressed in Mahaprajapati's words, again echoing the imagery of a wedding. Whether the five hundred women participated is not made clear when Mahaprajapati accepts the new rules:

> Then Mahaprajapati, having heard the venerable Ananda reporting the principles to be respected, with a mind of deep joy, respectfully took them on her head and said to Ananda: "Venerable sir, . . . When the woman sees the [wreath of] flowers arriving, she accepts it with great joy, and places it upon her head. Venerable sir, I am just like this,

with body, speech, and mind, I receive on my head the Tathagata's eight principles to be respected."

When Mahaprajapati accepted the principles to be respected, then she and the five hundred Sakyan women went forth, received the higher ordination and became nuns.[78]

A segue is in order here to report a contrasting story reported by Buddhaghosa in his *Dhammapada* commentary in which discord arose concerning the legitimacy of Mahaprajapati's ordination. It is unclear just when this took place, but the context here suggests Mahaprajapati took ordination separately without witnesses. Here we learn that some nuns did not feel that Mahaprajapati had received proper ordination, if indeed she had been ordained at all. Questions arose: Who witnessed her ordination? Who was her preceptor or teacher? Had she just assumed monastic robes "with her own hand"?[79] The rebellious nuns went so far as to refuse to hold religious observances with Mahaprajapati. They took their grievance to the Buddha, who heard them out and then roundly set them straight, by saying,

I myself conferred the Eight Cardinal Precepts on Maha Pajapati Gotami. I alone am her teacher; I alone am her preceptor.[80]

He went on to rebuke the nuns by pointing out the condition of their own negative minds:

They that have renounced the sins of [body, speech and mind], they that have rid themselves of evil passions, such persons should never entertain feelings of dissatisfaction.[81]

While this story serves an important purpose in clarifying the legitimacy of Mahaprajapati's ordination, it must be pointed out that the nuns' suspicion, if not animosity, in this story is completely out of character with the relationship we've seen thus far between the original five hundred nuns and their trusted, beloved leader. One thought is that the nuns in this story were not Sakya, but newly admitted nuns from other regions who had no particular allegiance to Mahaprajapati and who might well have felt resentment toward her and her close relationship with the scores of Sakya nuns, not to mention the Buddha himself.

Whatever its origin, this story serves to clear up any ambiguity about Mahaprajapati's standing and leadership position in the nuns' community. Indeed, among monastic women she alone had authorized, direct access to the Buddha. We are led to believe this was solely because he was her teacher and preceptor, but would we be wrong in surmising that it also had something to do with him being her son?

Returning to our story, the Buddha publicly put Mahaprajapati in charge of the nuns as a final step in establishing the women's monastic order:

> Nuns, so from now on in this life you should consider Mahaprajapati Gautami as responsible for the community, as the eldest of the community as the leader of the community.[82]

A tall order, but one that Mahaprajapati stepped into easily. Being "leader of the community" was an ever-expanding role she had known her whole life, beginning with Maya's death when she became queen of the Sakyas and head of the royal household. Already she was leader of the five hundred newly ordained nuns who had traveled with her from Kapilavastu. Now, as more and more women sought the monastic life, Mahaprajapati's authority and influence as chief nun would only increase.

By all accounts the monastic women's order burgeoned after Mahaprajapati and the Sakya women broke through the barriers that had held women back. Now women could choose between the paths of the *upasika* or *bhikkhuni*. For many of them, a life dedicated purely to religious practice held irresistible appeal. From the Sinhala legend, we learn:

> The number of females who were admitted to the profession after this period cannot be computed, but the chapters, both of priests and priestesses, increased so greatly that in all Jambudvipa it was scarcely possible to find a suitable place for the exercise of . . . solitary meditation.[83]

Similarly, according to Dhammapala,

> Thus the order of nuns was firmly established, and waxed in numbers in one place and another, in village, town, country, and royal city. Matrons, daughters-in-law and maidens hearing the wisdom of

Buddha, the Law and the Order, rejoiced at his system, and feeling agitation at the prospect of continuous rebirth, asked the permission of their husbands, parents and relatives, and joined the Order, taking the discipline to their bosom. And then, successful in virtuous works, and receiving instruction from the Teacher and the monks with energy and endeavor, they not long after realized arhatship.[84]

Mission accomplished! How joyous for the nuns and auspicious for the new religion that Buddhism's fourfold community was now complete. From a Buddhist standpoint, one could say that a lot of karma was spent getting women to that goal. Whether or not Mahaprajapati and the five hundred nuns saw it that way, we can imagine they were elated with the outcome of their efforts and with finally having a degree of control over their lives again. They had lost the families they had known, but now the monastic women's community was to become their new family with Mahaprajapati in the role, no longer of queen, but of preceptor and "mother" to them all.

As a postscript, it should be noted that this discussion has intentionally highlighted positive, informative details about the ordination of Buddhist women and, with equal intention, ignored—as much as possible—a tremendous amount of misogynist material that is found in the same narratives. The view here is that misogyny has no place in a true telling of the origin of the women's monastic order. It's not that we don't see that patriarchy, often misogyny, existed in early Buddhism, or that these elements became amplified by later editors and flowed into the androcentric narratives that have come down to us. But if we are to valorize the first Buddhist women and imagine how they might have told their own stories, we can begin by no longer dignifying the literature that disparages them.

One case in point is worth brief mention. Several of the *vinaya* accounts of women's entrance into the monastic order conclude with a cascade of negative remarks about women generally, including one instance where the Buddha even accuses Ananda of being under the influence of Mara for stirring up the vexing conundrum of female ordination in the first place.[85] We also find the Buddha enumerating a list of five "obstructions"[86] meant to underscore women's inferior status. These are mostly silly; for example, a woman cannot become the "heavenly ruler Indra."

But let's take another look. There is a ring of familiarity here. Are we seeing a parallel, however inverted, between this list of five and another list of five from a previous story? Recall the first time Mahaprajapati led the women on a protest march to the Nigrodha Grove, where their purpose was to request the Buddha's permission for women to attend dharma teachings. Along the way, the women were pummeled with misogynist insults from Sakya men about their unworthiness and their inability to grasp the dharma. Not only did the Buddha put a full stop to that cruel nonsense, but he went on to enumerate a list of women's *five virtues* as a public corrective to the men's abject sexism.

Following the parallelism of these two closely related accounts, could the Buddha have originally repeated the women's *five virtues* in these ordination narratives? It's easy enough to imagine. Repetition is a common feature in the texts. Once again, we have a story of "uppity" women triggering a maelstrom of gynophobic projections from the men. It's also easy to imagine a misogynist editor's sleight of hand as he later recounted this event, leaving in a list of five items spoken with supposed authority by the Buddha, but changing out the details of the five virtues to deliver a misogynist's agenda of the five obstructions intended to highlight female inferiority. We imagined this sort of textual alteration with the eight heavy rules. Could this be another example? In any case, here we see another glaring example of extremely mixed messages about the Buddha's view of women in the early texts.

Amid the gloom of all this early misogyny, a jubilant shout-out must go to Ananda in his role as a stalwart champion of women among all the early monastic men. As he is described in the *Samyutta Nikaya*,

> Ananda was the most popular teacher of the nuns; he often taught them and was also in charge of arrangements for regularly sending teachers to them. He was also a popular teacher among laywomen. His services were often sought for consoling the sick, advising, for example, practice of the four applications of mindfulness.[87]

Ananda's positive engagement with women worked while the Buddha was alive, but he swiftly paid the price shortly after the Buddha's *parinirvana*. At the First Council attended by five hundred monks, the grumpy disciplinarian and apparent misogynist Mahakasyapa grilled Ananda on a number of perceived infractions, including the "wrongdoing" of allowing women (again, "weeping") to be among the first to pay homage to the Buddha's corpse. Equally egregious, according to Mahakasyapa, was Ananda's wrongdoing of advocating the ordination of women. While otherwise defending himself on the basis of confusion or unmindfulness, here Ananda took a vigorous stand in his own defense. Invoking family ties, he cited Mahaprajapati's act of mother's love, taking the infant Bodhisattva to her breast when Maya died:

> Honored sirs, I made an effort for the going forth of women in the *dhamma* and discipline proclaimed by the Truth Finder, thinking, "This Gotamid, Prajapati the Great is the Lord's aunt, foster mother, nurse, giver of milk, for when the Lord's mother passed away, she suckled him."[88]

Ananda never forgets—or lets us forget—the deeper connections of his family. His experience of the blessed Tathagata far exceeds Mahakasyapa's, reaching back to childhood stories and memories growing up in Kapilavastu. Isn't Ananda, in essence, pointing out that Mahaprajapati saved the Buddha's life that long-ago day in Lumbini's Grove? Where would they all be without her? Where would Buddhist women be? Indeed, where would Buddhism be today, if not for Mahaprajapati?

# 9

# Mahaprajapati: Foremost in Seniority

While history—even more so, herstory—generally esteems Mahaprajapati's incomparable role in founding Buddhism's order of nuns, she largely disappears from the narratives once that task is accomplished. The androcentric canonical literature tells us little more about her, even though she clearly held a position of tremendous stature and responsibility during the Buddha's ministry. When she is mentioned at all, her appearance is rarely more than a cameo, and its place in the overall timeline is unclear. What is clear, however, is that the first Buddhist women remembered and revered her. As the nun Dharmadatta said to her retinue at the time,

> Sisters, the fact that the Lord has permitted *bhiksunis* to go forth, take ordination, and engage in bhiksunihood: this is all due to Mahaprajapati Gautami.[1]

We know that Mahaprajapati lived out her years as a nun, according to her own testimony, to the age of 120. That number seems unlikely, but figuring she predeceased her son by only a few months or years at most, she probably lived well into her nineties. A handful of stories come to us from that time.

Foremost among Mahaprajapati's responsibilities was to see to the dharma education of the nuns. Early on she would take them before the Buddha to receive teachings, which he would give willingly without being asked.[2] She was also preceptor to many of the nuns she ordained. The entire list is unknown, but at least thirteen nuns can be counted as her disciples: Dantika, Bhadda Kapilani, Gutta, Subha, (another) Subha, Utpalavarna, Gupta, Nilopala, Bhadrakundalakesa, Mithila, Patacara, Sukla, and Suvarnaprabha.[3]

The following story, known in the Pali canon as the *Nandakovada Sutta*, appears with slight differences in a number of variants. We will examine one found in the *Samyukta-agama* because, according to Analayo, it depicts the nuns in a more favorable light and is likely closer to the original rendering.[4] Further details have been sourced from Buddhaghosa's *Manorathapurani*. In this story, Mahaprajapati has already attained arhatship, while the five hundred nuns have not.

The story opens as Mahaprajapati brings the women to the Buddha for teachings. After paying homage to him, she says,

> The Gracious One should advise the nuns, reverend Sir, the Gracious One should instruct the nuns, reverend Sir, the Gracious One should give a Dhamma talk to the nuns, reverend Sir.[5]

Several of the women are identified in this text as "great disciples," so eminent in fact that they are named individually: Chanda, Mintuo, Moluopo, Patacara, Alavika, Khema, Nanmo, Kisagotami, Uppalavanna, and finally Mahaprajapati Gotami.* From Dhammapala's commentary on the *Therigatha*, we know that several of these women were not Sakya, which tells us that the *bhikkhuni* community had already drawn strong representation from different regions and castes in India.† The text reads,

> Then the Blessed One taught the Dharma to Mahaprajapati Gotami [and the other nuns], instructing, teaching, illuminating, and delighting them.[6]

---

* Here Analayo has transcribed the names Mintuo, Moluopo, and Nanmo from the pinyin (*Samyukta-agama*, 156).

† However, the Pali commentaries, which don't list women's names, identify these five hundred as the original Sakya women who followed Mahaprajapati from Kapilavastu.

After the women leave, the Buddha confides in his monks that he is getting old and is no longer able to teach the nuns. Giving over this responsibility, he instructs that monks who are "senior virtuous elders" should alternate teaching the *bhikkhunis* among themselves. (While his aging was no doubt a factor, being appointed by the Buddha to teach was an exceptional honor and privilege, as well as part of their higher training. Recall that part of the Buddha's original mission was to produce a generation of teachers qualified to carry on teaching the dharma after his death.)

The new system works well until it comes to the monk Nandaka's turn. Nandaka doesn't want to teach the nuns, so he doesn't show up. Arriving at the appointed time, Mahaprajapati and the five hundred nuns sit instead before the Buddha, who willingly gives them a teaching. Once again, the women depart, rejoicing and delighting in the dharma.

Now the Buddha calls for Nandaka and reprimands him for shirking his assignment, insisting that he must teach the nuns:

> You should give instructions to the nuns, you should teach the Dharma to the nuns. Why is that? I myself give instructions to the nuns, so you should also do it. I teach the Dharma to the nuns, so you should also do it.[7]

Without comment, this time Nandaka accepts the Buddha's directive. On the following day he teaches the *bhikkhunis* quite effectively, just as the Buddha would have done, "instructing, teaching, illuminating and delighting them." The Buddha is very pleased and instructs Nandaka to teach the nuns again. The second day Nandaka's efforts are again outstanding, so outstanding in fact that each of the five hundred *bhikkhunis* achieves arhatship on the spot.

Afterward the Buddha confirms the nuns' supreme achievement before his assembly of monks. Using imagery of the full moon, he says,

> It is just as when people look at the bright moon on the night of the fifteenth day and have no doubt whether it is full or not full, since the moon is completely full.
>
> In the same way, the clansman Nandaka has given proper instructions to the five hundred nuns, their liberation is complete. If it were time for the passing away for them, nobody could proclaim the

course of their destination. It should be known that [they reached] the end of *dukkha*.[8]

The story concludes with the affirmative note that the assembled monks were delighted by the news of the nuns' full awakening.

Let's unpack this story. Why was Nandaka so reluctant to teach the nuns? There is usually a backstory to these quirky details. Here the commentaries provide some humorous insight. It wasn't laziness or indigestion that held Nandaka back. No, his problem was more knotty than that. Stepping into the mysterious realm of karma and past-life stories, we find out that Nandaka was previously Mahaprajapati's husband. Further, as past lives cascaded forward to the present, all five hundred women were once his harem wives.[9] Poor guy—a room full of ex-wives. No wonder he didn't want to get out of bed that morning. One perk of being an arhat was that he was omniscient, so he remembered his past lives completely. Nandaka's unwillingness to teach arose from the concern—and potential embarrassment—that other monks with similar psychic powers would catch on and tease him or accuse him of maintaining worldly attachment to his former consorts.*

Let's look into this colorful story a bit further. As with all realized beings, Nandaka's karmic journey began with the aspiration to awaken. This took place during the era of Padumuttara Buddha, when Nandaka heard that buddha praise an eminent disciple as Foremost among Those Who Exhort Nuns. It's not clear why, but Nandaka ardently determined to be that disciple in a future life and straightaway began to make worthy offerings toward his goal. In a charming twist, he spent several lifetimes as a songbird that delighted subsequent buddhas with beautiful melodies, thus setting up the karmic causes for his future gift of eloquent speech that would instruct, delight, and inspire the nuns.

We have to remember that the Buddha, too, was omniscient, even more so in the sense he knew *everyone's* past lives, not just his own. Thus his insistence that Nandaka teach the nuns would have been a double act

---

* Analayo points out that this explanation is a bit contrived, since past-life recollection is typically the ability to recall one's own past lives, not those of others (*Samyukta-agama*, 177).

of kindness, knowing first that it would mark the fulfillment of Nandaka's long-held aspiration, and second that the women would rapidly achieve their goal of full awakening if their karmic connection to Nandaka were finally extinguished through his excellent oratory and their attainment of arhatship.

But what about the part where Nandaka was Mahaprajapati's husband? In a past life she was a chief slave and the leader of five hundred female water carriers whom she rallied to enlist their husbands in building shelters for five hundred solitary buddhas. The women provided food and all the amenities of comfort for these buddhas during the three months of the rainy season. Nandaka was Mahaprajapati's husband at that time and the chief slave of the five hundred husbands. Together the entire group generated tremendous merit serving the five hundred buddhas, which bound them all karmically toward their shared goal of arhatship. We're told Mahaprajapati and Nandaka spent many more rebirths as a married couple in close companionship with the others, particularly in a lifetime when Nandaka was a king and Mahaprajapati and the five hundred women were his harem wives.

Such tangled webs these imaginative past-life stories weave while filling us in on seemingly minor events in the early narratives! This one is exceptional because it elevates Nandaka, however grudging and otherwise undistinguished under Gautama Buddha's watch, to the ranks of a true champion of the first Buddhist nuns. After all, his long-ago vow to exhort nuns to the dharma launched his soteriological journey, and now he could take credit for at least five hundred nuns attaining arhatship through his gifted teachings.

This obscure, deeply embedded detail of Nandaka's original aspiration reflects rare philogyny in the early literature, as it valorizes female monastics and the importance of their religious education. Further—and this would be more curious than significant—we learn that Nandaka was Mahaprajapati's ex-husband. As an arhat, she would have been aware of this detail when she brought the nuns to him for teaching. No longer married, but karmically in tandem in this story, Mahaprajapati and Nandaka jointly tended to the first five hundred nuns' attainment of full awakening in the Buddha's ministry.

This brings us to Mahaprajapati's own arhatship, which allegedly took place shortly before the events just related. There is not much to this story, as we're simply told that she went to the Buddha one day in Vaishali and asked him for a teaching:

> Bhante, it would be good if the Blessed One would teach me the Dhamma in brief, so that having heard the Dhamma from the Blessed One, I might dwell alone, withdrawn, heedful, ardent and resolute.[10]

In response he gave her a brief teaching known as the *Samkhitta Sutta,* which summarizes those actions and emotions to be rejected and those to be embraced. For example, passion and laziness are to be abandoned, while their opposites—dispassion and diligence—are to be cultivated. The Buddha concluded with the words, "This is the Dhamma; this is the discipline; this is the teaching of the Teacher,"[11] and from this she attained arhatship. Dhammapala tells us further that the Buddha gave Mahaprajapati a meditation subject, and she remained "diligent in mental development" until she attained arhatship."[12] From the texts it would seem that both Mahaprajapati and the five hundred nuns became fully awakened soon after their ordination was granted.

Mahaprajapati's preeminence is highlighted in lists of outstanding nuns that appear in several canonical texts. These lists are generally part of a larger survey, generated by the Buddha, of all four assemblies—nuns, monks, laywomen, and laymen—that was meant to highlight foremost disciples as role models or "inspiration" for other disciples to emulate in their own daily lives and practice.[13] The *Anguttara Nikaya* cites a list of thirteen esteemed nuns, where Mahaprajapati appears as number one and is designated Foremost in Seniority.[14] Also at the top of the list in the *Ekotarrika-agama,* in which fifty-one nuns are listed, Mahaprajapati appears as Foremost of Those *Bhikkhunis* Who Have Gone Forth to Train for a Long Time.[15] Both instances refer to the longevity of Mahaprajapati's discipleship, including her years as a laywoman-cum-stream enterer who spearheaded the creation of the nun's monastic order.[16] Possibly also implied by "seniority" here would be her leadership position among the nuns and her advanced age and status in the community as an elder, suggestive of a matriarchal role, or even further, mother of the Buddha.

Dhammapala locates the Buddha's announcement of Mahaprajapati's foremost status in the Jeta Grove in Sravasti, spoken in the presence of a large assembly of nuns and monks.[17] As an arhat, she is described as spending her time enjoying the fruits of awakening, which have brought her tremendous happiness and a profound sense of gratitude for her Teacher. Joyously she expresses her thanks to the Buddha in this public forum by praising his many excellent qualities. Displaying her own perfect knowledges,* she speaks these verses, found in the *Therigatha*, to her son:

> Buddha, hero, homage to you, Best of All Creatures, who released me and many other people from pain.
>
> All pain is known. Craving as the cause is dried up. The noble eightfold way has been developed. I have attained cessation.
>
> Formerly I was a mother, son, father, brother, and grandmother. Not having proper knowledge, I journeyed on without expiation.
>
> I have indeed seen that Blessed One. This is my last body. Journeying on from rebirth to rebirth has been completely eliminated. There is now no renewed existence.
>
> I see the disciples all together, putting forth energy, resolute, always with strong effort. This is homage to the Buddhas.
>
> Truly, Maya bore Gotama for the sake of many. He has thrust away the mass of pain of those struck by sickness and death.[18]

This scene in the Jeta Grove is further elaborated in the Sinhala tradition, where Mahaprajapati concludes her panagyric to the Buddha with blessings for his long life:

> May your glory increase continually. By means of your mother, Mahamaya, who brought you into this world, blessings without number have been conferred. . . . May you live long; may you never decay or die; may you exist a whole kalpa, that you may continue to bless the world.[19]

Her words are met with a noisy outpouring of approval from the assembled nuns and monks. Indeed, her prayers for their beloved Tathagata echo their own. When the voices die down, the Buddha gently admonishes them all with a beautiful metaphor:

---

* Seeing clearly her own past lives and karmic freedom from rebirth.

The ornaments of a Buddha are his [monastic disciples], as dutiful nobles are the ornaments of a king, and stars of a moon; the Buddhas desire to see their [disciples] many in number.[20]

With that the Buddha instructs his assembled disciples to say, "May the pure [monastic community] continue and increase," but he does not want them to express wishes for his own long life.[21]

A similar passage in the *Theri-apadana* appears as a flashback. Here Mahaprajapati recalls how once she wished the Buddha long life after he sneezed. The Buddha scolded her, saying,

Buddhas are not to worshipped
as you're worshipping, Gotami.[22]

She asked him to explain his meaning, and he responded,

See my followers, united,
vigorously energetic,
constantly firm [in their] effort—
that is worship of the Buddhas.[23]

This story of the sneeze has been androcentrized in the *vinaya* section of the Pali canon, where a chorus of monks wish the Buddha long life, and there is no mention whatsoever of Mahaprajapati.[24]

We're seeing that the Buddha's abiding concern, as always, was the spiritual growth and well-being of his disciples. In the short term, it was obvious that they benefited personally from his teachings. Taking a longer view, he recognized the importance of firmly and purely establishing the foundation of his teachings, with the goal of the dharma flowing forward for the benefit of future generations. It was the survival of his legacy, not his physical form, that concerned him, and that was up to his disciples after he was gone. Thus the Buddha vigorously exhorted them that the best way to honor him was to apply themselves in their practice.

In a striking sutra in the *Majjhima Nikaya*, the Buddha responds to questions from a disciple as to whether anyone other than himself had attained the highest realizations. With gusto the Buddha affirms that countless disciples in each of the four assemblies had done so. Using similar language for each, he says of the nuns,

> There are not only one hundred . . . or five hundred, but far more *bhikkhunis*, my disciples, who by realizing for themselves with direct knowledge here and now enter upon and abide in the deliverance of mind and deliverance by wisdom that are taintless with the destruction of the taints.[25]

And so, according to the Buddha's own testimony, his legacy was well on track. As we have seen, Mahaprajapati had a lot to do with this in every way. Imagine removing her from the equation, and it quickly becomes clear that the Buddha could not have established a fourfold assembly without her. Sharing her son's goals and peerless virtue, Mahaprajapati opened the door for women, selflessly guiding, mentoring, and teaching them such that dharma took root in their lives, bringing them the fruit of freedom and, for many, the vocation to teach others. Decades later, shortly before entering nirvana simultaneously, the five hundred nuns lovingly acknowledged Mahaprajapati's great gift to them, saying,

> O Gotami, you have been sympathetic to us all for a long time. Established through your meritorious deeds, we have reached the annihilation of our taints.[26]

## 10

# A Patchwork of Stories

Now we will tell a few short stories of Mahaprajapati's years as a nun. Overall, there is little material to work with since the texts are mostly silent about the last decades of her life. Most commonly, stories about her are little more than frame stories for the Buddha's implementation of a monastic rule. Nonetheless, the power of her discrete influence and exemplary character shine through in the brief narratives that follow, as do colorful glimpses of the religious landscape in which she lived.

First we need to address the elephant in the room. Why is there so much silence surrounding Mahaprajapati, especially once she had become a central figure—indeed the central female figure—in all of early Buddhism?

Let's take a walk in the sandals of the monks who bore witness to the sweeping changes brought about by the onrush of women entering the monastic order. After all, their side of the story is the one that was eventually captured in the canonical narratives and comes down to us today. It's pretty obvious they weren't too happy about sharing the monastic institution with nuns. Laywomen didn't seem to concern them, and wealthy laywomen paid the bills (think: Visakha). But hundreds of women in one stroke ordaining as nuns must have been extremely disruptive and felt threatening to the monks' own, still-evolving, monastic lifestyle. No longer an all-guy sangha with their revered Teacher at the center, the new normal for monks meant that the Buddha would be dividing his time and attention between them and these seemingly disorganized, unwelcome, and—to true misogynists—unworthy women. The founding of the monastic women's order no doubt changed the monks' day-to-day lives and conversations considerably. Patriarchal instincts die hard, and these first monks—many of whom must have spotted their wives in the mix—would easily have been triggered to respond with confusion and resentment if not hostility.

Mahaprajapati was an obvious and easy target. First, she was a female who had the audacity and courage to breach social norms for women with the goal of nurturing her own religiosity and fulfilling her own soteriological potential—an ambition heretofore supposedly reserved for men. Further, she brought along five hundred women with the same purpose, and even more women followed, many of whom rose rapidly in the ranks and became exceptional representatives of the dharma in their own right (for example, Utpalavarna, Ksema, and Dharmadinna). An immediate impact would have been economic, since the droves of women arriving in central monastic areas such as Vaishali and Sravasti required shelter, food, and clothing from the first day, setting up competition for requisites that lay donors had thus far only furnished to monks. All this and more would certainly have given rise to monks' resentment of the female interlopers.

To boot, Mahaprajapati was the Buddha's mother. What were they to make of that? This detail must have been a complicating factor for his disciples. The Sakya monks obviously knew Mahaprajapati well; many had known her their whole lives as their queen. Previous feelings of affection and allegiance toward her must have become confused. What would be her new role, especially in relation to her son and the monastic hierarchy? Non-Sakya monks wouldn't have known what to make of her and no doubt would have been perplexed by the Buddha's mother showing up in India and taking the helm of the women's monastic order, becoming de facto co-leader with the Buddha himself. Like it or not, Mahaprajapati's presence was a game changer, one that had the fullest impact because she was the Buddha's mother, highly respected and beyond reproach in every way. The mostly deafening silence surrounding her in the early records makes it pretty clear where monks stood on the subject, perhaps confused as much as resentful.

Turning to the nuns' side of the story, their experience would have been entirely different. To them, Mahaprajapati was their *shero*. Trusted and beloved, she became their voice and the instrument of their agency. She made their dreams a reality. Not only did they attain their long-held aspiration to ordain as disciples of the Buddha, but their respected preceptor had the ear and attention of the great Teacher himself, in many ways a female counterpart to Ananda. This must have given the nuns a tremendous sense of confidence and protection as they adapted to huge life changes in a strange new land. Because of Mahaprajapati, these women had come to the dharma as *upasikas* years earlier in Kapilavastu and now were well trained and prepared as *bhikkhunis*. With her as their leader and voice, their reception as the newest arrivals and final complement to the fourfold community brought power and legitimacy they otherwise would not have had.

No doubt these first Buddhist women had many stories to tell about Mahaprajapati and their lives together at the inception of Buddhism. They would have had firsthand accounts of the Buddha and the living experience of his teachings and ministry. The absence of their voices (exceptions as always in the *Therigatha* and *Theri-apadana*) is a huge loss, one that has skewed Buddhist history toward the androcentrism and misogyny that persists today.

In no particular order, the brief stories that follow offer a periscope view into Mahaprajapati's life and the milieu in which she lived. Like vintage patchwork pieces, each story reveals a tiny glimpse into her world while inviting us to imagine the larger whole. Many questions arise. What does each story tell us? Why was it remembered? Is it at all relatable or relevant today? How different would it feel to hear it told in Mahaprajapati's voice rather than the voice of the narrator? Questions such as these release ancient stories from the confines of the past while suggesting abundant ways they can be reimagined and repurposed.

## Mahaprajapati's Mastery of the Dharma

Here we see the Buddha's confidence in Mahaprajapati and his egalitarian view of women.

The Buddha makes his esteem for Mahaprajapati's command of the dharma clear when he appoints her judge and mediator in a philosophical dispute between "contentious, quarrelsome" monks arriving from Kosambi. Her instruction is to hear out the arguments of both sides and rule without bias solely on the accuracy of the disputants' knowledge of the dharma. He says to her,

> Gotami, hear dhamma on both sides; having heard dhamma on both sides, choose the views and the approval and the persuasion and the creed of those monks who are there speakers of the dhamma. . . .[1]

To ensure the perception of fairness, the Buddha similarly appoints a representative from the other three assemblies—a monk, a layman, and Visakha (a renowned laywoman disciple)—who are to submit their rulings independently. That the Buddha's choice of judges to evaluate the accuracy of the dharma consisted of two women and two men is extraordinary and unambiguous evidence of his egalitarianism and respect for women. Of this story Horner observed,

> Both Mahaprajapati and Visakha were considered to be endowed with as reliable powers of discretion as the men, and to possess as thorough a knowledge of the Dhamma as the men. . . . A religion which allows this amount of independence of judgment to its women members, and does not differentiate between the capacity of the two sexes, is ennobled, for the women rise and justify the faith which is placed in them.[2]

## The Rape of Bhadra

The following sad story from the Kanjur tells of the rape of Bhadra, the wife of Mahakasyapa and one of Mahaprajapati's disciples.

Bhadra and Mahakasyapa are forced by their families into marriage despite each of them wanting a monastic life. By mutual agreement they do not consummate the marriage and soon part ways. Mahakasyapa ordains as a disciple of the Buddha, and Bhadra joins a Jain sect of monastic women. Unfortunately, during this time Bhadra is raped. Seeing each other again a short time later, Mahakasyapa asks her why she appears so distraught. Hearing her story, he urges her to take refuge in the Buddha. But Bhadra hesitates, disillusioned by the religious life she has just fled. Finally convinced, she takes ordination with Mahaprajapati and becomes a nun.

But Bhadra's troubles are not over. An evil minister, captivated by her beauty and wishing to ingratiate himself with the king, has her kidnapped while she is collecting alms in the village. Forcefully bathed in exotic perfumes and dressed in fine ornaments, she is brought before the king who rapes her and pleasures himself with her as he wishes.

Meanwhile Mahaprajapati notices Bhadra's absence from the nun's assembly. Concerned, she sends the nun Utpalavarna to locate her. Known for her magical abilities, Utpalavarna finds Bhadra in the king's palace and instructs her in how to employ magic to escape. Bhadra appears instantly in the nuns' assembly hall in the presence of her preceptor, Mahaprajapati. However, the other nuns mock her because she is still wearing the jewels and fancy clothes forced on her by the king. With insight into how to correct this awful situation, Mahaprajapati instructs Bhadra to don her clerical robes and return the costly items to the king. Now in control, Bhadra magically returns to the king's bedchamber where he, aroused, seeks to embrace her. She flies into the air and rebukes him. The king now falls at her feet and begs forgiveness, which she grants.[3]

### The Crude Brahman

Violence of a different sort takes place in the following story, also from the Kanjur. Of note is the female householder's immediate reverence upon recognizing Mahaprajapati as the Buddha's mother.

Mahaprajapati enters a home on her alms rounds just as a brahman is leaving. He is upset that he has been refused alms and lurks nearby to see if she will get anything. As the housewife spots Mahaprajapati, the former jumps to her feet exclaiming, "The esteemed mother of the Buddha has come!" Hastily she sets out a cushion and fills Mahaprajapati's bowl with the finest, most delicate food. The lurking brahman sees this and becomes very angry. Approaching Mahaprajapati as she is leaving, he asks to see what alms she received in her bowl. Without hesitation she shows him, at which time the crude brahman intentionally drools directly into the bowl. Mahaprajapati says,

> Son, why have you spoiled the alms? If you had asked, I would have given it to you.[4]

The nuns report this event to the monks, who report it to the Buddha, who takes it very seriously. After some consideration, he says,

> Other common men too will inflict violence on women and produce a great deal of non-virtue, just as this ignorant brahman man has done. That being the case, I permit *bhiksunis* to keep a cover on their begging bowls.[5]

And from this a *vinaya* rule was introduced allowing covers on alms bowls.

### Kindness toward Rahula

This sweet story speaks to enduring Sakya family ties even after everyone has ordained. It also underscores the reverence the king felt toward the Buddha's family members. Here kindness takes precedence over the daily practice of paying homage to the Buddha.

A senior monk has physically ejected Rahula, the Buddha's son and a novice monk, from the monastery. Rahula sits outside distraught and weeping as his grandmother, Mahaprajapati, approaches with a retinue of five hundred nuns. They are on their way to pay homage to the Buddha. Seeing her grandson thus, Mahaprajapati postpones her plans and sits down to comfort him. Soon more disciples arrive to pay homage to the Buddha, first King Prasenajit, and then the esteemed merchant and patron Anathapindada with their retinues. Thinking it would not be right to pass by the Buddha's own son and mother, they too sit down, joining company with Rahula, Mahaprajapati, and the five hundred nuns outside the monastery. The story concludes with the Buddha explicating proper corrective discipline for monks, including those who wrongly expel others from the monastery.[6]

### Allowing Women Equal Access

Here the Buddha calls out monks for instituting petty sexism within the monastic order.

Without the Buddha's knowledge, some monks implement a rule that bars nuns from the monastery. Mahaprajapati arrives to pay her daily homage to the Buddha, and for the first time, she is not allowed entrance. Noticing her absence (although knowing full well what is going on), the Buddha inquires of the monks, "Has Mahaprajapati Gautami fallen ill?" He sets things right by amending the monks' rule to allow nuns entrance to the monastery after the formality of request and permission.[7]

## Mahaprajapati Falls Ill

These twin stories demonstrate the Buddha's kindness and flexibility in seeing to the comfort and needs of his disciples, in this case, his mother.

Mahaprajapati has fallen ill and is confined to her bed. A nun asks her what she normally does to care for herself while convalescing. Mahaprajapati responds that as a laywoman she always wore a hat indoors, but this was not allowed for nuns. When the Buddha hears this news, he changes the rule to allow nuns to wear hats indoors when they are ill.[8]

Another time Mahaprajapati falls ill and is confined to her bed. When the Buddha hears about her illness, he goes to see her and inquires how she is feeling. Mahaprajapati responds that previously monks were allowed to give dharma teachings in the nuns' residence, but ever since the Buddha implemented a rule prohibiting it, there was no comfort to be had. Hearing her longing for the dharma, out of compassion, the Buddha gives his mother a bedside teaching on the spot. After that, the rule is amended to include the exception that monks could enter the nuns' residence to teach nuns who were ill.[9]

## Majaprajapati Advocates for the Nuns

The challenge of blending female and male communities comes down to the details, as we see in the following story from the Kanjur.

Seats in the assembly hall normally had covers on them. Occasionally the covers became soiled with blood from menstruating nuns. In this story the monks complain to the Buddha, who instructs that all the covers be removed. Mahaprajapati arrives for a teaching and notices her seat has no cover. The following exchange ensues:

[Mahaprajapati]
 Noble Ones, back when I was living at home, we never had any seats that lacked a covering.

[Monks]
> Gautami, the Blessed One does not permit them. He has spoken and said, "Do not give the *bhiksunis* who come to listen to the Dharma covered seats."

[Mahaprajapati]
> Noble Ones, have I committed the same wrong as the *bhiksuni* who had not established herself in mindfulness?[10]

After that the Buddha permitted seat covers for nuns who had established themselves in mindfulness. It's striking in this story how Mahaprajapati immediately identifies with and advocates for the younger nuns, not judging or setting herself apart.[11]

### Mother and Daughter Excel in Debates

While patriarchy weighs heavily in many early stories, we also find dramatic exceptions—wholehearted philogynist narratives where women have intelligence, wit, and agency that often prove superior to men's. Where did these stories come from? Are we seeing remnants of a women's literature that spilled beyond the bounds of the *Therigatha* and *Theri-apadana*? In the following story we find a woman who is pregnant, and rather than craving pickles, she can only be sated by debating religious scripture. The story goes as follows.

As soon as the queen of Taxila becomes pregnant, she develops fervent thoughts: "If only I could debate all the other scriptural exegetes myself!" The king is puzzled and takes her to soothsayers, who augur that the child in her womb will understand all religious treatises and defeat all contenders in debate, but only if the queen has her pregnancy craving satisfied (otherwise the baby will be born without limbs). The king is happy to comply, but this is tricky since the queen is asking to participate in a field of scholarship that is only open to men. Arriving at a solution, he installs his wife behind a curtain with all the male debaters, observers, and judges on the other side. The queen roundly defeats her opponents, and her pregnancy cravings cease.

Soon a beautiful daughter is born whom they name She Who Gathers. As she grows older, she masters reading and writing, again behind a curtain since such skills are forbidden to girls. As She Who Gathers comes of age, like her mother, she confounds all the scriptural debaters in Taxila (from behind a curtain). When the marriage question comes up, she tells her father that she will only marry a man who can defeat her in debate. The word spreads quickly, and she defeats all her suitors.

One day a handsome young debater named Rui hears of She Who Gathers by reputation and determines to win her hand through debate. Once she lays eyes on him, she knows he is the one and lets him defeat her. They have a son, Katyayana, who grows up equally accomplished in scriptural debate, but when he is undefeated, he becomes very vain and arrogant. One day, hearing of the Buddha's superior dharma, Katyayana requests permission from his parents to travel to India to see for himself. Also inspired to meet the Buddha, his parents give up household life and journey with their son to Sravasti, where they all come before the Buddha and request ordination. Father and son are ordained on the spot with the Buddha's words, "Come monks!" Mahaprajapati ordains She Who Gathers and gives her dharma teachings. Shortly thereafter She Who Gathers attains arhatship.[12]

### On Choosing Dharma over Marriage

In this story, we again see a young girl's passion for the dharma.

Kasisundari is a princess born to the queen and king of Benares. She grows up flourishing "like a lotus in a lake," with every manner of luxury and affection from her family. As a girl she finds faith in the dharma and, with her parents' permission, offers respectful service to the three jewels of the Buddha, dharma, and sangha. When she comes of age, suitors hear of her exceptional beauty and vie for her hand. In particular, six vassal kings send envoys to the king demanding his daughter in marriage.

The king is overcome with confusion and sorrow as he sees no way out of this competition for his daughter's hand without inciting war. Kasisundari comes across her father brooding and inquires what is wrong. After he explains, she asks his permission to choose her own husband, which he readily grants. Hearing the news, the six vassal kings are arrogantly confident they will be Kasisundari's choice, so they agree to an open competition. In a long row outside the city of Benares, they each build a towering structure topped by an ornately decorated lion throne. On these they each perch the day of the contest, garishly outfitted and ornamented to catch Kasisundari's attention.

Dressed as a bride, Kasisundari rides from the city astride a fine mount, carrying a colorful victory banner and followed by a retinue of young women on horseback. Spurning the kings, Kasisundari turns toward Deer Park where the Buddha is residing. Casting her bridal bouquet in that direction, she calls out, "I take refuge in the Buddha!"

To the astonishment of the onlookers, she and the young women ride off in the direction of Deer Park. Coming before the Buddha, Kasisundari pays proper homage, professes her aspiration to lead the religious life, and requests permission to ordain. The Buddha welcomes her and summons Mahaprajapti, who ordains Kasisundari as a novice nun, then confers on her full ordination and transmission of the scriptures.[13]

### The Bethrothal of Dharmadinna

This story introduces us to Dharmadinna, one of early Buddhism's most influential nuns. It comes from the Kanjur and differs considerably from her life story as told in the Pali tradition.

Two close friends named Lord of Deer and Given, both chief ministers in King Prasenajit's court, vow they will strengthen their bond of friendship by marrying their future children to one another. So Given's firstborn daughter is betrothed to Lord of Deer's son, Vaisakha.

But the poor baby girl is prone to crying endlessly. No matter what her parents do, nothing will console her. One day Mahaprajapati comes to their house to give the family a dharma teaching. As soon as she begins to speak, the baby quiets down. But after Mahaprajapati completes her discourse and leaves, the baby begins to wail again. The parents realize that their baby girl only wants to hear more dharma, thus at the elaborate feast celebrating her birth, they give her the name Dharmadinna (Given by Dharma).

As a child, Dharmadinna is precocious and never misses an opportunity to make offerings to nuns and monks or to attend dharma teachings. Soon she takes refuge and, still living at home, reaches the resultant state of nonreturner, even performing miracles. Deeply cherishing the truth of dharma, Dharmadinna requests her parents' permission to ordain as a nun.

This poses difficulties because Dharmadinna is already betrothed to Lord of Deer's son. Her parents do not have the power to reverse their pledge. At the same time, they sincerely want happiness for their daughter. Thus, they devise a plan by which Dharmadinna can make the plea on her own behalf in the presence of the Buddha and Lord of Deer's family.

With this plan, Given invites the Buddha and his assembly of nuns and monks to an elaborate midday meal. Lord of Deer, who is also invited, shows up with his son Vaishaka and surrounds Given's house with sentries. At the end of the meal and a discourse by the Buddha, Dharmadinna stands up to leave with the company of nuns. Immediately Vaisakha cries out to the guards to capture her. Dharmadinna rises up into the sky, making a display of miracles. Humbled by her devotion and accomplishments, Vaisakha falls to his knees begging for forgiveness and releases her from their marriage pact.

But the path of dharma is never easy for women. Dharmadinna receives her novice ordination in the nunnery and sometime later prepares to receive full ordination in the Jeta Grove. Meanwhile, evil men learn she is no longer pledged in marriage and conspire to kidnap and rape her. Word of this gets to the nuns, who determine that Dharmadinna is at great risk. They postpone her ordination and send her home to her family for safety.

Now the nuns bring this terrible dilemma directly to the Buddha (probably via Mahaprajapati, although she is not named here). What should they do, and how can Dharmadinna complete her ordination safely? Always resourceful and compassionate, the Buddha determines she can be ordained by messenger. As soon as the nuns receive clarification from the Buddha, they confer full ordination on Dharmadinna by message, exactly the way it was given in the scriptures. Shortly thereafter, Dharmadinna attains arhatship.[14] The Buddha later declares Dharmadinna to be Foremost among Those Who Teach—a very high honor, indeed. From then on, the option of being ordained by messenger was open to anyone similarly caught by danger.

## Hardship for the Nuns

Both from the Sanskrit tradition, the similar stories that follow reveal how much more difficult life was for nuns than for monks.

Mahaprajapati, accompanied by five nuns, arrives at the Jeta Grove in Sravasti at nightfall. Having nowhere to sleep and prohibited from entering the all-male monastery, the women sleep outside on the bare ground. The following day the Buddha sees that the nuns' robes are dirty, and he inquires as to the cause. Once Mahaprajapati explains, he permits monks to provide bedding for nuns.[15]

In the second story, a senior monk named Nanda is giving teachings to the nuns in the Jeta Grove.* He gives an excellent teaching and then falls silent. Eager to hear more, Mahaprajapati urges him to continue. Again, Nanda speaks eloquently on the dharma and then becomes quiet. So enthused is Mahaprajapati that she again exhorts him to go on. And so it is, over and over, until late in the evening when Nanda's teaching finally concludes.

By this time, it is dark and the gates to the city are locked. Mahaprajapati and the nuns have no choice but to camp on the bare ground. In the morning they enter the city bedraggled, with dirty robes. Swift as tongues will wag, townsfolk begin to gossip that the nuns slept with the monks outside the city and are only now returning. Scandal was something the Buddha was wary of and always tried to avert. Hearing about this incident, he implemented the rule that monks could not teach nuns after dark.[16]

### Three Stories Concerning Robes

Robes appear as central motifs in the following three stories, where we see Mahaprajapati's motherly kindness and humility, as well as her advocacy on behalf of the women. Most importantly, we see the Buddha's vigilance guarding against monks interfering with the nuns' monastic training.

Mahaprajapati is shepherding five hundred nuns to a teaching with the Buddha. Along the way they encounter a company of monks going to the same teaching. One of them is wearing a particularly ragged robe. Drawn by kindness to speak to him, Mahaprajapati inquires why he is wearing such a poor robe. "Because I don't have any other," is his reply. Mahaprajapati points to her own fine robe and asks if he would like it. When he accepts her offer, she suggests they exchange robes. Now dressed in a poor, ragged robe she proceeds with the nuns to the teaching.

The Buddha immediately notices her decrepit robe and asks about it. She explains what happened, and he remains silent. After the teaching, Mahaprajapati and the five hundred nuns return to the nunnery. The Buddha

---

* This is probably the elder Nandaka from our earlier story.

now calls upon the aforementioned monk and asks him if it is true that he exchanged his poor robe with Mahaprajapati's excellent one. Hearing the affirmative, the Buddha scolds him as silly and greedy. Due to this and similar instances, the Buddha enacted a rule that monks could not accept robes from nuns. This was later amended to say that a monk could not accept a robe from a nun unless she was a family member.[17]

In a second story, Mahaprajapati goes before the Buddha, and he says to her, "Gotami, I hope that the nuns are zealous, ardent, (with) a self that is striving." Unfortunately, she has come to report the opposite—that the nuns are neglecting their religious studies because six monks are requiring that they wash, dye, and comb wool to make them new robes. After she explains this, the Buddha gives her a dharma teaching that "gladdens" her, and she departs. Immediately the Buddha summons the offending monks and questions what they have been up to. Hearing Mahaprajapati's story confirmed, he strongly rebukes them for their inappropriate behavior, saying,

> Foolish men, those who are not relations do not know what is suitable or what is unsuitable, or what is pleasant or unpleasant. . . . Thus you, foolish men, will have sheep's wool washed and dyed and combed by nuns who are not relations.[18]

The third story brings us back to family ties in Kapilavastu. One day in Sravasti the monk Udayin asks Mahaprajapati to wash and dye his robe. She immediately does so and returns it to him, whereupon he blesses and thanks her. Soon after they are both before the Buddha, who notices the dye stains on Mahaprajapati's hands. When he inquires as to their cause, she explains that she washed and dyed Udayin's robe. The Buddha remains silent. After she leaves, the Buddha makes an example of Udayin in the assembly, admonishing his male disciples that nuns should not serve monks because their time was better spent pursuing their own religious study and practice. Later he makes a rule that a nun should not wash a monk's robe whether she is a relative or not.[19]

The last story is striking because the monk Udayin* was Sakya and, together with Chandaka, he was the Buddha's closest childhood friend. The

---

* Also known as Kalodayin.

*Mahavastu* tells us they made mudpies together as little boys.[20] In all stories of Udayin, he was extremely beloved and trusted by Siddhartha's family, including the king. This type of intimacy might explain Udayin's seeming audacity in asking Mahaprajapati—the Buddha's mother and his former queen—to wash and dye his robe, a job typically asked of servants but also of mothers. However apparently sexist, his request and Mahaprajapati's quick acceptance suggest a lingering affection between them going back to palace life in Kapilavastu, where she would have known him as a little boy. In any case, the Buddha puts a stop to it, pointing out that Mahaprajapati's responsibility now is to her religious study.

# 11

# The *Parinirvana* of Mahaprajapati

*This Gotami who carefully reared up the body of the Sage, has gone to peace . . . just like stars when the sun rises.[1]*

At last we come to a true treasure in our quest to learn more about Mahaprajapati: her own autobiography or *apadana* told in 189 verses. It is located among forty nuns' autobiographies in the *Theri-apadana* section of the *Khuddaka Nikaya* of the Pali canon. Side-by-side with this collection are 550 *Thera-apadana*, or autobiographies of monastic men. Most of this material lay largely untranslated and overlooked until recent decades when scholar Jonathan Walters brought the entire corpus to the world in English. What a surprise and delight to hear the voices of so many early Buddhist women telling their own stories in their own words, piercing the din of misogyny and androcentrism that suffused their world and that of the male redactors who authored later Buddhist texts!

While much can (and has) been said about women being marginalized in early Buddhism, no other world religion has produced a body of women's literature that dates from its origins. That these earliest autobiographies endured until now lends credence to the power of their female authors' experiences of the Triple Gem and reported soteriological accomplishments.

It further speaks to the dedication of subsequent generations of Buddhist women who looked to their predecessors as role models, remembering their stories and drawing inspiration from those earlier lives as they forged their own spiritual paths.[2] With so much to offer, it's particularly regrettable that this women's literature was never integrated into early canonical narratives, instead being sequestered in a separate "women's quarters" in the *Khuddaka Nikaya* or "miscellaneous" section of the canon. But better there than nowhere at all.

So why have these remarkable women's autobiographies remained hidden (in plain sight) for so long to Western scholarship? Tiresome themes of androcentrism return, but let's say there is more to the story than that. We're in an era where women's voices are returning in many traditions and cultures, speaking to us from the past with sacred intelligence that can help bring needed transformation to today's troubled world. Perhaps we're only just ready to hear these ancient female voices anew, as patriarchy's fields lay fallow and seeds of the sacred feminine return with the promise of new life. Perhaps these hidden stories are reemerging because they are ripe for our time.

The *Theri apadana* are distinctively Buddhist in that they relate each nun's spiritual path to arhatship across the trajectory of not one but countless lifetimes, connecting karmic dots along the way. As such, these women's personal stories provide a soteriological blueprint for both lay and monastic women since—according to this Buddhist paradigm—the struggles and good deeds of lay life bring one eventually to monasticism as the final stepping-stone to nirvana. The stories are remarkable for many reasons, but noteworthy here is that the women narrators have integrated their lay and religious careers into a karmic whole, emerging as "both and neither" *upasikas* or *bhikkhunis*. Instead they are simply awakened women who have finally attained their long-held goal of liberation from samsara.

Mahaprajapati's *apadana* is unique in several ways. While told mostly in the first person, it concludes with her death and funeral, unlike the other *apadanas* where the nuns are alive and well as they tell their own stories. Also, Mahaprajapati's entire company of five hundred nuns, all arhats, are included in her *apadana* and decide to pass into nirvana with her. This is an amazing detail. True to her lifelong (lifetimes-long) persona, Mahaprajapati's personal story is presented as a collective account of 501 women bound until liberation by karmic friendship and interconnection. It serves as both remembrance and tribute not just to Buddhism's most famous nun but to all her disciples. Further, Mahaprajapati's story is textured by other speakers: a narrator, nuns, laywomen, Ananda, even goddesses and the Buddha himself all take turns speaking in this long, biographical narrative, which concludes with the Buddha's eulogy upon her death. It took Mahaprajapati countless lifetimes to arrive at this moment of telling her story, yet the *apadana* itself is said to span the events of just one day.

So dearly beloved and revered was Mahaprajapati in the first centuries of Buddhism that her *apadana* (and probably others) was celebrated as a popular and widely transmitted performance piece, recited and performed in large festival settings.[3] By this we see her remarkable founding role was not just remembered but continued to serve as a model and inspiration to new generations of Buddhist girls and women, assuredly also boys and men.

The following summary weaves elements from the Walters' translation, Dhammapala's commentary, and related fragments that appear in the Kanjur and Sinhala tradition.

## The Last Day of Mahaprajapati's Life

Arising early in the morning, Mahaprajapati visits her son, the Blessed One, who has just arrived in Vaishali and taken up residence in the Kutagara-sala monastery. After their meeting, sitting in meditation, she reflects, "The Buddha is the glory of his disciples, and the disciples are the glory of the Buddha,"[4] recalling his similar words earlier after she wished him long life in the Jeta Grove. Contemplating this phrase deeply, she notes the harmony within the monastic community and foresees that this will change.[5] With her superior insight, she scans the karmic field of the assembly's chief disciples to see who will be among the first to pass into final nirvana. Sorrow arising in her heart, she foresees the impending demise of loved ones, including her son, the Buddha. Quickly a resolve arises within her: she must be the first to die and will request the Buddha's permission to do so that very day. In the Sinhala account she reflects,

> I am now 120 years of age, though in appearance I am as young as when I was maiden of sixteen; my teeth are perfect and my hair is not grey; but it is meet that the child should see the departure of the

parent, and not the parent the departure of the child. I will therefore request that I be the first of the faithful to be admitted to the city of peace.[6]

However studied in the impermanence of all phenomena, however awakened in arhatship, in this moment Mahaprajapati expresses the very relatable human emotions of a mother. Acknowledging the suffering her son's death would evoke while applying a parent's wisdom, she knows it is the natural order of things that she pass away first. As foremost nun, she feels too that it will be best for the harmony within the monastic assembly if she departs while the Buddha is still living.[7]

This touching episode is expressed somewhat differently in the Pali canon's *apadana* version, where we see that Mahaprajapati dreads losing not just the Buddha, but her son Nanda, grandson Rahula, and nephew (or grandson) Ananda. Here Mahaprajapati says,

> I cannot bear to look upon
> the Buddha's final passing,
> nor that of his two chief disciples,
> nor Rahula, Ananda, and Nanda.
>
> Ending life's constituents
> and letting go, I shall go out:
> permitted by the greatest sage,
> by [him] who is the whole world's lord.[8]

With her reflections, miracles take place: the earth quakes, thunder roars, and goddesses in the heavenly realms, "weighed down by grief,"[9] begin to wail and weep, their tears cascading as rain to the earth.

Concerned by these dramatic portents, the five hundred nuns know something is up. Led by Ksema, they go immediately to Mahaprajapati, who informs them of her decision to pass into nirvana that very day. As always with one voice, the nuns respond that they wish to attain nirvana with her. After all, they left their households together, ordained together, and lived many years in community with each other. "Queen-mother" Mahaprajapati had always been their beloved guide and preceptor.[10] The nuns say,

If this is what you want, [noble lady]—
the unsurpassed pure going out—
then, pious one, with his assent,
we all will go out too.

Along with us you left home
and also left the world.
Again together all of us
to great nirvana city go![11]

Together the women depart the nunnery to inform the Buddha of their intention, but not before Mahaprajapati pauses at the door to comfort the indwelling goddesses who are weeping inconsolably. The goddesses say,

Alas, meritless women are we,
this ashram has become empty:
the victor's heirs, no longer seen,
are like the stars at daybreak.

Gotami goes to nirvana,
so do her five hundred;
She's like the Ganges flowing toward
the sea, with [five hundred] tributaries.[12]

As Mahaprajapati and the five hundred nuns walk along the road, they are similarly beset by laywomen from the village who have just heard the news and are very unhappy about Mahaprajapati's decision. Unlike the goddesses who are sad, these women are deeply distressed. No doubt they have enjoyed and benefited greatly from the presence of the nearby nuns' community and Mahaprajapati's wonderful dharma teachings. Insisting, "Nirvana is not proper for you," these laywomen lament Mahaprajapati's departure, fearful of being left "destitute."[13]

Unyielding but kind, Mahaprajapati responds that the Buddha and his teachings will remain, but that she has accomplished her goal and is ready to depart worldly existence. She wisely questions why the final freedom of nirvana should be lamented rather celebrated. Isn't attaining nirvana the whole point of the dharma teachings? Rather than grieve for her, they should strive to emulate her and continue diligently to follow the Buddha's path. Mahaprajapati says,

> My wish I've had for very long
> today will be fulfilled.
> This is the time for drums of joy!
> Why are you crying, children?
>
> If you all have love for me,
> and if you all appreciate
> the dharma's great stability
> then strong and fervent you should be.
>
> The great Buddha made women nuns
> only at my beseeching.
> So if you love me, be like me,
> and follow after him.[14]

And so, resolute as always—twice in Kapilavastu and again in Vaishali as they sought ordination—the five hundred women led by Mahaprajapati go before the Buddha with a fervent shared request. The *Ekotarrika-agama* names some of these nuns: Ksema, Utpalavarna, Kisagotami, Sakula, Sama, Patacara, Bhaddacala, Bhaddakaccana, and Vijaya.[15]

After paying homage to her son, Mahaprajapati begins her entreaty by invoking the metaphor of dharma and mother's milk that we heard previously. As his mother, she nurtured him with milk from her breast; as her dharma father, he nurtured her with "dharma-milk." She sheltered him from the "sun and the storm," while he sheltered her from the "perils of existence."[16] The reciprocity between them over this supreme final lifetime together erases any notion of filial indebtedness, as Mahaprajapati opines that she has received from him the greatest gift of all. Further, Mahaprajapati acknowledges his gift to her, not in the stock words of a devoted disciple but from the unique vantage point of having traveled her (and his) final lifetime as his mother:

> I suckled you with mother's milk
> which quenched thirst for a moment.

From you I drank the dharma-milk
perpetually tranquil.

You do not owe a debt to me
because I brought you up.
Great Sage, to get a son like you
sates all desire for sons. . . .

Women can obtain with ease
the names, "Chief Queen," "King's Mother."
The hardest name of all to get
is "Mother of the Buddha."

Oh Hero, I attained that name![17]

There is no equivocation here. Not "aunt," or "wet nurse," or "foster
mother," or any of the other distancing appellations for Mahaprajapati
that we invariably find in the androcentric literature. Here, held in a story
remembered and recorded by women, Mahaprajapati is explicitly named
the Buddha's mother.

Mahaprajapati now advises her son of her wish to pass into nirvana that
very day. The beautiful passages that follow capture the intimate poignancy
of her last acts as she prepares to leave all earthly ties behind. Still addressing
her son, Mahaprajapati asks permission to gaze upon his beautiful body,
which radiates the thirty-two marks of an enlightened being "like a heap of
gold." Putting her head on his feet, she says,

I will bend to worship [your feet],
my son, with all my love. . . .

I'm bowing to the sun for [humanity],
the banner of the solar clan.*
After this, my final death,
I'll not see you again.[18]

---

* Referring to their Sakya lineage.

After countless lifetimes in karmic relationship with one another, Mahaprajapati is saying her final good-bye to her son. With release into the expanse of nirvana, she will not take rebirth or ever see him again.

An important step in saying good-bye to a buddha is asking forgiveness for any and all wrongdoing—a Buddhist confessional of sorts. Here Mahaprajapati specifically asks her son to forgive her if there was any fault in her repeated requests for women's ordination. Acknowledging the tremendous responsibility he gave her to teach dharma to nuns, she further asks forgiveness for any errors she may have made or bad advice she may have given during her years of guidance and teaching. These remarks are slightly different in the Sinhala version of this passage, where she describes her role as "the chief of women," implying that her responsibilities extended to oversight and teaching of the laywomen's community as well.[19]

Hearing her out, the Buddha gently responds that no forgiveness is needed, as those who have seen nirvana require no forgiveness. In the Sinhala version, he says,

> The gold from the great jambu tree in the Himalayan forest needs not be refined; nor does the queen-mother need to be forgiven, as there is nothing to forgive. It is not requisite that those who have seen nirvana should forgive each other. Yet as you have requested it and it is the custom of Buddhas thus to forgive, what you seek is granted, as what you ask for is good.[20]

Sanctioning her request with the words, "Know that it is the right time, O Gotami,"[21] the Buddha gives her permission to be the first of his disciples to enter nirvana. His words imply that he regards her as foremost among all his disciples, not just the women:

> Therefore be the first to enter nirvana; and thus obtain the preeminence over all my other [disciples], as all the stars are eclipsed by the superior light of the full moon.[22]

Following their beloved preceptor's lead, the five hundred nuns now come forward and venerate the Buddha's feet. Mahaprajapati's actions and testimonial implicitly fulfill their own end-of-life obligations.

In a sweet twist we find only in the Pali canon version, Mahaprajapati now turns to her other "children"—Rahula, Ananda, and Nanda—to inform them of her intention to enter nirvana and seek their approval to do so. While it is not the same as asking the Buddha's permission, it is her way of saying good-bye to them, a mother's way of giving her children a final teaching and opportunity to speak. Hearing her words as arhats, Rahula and Nanda remain steadfast, rooted in a profound understanding of life's impermanence and the futility of clinging to conditioned things ("worthless as banana wood"[23]), even the loss of a cherished loved one. On the other hand, like the rest of us, Ananda is not awakened. Overcome with grief at Mahaprajapati's words, he bursts into tears. For him, her announcement is a double blow because he knows that her passing augurs in short order the passing of the Buddha. Unable to bear the thought of such loss, he weeps inconsolably.

Wise in her way of comforting him, Mahaprajapati points out to Ananda his own supreme accomplishments that have set in motion his future arhatship. Praising him as "Protector of the Buddha's Teachings,"[24] she declares his knowledge "deep as the sea."[25] By assisting her in requesting ordination for women, she says, he has attained immeasurable merit, not just by helping her but by enabling multitudes of women to reach their goal of nirvana. Mahaprajapati is telling Ananda to keep his eye on the ball: this is no time to get caught up by the emotions of samsara's impermanence, which you know to be inevitable and the cause of suffering. Nirvana is an occasion for laughter and celebration, not grief. Isn't this what we've all been striving for? Isn't this what the dharma is all about?

With this final dharma pep talk, Mahaprajapati reciprocates the immeasurable gift Ananda gave her and all Buddhist women (then and now). In her motherly (perhaps grandmotherly) way, her farewell is a loving teaching and direct empowerment to help Ananda transform his worldly clinging into a reenergized focus on his own soteriological journey. Soon both his "parents" will be gone. He has everything he needs to fulfill his goal. Now is the time for Ananda to stand on his own and become a lamp unto himself.

Mahaprajapati further contemplates the chosen timing of her departure. Leaving before her son requires tying off other personal, karmic loose ends. With insight, she observes the overall harmony of the monastic community and feels satisfied that the Buddha is "pleased by the monks and nuns at peace."[26] Recalling the sneezing incident in the Jeta Grove, when he admonished his disciples not to pray for his long life but to honor him through their own spiritual accomplishments and living in harmony, she takes satisfaction knowing that in just over four decades her son had accomplished his goal and the dharma would flourish after his death.

Tremendous responsibility for this ambitious outcome had fallen to Mahaprajapati. In the patriarchal culture of the time, it would have been impossible for the Buddha to fulfill the female half of his commitment to a fourfold assembly alone, without a woman to take the lead on his behalf. It worked out well that it was his mother, since a woman of different or unknown provenance might have given rise to even more controversy and patriarchal pushback than Mahaprajapati had already been subjected to.

It is easily asserted that Mahaprajapati as leader of the nuns, together with a dozen or so other foremost nuns, can be given credit for the formation of a quarter of the Buddha's fourfold community. But what about the laywomen? There was no designated leader of laywomen. Where Mahaprajapati's role as advocate, mentor, and teacher extended to all women, it can be further asserted that actually *half* of the fourfold assembly came into wholeness because of her. Self-described as "the chief of women," she took on the groundbreaking role of representing Buddhist women, first as a laywoman herself, then as a nun, serving both communities in the role of a wise and powerful mother figure until the end of her life. We saw clear evidence of this when laywomen fell at her feet weeping with the words, "Do not abandon us without a protector."[27]

Returning to the *apadana*, more episodes in this wonderful drama continue to unfold. The Buddha has given Mahaprajapati permission to depart, but first he asks her to publicly display miracles as evidence of her awakened state. Ordinarily, exhibiting supernormal powers is forbidden because they are only side effects of the much more significant state of arhatship. But here the Buddha makes an exception. He knows Mahaprajapati has attained arhatship and wants to be sure there is no doubt in anyone else's mind. It is important to him that her legacy be untainted by the biases of those with ordinary minds who might not recognize her supreme accomplishment.

Varying accounts of this episode suggest different reasons the Buddha gave Mahaprajapati this instruction. In Walters's translation, the Buddha offers it as a corrective to misogynist ignorance, saying,

> Yet still there are these fools who doubt
> that women too can grasp the truth.
> Gotami, show miracles,
> that they might give up false views.[28]

The parallel Sinhala passage similarly reads,

> Before her departure, [Gotami] was directed by the Buddha to
> exhibit some miracle in the presence of the faithful, that the error of
> those who supposed that it was not possible for a woman to attain
> nirvana might be removed.[29]

Pruitt's translation of the *apadana* in Dhammapala's commentary expresses
a different but equally significant reason: the Buddha recognized the
importance of Mahaprajapati as a role model for women. Proof of her
arhatship was needed to incentivize and inspire girls and women on the
dharma path. Here the Buddha says,

> O Gotami, in order to overcome their wrong views, show your
> supernormal power[s] to the young women who comprehended the
> Dharma [but] who have become confused.[30]

In all ways, the Buddha's egalitarianism, if not his advocacy of women's
soteriological potential, shines through in these remarkable passages. How
differently the women's literature recalls the Buddha's teachings and tells the
story of early Buddhist women!

Miracles provide an outer display that can help the ordinary mind fathom
the ineffable vastness of the enlightened mind. Mahaprajapati's display of
miracles, performed before crowds of assembled monastics and layfolk, is
mind-boggling indeed. The powers of her mind far surpass anything the
ordinary mind can conjure. The texts go on with magnificent imagery and
detail, beginning with her prostrating to the Buddha and flying up into the
sky. A few samples of her resplendent performance follow:

> With the tip of her finger she covered the sun and the moon. She
> wore a thousand suns and moons like a garland. . . .
> She carried the waters of the four oceans in one hand and rained

them forth like the great rain produced by the rain cloud at the end
of an age. . . .

She made a wheel-turning monarch and his retinue appear on the
surface of the sky. She showed a Garuda,* an elephant, and a roaring
lion.[31]

Thus, Mahaprajapati demonstrates her awakening for all to see. Proclaiming
that she has arrived at her goal, she returns to the earth in ordinary form,
humbly pays homage again to the Buddha, and sits by his side.

The assembled witnesses erupt in cheers and praise. They then ask, "How
did you attain this astonishing, unequalled level of accomplishment?"
Deeply respectful and in awe, they request that Mahaprajapati tell her
story.

As we've seen, in the realm of karmic imagination all biographical stories
begin in previous lifetimes. All arhats and bodhisattvas have perfect recall
of past lives and thus know exactly the karmic trajectory that brought them
to their awakened state. While all lifetimes are said to be beginningless, the
starting point in Buddhist hagiography is the lifetime that gives rise to the
aspiration to awaken. Like a tiny seed that will one day yield a giant sequoia,
the moment of aspiration takes root in the karmic continuum and inviolably
persists until its ultimate fruition. Needless to say, countless zigs and zags,
advances and reversals, sufferings and virtue form the trunk, limbs, and
blossoms of this relentless soteriological progression. Each awakened being
has their own unique story of spiritual development.

Mahaprajapati relates to her rapt audience the inspiring story of her
spiritual journey. The following is a summary, written in Mahaprajapati's
voice by the author:

> *It began in the time of Padumuttara Buddha, one hundred thousand*
> *world cycles ago. At that time, I was born into a minister's family*
> *abounding with riches and prosperity. One day as a young girl,*
> *accompanied by my father and a retinue of servants, I saw the Blessed*
> *One give a public teaching. To me he appeared like "the autumn sun*
> *resplendent with a network of rays," his dharma as pure as gentle rain.*

---

* A mythical bird, often depicted as Vishnu's mount.

*The moment came when, in front of multitudes, he declared his elderly aunt chief of nuns.*

*Immediately the aspiration arose in my heart that I would achieve that position in the era of a future buddha. This would be my chosen path to final awakening. For the next week I tirelessly made offerings to the Blessed One and his disciples until finally I approached him and paid homage at his feet. It was then that I told him of my aspiration.*

*Praising me in front of all, Buddha Padumuttara prophesied that my aspiration would be fulfilled during the era of Gautama Buddha. I rejoiced to hear his words: "This one will be the aunt of that Buddha, a foster mother of his life, and she will attain preeminence for long standing among the nuns."*[32]

*And so, I journeyed through countless more lifetimes, accompanied by a retinue of five hundred female friends who similarly aspired to awaken. Once we were all born as slaves in the realm of King Kasi. I was the eldest and chief of the women. At one time five hundred pratyekabuddhas entered our village seeking alms. We were very pleased to honor them as our guests and formed a guild with our husbands that provided these holy buddhas with food and shelter for four months. Before their departure, we gave each a fine new set of robes. From that lifetime as slaves, we continued our journey, together with our husbands.*

*In this life we were all born in the clan of the Sakyas, and I became the foster mother of the Bodhisattva when my sister, Maya, sadly died in childbirth. As my son went forth, becoming the Blessed One, I too went forth, together with those five hundred wise women. Together still, we have now attained peace and happiness, the fruits of complete liberation. Our husbands too, who performed meritorious deeds with us, have attained complete liberation. Our karmic journey is complete. Together we have achieved our long-held wish for awakening through the compassion of the Blessed One.*

Now the five hundred nuns take their turn demonstrating their supernatural powers for the entire assembly to see. Rising up into the sky, blazing forth "like stars," they too perform myriad miracles. This delights their vast audience and the Buddha watching from below. Returning to their seats in the assembly, the nuns speak with one voice, praising Mahaprajapati and then the Buddha, crediting them both with their attainments. Finally, they request the Buddha's permission to pass into nirvana together, to which he responds, "Know that it's the right time!"[33]

As Mahaprajapati and the five hundred nuns depart for their nunnery, the Buddha and his entourage accompany them to the gates in a show of respect. Falling at his feet for the last time, Mahaprajapati is both disciple and mother as she speaks her final words to her son:

> This is my last look
> at the lord of the world;
> your face, a fountain of ambrosia,
> won't be seen again.

> No more homage to your soft feet;
> I won't touch them again.
> O hero, chief of all the world,
> today I go to [final peace].[34]

And so Mahaprajapati's long-held karmic ambition is nearing fulfillment. She enters and takes her seat in the lotus posture. In a final, touching scene, a profusion of laywomen rush forward, wailing, pounding their fists. "Crying piteous tears," they beseech her not to leave. One woman, beside herself with grief, falls at Mahaprajapati's feet. Gently stroking the top of her head, Mahaprajapati comforts her, speaking soothingly, as a mother would to a child:

> Enough, enough depression child;
> free yourself from Mara's snares!
> Everything existent changes;
> shaking, it's lost in the end.[35]

Mahaprajapati sends the women away and enters the first state of meditative absorption. With adept mental prowess, she travels the spheres of consciousness to the farthest reaches, reverses the order, then ascends again until finally, like a flame that has gone out, she is released into the limitless expanse of nirvana.

Miracles rock the universe as the earth quakes, oceans roar, lightning falls from the sky, and flowers rain down on the earth. Now the five hundred nuns follow their fearless Mahaprajapati, and like flames, they too go out.

With sadness, the goddesses lament:

> The death of [Gotami] and the [nuns] is like the passing away of the moon and the stars from the sky; the number of the faithful is diminished.[36]

All the gods of heaven and earth observe with awe the nuns' passing away. With the power of impermanence spectacularly manifest before their eyes, their own understanding of the Buddha's most essential teaching strikes deeply in their hearts. They all wail:

> Indeed, formations are impermanent, just as [Gotami] is dispersed.
>
> These [nuns] who carry out the Teacher's teachings and who surrounded her, they are all quenched, like the flame of a lamp without fuel.
>
> Alas, ties end in separation. Alas, all conditioned states are impermanent. Alas, life ends in destruction.[37]

Now the Buddha summons Ananda, saying, "Go now, Ananda, tell the monks my mother's reached nirvana."[38] Fighting tears, Ananda dutifully calls for disciples to gather:

> Now assemble, all you monks, . . .
>
> This Gotami who carefully
> reared up the sage's body,
> is gone to peace, no longer seen,
> just like the stars at sunrise.
>
> Her destination now is reached;
> her name alone remains.
> Even the Buddha, who has five eyes,
> cannot see where she went.

Each who has faith in the Well-Gone One
and each who is the Sage's pupil
ought to come, that Buddha's [heir],
to honor the Buddha's mother.[39]

And so Ananda calls out that all disciples of the Buddha should assemble to pay homage to Mahaprajapati. By the power of the Buddha, anyone who wished to be present appears in a moment of time without effort; thus multitudes quickly form the largest assembly ever gathered during the Buddha's ministry.[40]

### Funeral of Mahaprajapati and the Five Hundred Women

Let's take Mahaprajapati's instruction to heart and celebrate her marvelous victory over life's suffering grasp. Unique among women, after lifetimes on the dharma path, she lived her final life as Gautama Buddha's loving mother and the revered leader and teacher of countless religious women. Her aspirations fulfilled, "all fetters destroyed," at the age of 120 she chose the time and method of her religious death, departing together with five hundred lifelong companions and leaving no trace, "like stars at dawn."[41]

Hear Mahaprajapati's call for laughter! Drums of joy! No doubt the ancient festivals that produced this drama celebrated her life in such a jubilant manner. Hers is an inspiration to all spiritual seekers, wherever they are on the spiritual path. Laywomen and girls can look to Mahaprajapati's past lives and find guidance about how to live a life of generosity, loving kindness, and pure moral conduct. Monastic women see a role model for deep constancy and dedication to the Buddha and the dharma, a practitioner of such accomplishment that Mahaprajapati became a great teacher herself, ensuring that the dharma would flourish into the future, especially as a path for women. And then there are the mothers! Mothers from all walks of life can find in Mahaprajapati a kindred soul who struggled to raise a difficult child, her heart always riveted unconditionally to his throughout his arduous and then glorious life journey.

The Buddha saw fit to publicly honor his mother and the five hundred nuns by mounting a grand funeral—so public, in fact, that the entire universe participated. There is nothing quite like these final obsequies in all of Buddhist literature, including the rites marking the Buddha's own passing into *parinirvana*. As Mahaprajapati's *apadana* says,

> The Buddha's final nirvana
> was not of such a kind as this.
> Gotami's final nirvana
> was extremely miraculous.[42]

It's worth noting that the Buddha did not choose his death in the same way Mahaprajapati chose hers. His was a natural-appearing, human demise where, at age eighty, he succumbed after an illness, possibly food poisoning.* Also significant is that Mahaprajapati did not pass into nirvana alone, but together with five hundred women companions whose lives intersected through support and caring for one another on the path to awakening over many lifetimes.

Returning to our story, funeral preparations are in full swing.† According to the *Mulasarvastivada Vinaya*, inspired by affection for the Buddha's mother, monks bring finely scented wood to Mahaprajapati's residence, where her corpse and those of the five hundred nuns lie in repose. The Buddha, accompanied by senior disciples and a large entourage, also arrives. Among the gathering throng is King Prasenajit attended by a full complement of wives, ministers, citizens, and country folk, in addition to regional kings with their retinues and hundreds of thousands more people who come from every direction to pay homage to Mahaprajapati and the nuns.[43]

The gods now produce 501 glorious, golden, pinnacled "huts" to contain the corpses, while Prasenajit provides gem-studded biers to carry them to the cremation site. Celebrants (no doubt mourners too) form a colorful procession, holding up flowers, parasols, garlands, banners, and canopies. They swing incense burners and dance to the rhythms and melodies of myriad musical instruments. How pleased Mahaprajapati would have been to see such celebration of the fruition of dharma's purpose!

---

* As Bodhisattva, however, his very "human" death would be viewed as entirely intentional.
† The following summary weaves highlights and unique details from several accounts.

A colorful variant from the Chinese-Sanskrit tradition has a local general, Yasa, making all the funeral arrangements. Since the bodies of the 501 nuns are locked inside their nunnery, he has someone erect a ladder to climb in a window and open the door, allowing entry to five hundred men who carry the corpses away. Inside the residence, two novice nuns, who thought the women had all been sleeping, are shocked by the truth of what has just taken place. They attain instant realization of impermanence and thereby arhatship. One of these novice nuns is named Nanda. Could she perhaps be Mahaprajapati's daughter, Sundarinanda?[44]

Now, the Pali *apadana* tells us the guardian *devas* of the four directions were Mahaprajapati's pallbearers.[45] A Sanskrit account differs significantly here, telling us that her pallbearers were her "sons," Nanda, Aniruddha,* Ananda, and Rahula, and that the Buddha walked alongside them, his right hand supporting the coffin from underneath.[46] More authentic in tone and feeling, this latter account creates a striking visual narrative where male family members are shown performing the traditional, filial act of bearing a mother's coffin. Recalling that Mahaprajapati's *apadana* was composed as a public performance piece, it is not illogical to imagine that the Pali variant employed *devas* for this purpose because depicting the Buddha as a pallbearer (where he would be showing reverence as a son) could be misconstrued as demeaning under any circumstances for a buddha, even in relation to performing obsequies for his mother.

No higher honor could have been shown to Mahaprajapati than to have her beloved sons be her pallbearers.† Regarding the remaining five hundred nuns, monks (elsewhere gods) carry their biers "with sincerely respectful hearts,"[47] in a lengthy cortege winding its way to a secluded, open expanse where 501 cremation pyres have been prepared with fragrant wood sprinkled with perfumes. The entire universe manifests as a chapel containing this marvelous event—the sky a canopy with the sun, moon, and stars drawn in gold. Brilliantly colored flags dot the landscape, which is covered in a carpet of flower petals, as incense swirls heavenward, like offerings emanating from the earth.

Multitudes of divine beings heap flower garlands on the caskets. Leading the procession, they honor these foremost women with music, dance, and

---

* Usually identified as a nephew.
† Except of course to have her daughter, Sundarinanda, participate too.

song. The five hundred biers of "the Buddha's daughters"[48] follow first, with Mahaprajapati's bier surrounded by her son's disciples behind them. One variant has the Buddha walking in front of his mother's casket carrying incense and, assisted by his monks, adding precious, red sandal incense firewood to his mother's pyre.[49]

Conspicuous narrative discrepancies appear when it is time to light the funeral pyres. The Pali *apadana* is curiously silent about who performs this important ritual act, which in ancient India traditionally falls to the eldest son. In a Sanskrit variant, King Prasenajit and members of his entourage light the fires.[50] In another, the *devas* step forward to do this but are sharply halted by the elder monk Sariputra, who cites the filial responsibility of sons, including buddhas, to their parents:

> Because the parents give birth to the son, feed milk, carry in their arms and raise him for a long time, the son is indebted to his parents in many ways. Hence he should repay the debt. O gods, you should know that the natural mothers of the past Buddhas died before them. If the mothers of the future Buddhas also will die before them, the future Buddhas too will worship them likewise. You must know this rule. The Tathagatha should perform the funeral rites and worship the relics in person, not the gods.[51]

So the Buddha performs the funeral rites for his mother, just as he previously did for his father.[52] The Sinhala account tells us that all the corpses are completely consumed except Mahaprajapati's, which appears "like a heap of pearls."*[53] More graphic, her Pali *apadana* relates that charred bones remain, which serve as an upsetting reminder to Ananda of the impending demise of his beloved Teacher. Gathering her bone fragments in an alms bowl, he brings them to the Buddha.

What follows is an exquisite eulogy to Mahaprajapati delivered publicly by the Buddha. While the Sanskrit sources state simply that he delivered a teaching on impermanence, in her Pali *apadana*, the Buddha holds up Mahaprajapati's bone fragments as an outward sign of impermanence while

---

* A sign of sainthood.

lauding the supreme accomplishment of her complete inner realization of that profound teaching, the cornerstone of dharma and gateway to nirvana.

Recalling that Mahaprajapati is the first among his senior disciples to pass away, this is a critical teaching moment for the Buddha. He too is reaching the end of his life, the end of his ministry, the end of his final rebirth in which his mission to establish dharma in the world is almost complete. How essential it must have felt to his purpose to have arhats precede him in death, leaving no doubt in the minds of the unawakened that dharma truly works, that nirvana is possible, that the path truly leads to freedom from suffering, just as he had laid out in his first teaching of the Four Noble Truths in the Deer Park over four decades earlier. Surely Mahaprajapati knew this too and wanted to offer her paradigmatic death not just for her son but for the assembly, according to her own intention to further the dharma in the world, helping to secure its continuity and its resilience into the future.

Only the Buddha could see without doubt her awakened mind, thus it became paramount to him that others should see it too. In this way, he insisted upon a complete display after granting Mahaprajapati's request to die: from her miracles, to her past-life testimonial, to her dramatic going out. An exemplar across lifetimes and in her final death, Mahaprajapati was the first of all the Buddha's disciples to patently demonstrate the truth of his teachings. More than that, five hundred women simultaneously did the same thing. Misogynist doubters take note: in voluntarily opting for nirvana, it was women (hundreds of them) who pioneered the way for the Buddha's remaining disciples as well as future generations by displaying the profound result of the path.

More than demonstrable proof of women's soteriological potential, the great liberation of Mahaprajapati and the five hundred nuns was a transformative moment at the dawn of Buddhism. Endorsed and witnessed by the Buddha himself, it ratified the entire wealth of his teachings, demonstrating truly that "the Buddha is the glory of his disciples, and the disciples are the glory of the Buddha."[54] Women, it turns out, were the first to manifestly exhibit this truth.

In his eulogy, the Buddha calls Mahaprajapati "my mother," speaking tenderly as a son. He is also the Great Teacher, weaving events at hand into a profound homily for the benefit of his audience. "If you love me, be like me,"[55] Mahaprajapati had instructed her disciples earlier, and so her son carries her message into his encomium:

Even the trunk of a huge timber tree,
however massive it might be,
will break to bits, eventually.
Thus Gotami, who was a nun
is now gone out completely.

It is so marvelous a thing:
my mother who has reached nirvana
leaving only bits of bone
had neither grief nor tears.

She crossed this ocean of existence,
grieving not for others left;
she now is cool, she's well gone out:
her torment is now done.

Know this, O monks, she was most wise,
with wisdom vast and wide.
She was a nun of great renown,
a master of great powers.
She cultivated "divine ear"
and knew what others thought.

In former births, before this one,
she mastered "divine eye."
All imperfections were destroyed;
she'll have no more rebirths.

She had purified her knowledge
of meaning and the doctrines,
of etymology, and preaching;
therefore she did not grieve.

An iron rod aglow in fire
cools off and leaves no ash.
Just like the flame once in the rod,
it's not known where she went.

Those who are emancipated
cross [desire's] deluge;
those with solid happiness
do not get born again.

Therefore be lamps for yourselves;
go graze in mindfulness.
With wisdom's seven parts attained,
you all should end your woe.[56]

As her "lamp" has gone out, the Buddha urges his disciples to become lamps unto themselves. In this way his admonishment to them is to internalize the dharma Mahaprajapati modeled and taught during her life, heeding her presence now as an inner rather than outer teacher. Like a candle passing a flame to another candle, she was gone, but her blaze lived on in those she touched.

Of course, the Buddha's words presaged his own imminent death and his ardent wish to free his disciples of their dependency on him before that took place. Mahaprajapati and the five hundred women's intentional passing forged the way, demonstrating to a huge assembly of witnesses that in their final freedom they were no longer tied to anything, including their Blessed Teacher. The women's simultaneous "great going out" was their ultimate offering to him and to his legacy. At the same time, it prepared the first generation of disciples for the biggest loss of all—the Buddha's own *parinirvana*.

# Epilogue: Her Story Continues

The conclusion of Mahaprajapati's final lifetime is by no means the end of her story. But here different Buddhist schools and traditions would pick up the thread in different ways. To many, the metaphor of the flame going out signifies her final freedom from the grasp of suffering while achieving a state of peace that lies beyond the bonds of rebirth. Indeed, the Buddha claimed there are no adequate, conceptual means of expressing nirvana.[1]

Other Buddhist schools might suggest that Mahaprajapati's rebirths would continue, albeit in different form, that her arhatship was a stepping-stone to a higher buddhahood, achievable by all beings by engaging the path of the bodhisattva. In these schools, she would intentionally continue to take rebirth with the altruistic wish to free all beings from suffering just as she herself had become free. Scholar Jan Willis notes that many historically preeminent Tibetan women saints were said to be incarnations of preeminent Indian women saints, Mahaprajapati among them.[2] The notion of female lineages traceable back to Mahaprajapati and the first generation of Buddhist women is certainly an area inviting further research.

In the revered *Lotus Sutra*, the Buddha predicts future buddhahood for all disciples (*sravakas*) in his assembly. In one such passage he addresses Mahaprajapati, who stands before him as foremost nun with her entire cohort of nuns (here said to number six thousand), and says to her,

Are you [thinking] I have not mentioned your name and predicted for you Perfect Enlightenment? Gautami! I have already inclusively announced that the future of all *sravakas* is predicted. Now you, who desire to know your future destiny, shall in the world to come become a great teacher of the Law . . . and these six thousand nuns, all training and trained will all become teachers of the Law. Thus you will gradually become perfect in the bodhisattva way and will become a buddha entitled Loveliness Tathagata, Worshipful, All Wise, . . . Peerless Leader, Teacher of Gods and Men, Buddha, World-honored One. Gautami! This Buddha Loveliness and the six thousand [female] bodhisattvas will in turn be predicted to attain Perfect Enlightenment.[3]

With this we learn that Mahaprajapati's eventual buddhahood is ensured by her continuing to take rebirth as a teacher of the "Law" or dharma. Always together, the same path and future are promised to her assembly of nuns. Hearing the Buddha's prediction, the women rejoice and respond,

> World-honored Leader!
> Comforter of gods and men!
> We, hearing thy prediction,
> Have perfect peace in our hearts.[4]

These religious women have all vowed to take rebirth as bodhisattvas to teach the dharma in future lifetimes wherever it may be needed, for as long as it takes to free all beings. Not the same outcome as nirvana, in this account the bodhisattva path has brought Mahaprajapati and her company of women perfect peace of a different kind. Indeed, the Buddha's prediction appears to have borne fruit, since today as never before there are myriad accomplished Buddhist women teachers—lay and monastic—promulgating the dharma across diverse Buddhist cultures and traditions.

This survey would not be complete without looking to the *Gandavyuha Sutra*, which foregrounds female bodhisattva teachers in a lengthy narrative about the pilgrim Sudhana's journey across a sacred cosmic landscape in pursuit of ultimate truth. Of the fifty-two enlightened advisors he encounters along the way, twenty are women, including a prostitute, a queen, and several goddesses, among others. As Sudhana travels to the sacred site of Kapilavastu, he comes across Gautama Buddha's mother Maya and wife Gopa (Yasodhara), who, as supreme bodhisattvas, answer his questions and impart to him their singular wisdom. Nowhere in Sudhana's pilgrimage is Mahaprajapati mentioned.

But let's take a closer look. Perhaps once again she is present while remaining hidden from view. Different life stories often shed light on the same character in different ways. We learn that Sudhana goes to the Buddha's birth site, Lumbini, where he meets a bodhisattva night goddess by the name of Sutejomandalaratishri, who is attended by countless wood goddesses. Over the course of their discussion, Sutejomandalaratishri relates that she was present at the birth of every buddha, beginning countless eons before with the birth of the very first buddha, named Paragon of Virtue. In beautifully descriptive verse, she recalls the ebullience of the flowers in bloom and radiance of light emanating in all directions from the Lumbini garden as his mother, the queen, grasped the branch of a holy fig tree and gave birth, surrounded by a vast company of women. Sutejomandalaratishri goes on to reveal that the mother was Maya in a past life, while the baby's father was King Suddhodana. The women attending the birth were the wood goddesses surrounding her now, and she, Sutejomandalaratishri, was the baby's wet nurse. The bodhisattva describes her great joy the first time she held the infant buddha:

> He was born, shining with golden light. Taking that supreme person in my arms, I could not see the top of his head; Looking at his inconceivable body, I could not see any bounds. Adorned by marks of greatness, pure. His body was beautiful to behold; seeing him, like a jewel figurine, incomparable joy welled up in me. Thinking of his measureless virtues, an infinite sea of felicity grew in me; And seeing his ocean of miracles, I was inspired to seek enlightenment.[5]

From that long-ago moment of joy holding the baby buddha, the night goddess aspired to a soteriological path that included being wet nurse across eons to all buddhas, which would have included, of course, Gautama Buddha. For now, Sutejomandalaratishri continuously dwells in the Lumbini garden awaiting the birth of the next buddha. In between nurturing babies, she is a great teacher, expounding the dharma to a vast assembly of goddesses. Consummate wet nurse to buddhas, supreme dharma teacher and leader of women—who but Mahaprajapati comes to mind in this tale?[6]

Whatever aftermath to Mahaprajapati's long life rings true for the reader, it is how she is remembered in hearts and minds today that is important. Gentle sister and wise queen, loving mother to the Buddha, intrepid advocate and leader of women, peerless dharma preceptor, she helped her son lay the foundations of early Buddhism while realizing her own soteriological potential in myriad ways that continue to reveal themselves as her stories reemerge from the past. "If you love me, be like me," were her final words. Twenty-five hundred years later they continue to resound, offering wisdom we would all do well to contemplate and seek for ourselves.

# NOTES

## Introduction

1. W. Woodville Rockhill, trans., *The Life of the Buddha and the Early History of His Order* (London: Trubner, 1884), 34. See also Bhikkhu Nanamoli, ed. and trans., *The Life of the Buddha According to the Pali Canon* (Onalaska, WA: BPS Pariyatti Editions, 1992), 303.

2. Jonathan S. Walters, trans., *Legends of the Buddhist Saints: Apadanapali* (Walla Walla, WA: Whitman College, 2018), 4.17. Download available at http://apadanatranslation.org.

3. Karma Lekshe Tsomo, ed., "Mahaprajapati's Legacy: The Buddhist Women's Movement: An Introduction," in *Buddhist Women Across Cultures: Realizations* (Albany: State University of New York Press, 1999), 5.

4. Peter Skilling, "Nuns, Laywomen, Donors, Goddesses: Female Roles in Early Indian Buddhism," *Journal of the International Association of Buddhist Studies* 24, no. 2 (2001): 246.

5. Maurice Winternitz, *A History of Indian Literature* Vol. 2, *Buddhist Literature and Jaina Literature*, 1927, trans. S. Ketkar and H. Kohn (New Delhi: Oriental Books Reprint Corporation, 1977), 2:102.

6. Caroline A. Foley, "Women Leaders of the Buddhist Reformation, as Illustrated by Dhammapala's Commentary on the *Therigatha*," in *Transactions of the Ninth International Congress of Orientalists* (Indian and Aryan Sections), ed. E. Delmar Morgan (London: Committee of the Congress, 1893), 1:344.

7. Winternitz, *History of Indian Literature*, 2:112.

8. J. J. Jones, trans., *The Mahavastu* (London: Luzac & Company, 1949–56), 3:245.

9. Bhikkhu Bodhi, trans., *The Numerical Discourse of the Buddha: A Translation of the Anguttara Nikaya* (Boston: Wisdom Publications, 2012), 1188.

10. Dharmachakra Translation Committee, trans., *The Play in Full* [*Lalitavistara*], chap. 8 (84000: Translating the Words of the Buddha, 2013),

https://read.84000.co/translation/UT22084-046-001.html. (Hereafter, DTC, *Lalitavistara*, with chapter numbers.)

11. Monier Monier-Williams, *A Sanskrit English Dictionary* (Delhi: Motilal Banarsidass, 1974), 794.

12. Monier-Williams, *Sanskrit English Dictionary*, 658.

13. Monier-Williams, *Sanskrit English Dictionary*, 658.

14. R. L. Mitra, trans., *The Lalita-Vistara: Memoirs of the Early Life of Sakya Sinha* (Chs. 1–15). 1877. (Delhi: Sri Satguru Publications, 1998), 152n42, 161n3.

15. N. Dutt, ed., *Vinayavastu 16: Adhikaranavastu*, http://gretil.sub.uni-goettingen.de/gretil/1_sanskr/4_rellit/buddh/vinv16_u.htm, 2000; based on Raniero Gnoli, *The Gilgit Manuscript of the Sayanasanavastu and the Adhikaranavastu: Being the 15th and 16th Sections of the Vinaya of the Mulasarvastivadin*. Serie Orientale Roma, vol. 5 (Rome: Istituto italiano per il Medio ed Estremo Oriente, 1978).

16. Edward J. Thomas, *The Life of the Buddha as Legend and History* (Delhi: Motilal Banarsidass, 1977), 25.

17. Herman Oldenberg, *Buddha: His Life, His Doctrine, His Order*, trans. William Hoey (London: William and Norgate, 1882; London: Forgotten Books, 2012), 94n2. Citations refer to the Forgotten Books edition.

18. T. W. Rhys Davids and William Stede, eds., *The Pali Text Society's Pali-English Dictionary* (London: Cheapstead, 1921–1925), 432.

19. Mitra, *Lalita-Vistara,* 167.

20. *Buddhist Dictionary of Pali Proper Names*, http://www.palikanon.com/english/pali_names/dic_idx.html, s.v. "Mahapajapati Gotami." (Website note. Most of the entries have been taken from the *Dictionary of Pali Names* by G. P. Malalasekera, 1899–1973, which is available in printed version from the Pali Text Society, London.) See also Shoba Rani Dash, *Mahapajapati: The First Bhikkhuni* (Seoul: Blue Lotus Books, 2008), 18–19.

21. Walters, *Legends*, 4.17.

22. Charles Hallisey, trans., *Therigatha: Poems of the First Buddhist Women*. Murty Classical Library of India, vol. 3 (Cambridge, MA: Harvard University Press, 2015), 85.

23. T. W. Rhys Davids, trans., *Buddhist Birth-Stories (Jataka Tales): The Commentarial Introduction Entitled "Nidanakatha, the Story of the Lineage,"* rev. ed. (London: George Routledge & Sons, 1908), 184–87. See also Wendy Garling, *Stars at Dawn, Forgotten Stories of Women in the Buddha's Life* (Boulder: Shambhala Publications, 2016), 170–73.

24. Jones, *Mahavastu*, 2:195.

25. Jones, *Mahavastu*, 2:280–81.

26. Karen Muldoon-Hules, *Brides of the Buddha: Nuns' Stories from the Avadanasataka* (Lanham, MD: Lexington Books, 2017), 129–37.

27. Lozang Jamspal and Kaia Fischer, trans., "The Story of Kacankala," in *The Hundred Deeds* [*Karmasataka*], part 3, chap. 1 (84000: Translating the Words of the Buddha, 2020), http://read.84000.co/translation/toh340 .html.

28. Muldoon-Hules, *Brides*, 132.

29. Jamspal and Fischer, "Kacankala," 3:6.

30. Jamspal and Fischer, "Kacankala," 3:7.

31. Jamspal and Fischer, "Kacankala," 3:8.

32. Jamspal and Fischer, "Kacankala," 3:9.

33. Frank E. Reynolds, "Rebirth Traditions and the Lineages of Gotama: A Study in Theravada Buddhology," in *Sacred Biography in the Buddhist Traditions of South and Southeast Asia*, ed. Juliane Schober (Honolulu: University of Hawai'i Press, 1997), 29.

34. Richard Gombrich, "Feminine Elements in Sinhalese Buddhism," *Wiener Zeitschrift fur die Kunde Sudasiens* 16 (1972): 84.

35. Gombrich, "Feminine Elements," 90.

36. Gombrich, "Feminine Elements," 90.

37. Gombrich, "Feminine Elements," 90.

38. Gombrich, "Feminine Elements," 92.

39. Gombrich, "Feminine Elements," 81.

## Prologue: Her Story Begins

1. Reimagined from Susan Murcott, *First Buddhist Women, Poems and Stories of Awakening* (Berkeley, CA: Parallax Press, 2006), 44–45.

2. Reimagined from Murcott, *First Buddhist Women*, 117.

3. William Pruitt, trans., *The Commentary on the Verses of the Theris,* by Acariya Dhammapala (Bristol, UK: Pali Text Society, 2017), 194.

## Chapter One: Growing Up in Devadaha

1. Paul Bigandet, trans., *The Life or Legend of Gaudama, the Buddha of the Burmese* (London: Kegan Paul, Trench, Trubner, 1911–12), 1:11.

2. Bigandet, *Legend of Gaudama*, 1:12–13.

3. Rockhill, *Life of the Buddha*, 12.

4. Bhuwan Lal Pradhan, *Lumbini-Kapilawastu-Dewadaha* (Kathmandu: Tribhuvan University, 1979), 7.

5. Jones, *Mahavastu*, 1:299.

6. Jones, *Mahavastu*, 1:299–300.

7. Jones, *Mahavastu*, 1:300–1.

8. Pradhan, *Lumbini-Kapilawastu-Dewadaha*, 6–9.

9. K. D. P. Wickremesinghe, *The Biography of the Buddha* (Colombo, Sri Lanka: published by the author, 1972), 5.

10. Rockhill, *Life of the Buddha*, 114–21.

11. Bodhi, *Anguttara Nikaya*, 446, 570, 1194.

12. Bhikkhu Nanamoli and Bhikkhu Bodhi, trans. *The Middle Length Discourses of the Buddha: A New Translation of the Majjhima Nikaya*, ed. and rev. Bhikkhu Bodhi (Boston: Wisdom Publications, 1995), 493.

13. Bhikkhu Bodhi, trans., *The Connected Discourses of the Buddha: A New Translation of the Samyutta Nikaya* (Boston: Wisdom Publications, 2000), 2:1359.

14. Nanamoli and Bodhi, *Majjhima Nikaya*, 827.

15. E. B. Cowell, trans., "The Buddha-Karita of Ashvsghosha," in *Buddhist Mahayana Texts. The Sacred Books of the East*, ed. Max Muller (Oxford: Clarendon Press, 1894), 49:198.

16. Wilhelm Geiger, trans., *The Mahavamsa, or The Great Chronicle of Ceylon* (London: Oxford University Press, 1912), 12.

17. Rockhill, *Life of the Buddha*, 14.

18. Jones, *Mahavastu*, 1:301.

19. Geiger, *Mahavamsa*, 12.

20. Henry Alabaster, trans., *The Wheel of the Law: Buddhism Illustrated from Siamese Sources* (London: Trubner, 1871), 85.

21. Pradhan, *Lumbini-Kapilawastu-Dewadaha*, 42–43. See also National Geographic Society, "Archaeological Studies Confirm Early Date of Buddha's Life," November 25, 2013, https://phys.org/news/2013-11 -archaeological-discoveries-early-date-buddha.html.

22. Rockhill, *Life of the Buddha*, 14.

23. Walters, *Legends*, 4.17.

24. R. Spence Hardy, trans., *A Manual of Buddhism in Its Modern Development* (London: Partridge and Oakey, 1853), 136.

25. Jones, *Mahavastu*, 1:301–2.

26. Samuel Beal, trans., *The Romantic Legend of Sakya Buddha: From the Chinese Sanscrit* (London: Trubner, 1875), 23.

27. Rockhill, *Life of the Buddha*, 15.

28. Hermann Oldenberg, trans., ed., "The Bhikkhuni Lineage," in *Dipavamsa* [*The Chronicle of the Island*], chap. 18, v. 7, https://www.ancient-buddhist -texts.net/Texts-and-Translations/Dipavamsa/index.htm. (With many thanks to Charles Hallisey and Ven. Tathaloka for their help with this translation.)

29. John S. Strong, *The Buddha: A Short Biography* (Oxford: Oneworld, 2002), 41.

30. DTC, *Lalitavistara*, chap. 3.
31. Hardy, *Manual of Buddhism*, 137.
32. H. T. Rogers, trans., *Buddhaghosa's Parables* (London: Trubner, 1870), 178.
33. Pruitt, *Commentary*, 181.
34. Hardy, *Manual of Buddhism*, 306.
35. Beal, *Romantic Legend*, 23.
36. Walters, *Legends*, 4.17.
37. Mabel Bode, "Women Leaders of the Buddhist Reformation (from the *Manoratha Purani*, Buddhaghosha's Commentary on the *Anguttara Nikaya*)," *Journal of the Royal Asiatic Society* 25, no. 3 (1893): 526.
38. Hardy, *Manual of Buddhism*, 306.
39. Hardy, *Manual of Buddhism*, 137.
40. DTC, *Lalitavistara*, chaps. 5 and 7.

## Chapter Two: Birth of the Buddha

1. Ji Xianlin, trans. and ed., *Fragments of the Tocharian: A Maitreyasamiti-Nataka of the Xinjiang Museum, China* (Berlin: Mouton de Gruyter, 1998), 157.
2. Rhys Davids, *Buddhist Birth Stories*, 148.
3. Jones, *Mahavastu*, 1:113.
4. Jones, *Mahavastu*, 1:115–16.
5. Beal, *Romantic Legend*, 36.
6. DTC, *Lalitavistara*, chap. 5.
7. DTC, *Lalitavistara*, chap. 6.
8. Jones, *Mahavastu*, 1:117. See also Garling, *Stars at Dawn*, 50–51; and D. D. Kosambi, *Myth and Reality: Studies in the Formation of Indian Culture* (Mumbai: Popular Prakashan, 2013), 101.
9. Bigandet, *Legend of Gaudama*, 1:35. See also Patricia Eichenbaum Karetzky, *The Life of the Buddha: Ancient Scriptural and Pictorial Traditions* (Lanham, MD: University Press of America, 1992), 18.
10. DTC, *Lalitavistara*, chap. 7.
11. DTC, *Lalitavistara*, chap. 7.
12. Beal, *Romantic Legend*, 42.
13. Bigandet, *Legend of Gaudama*, 35.
14. Michael Edwardes, ed., *A Life of the Buddha, from a Burmese Manuscript* (London: Folio Society, 1959), 19.
15. Bigandet, *Legend of Gaudama*, 35.
16. Patricia Herbert, *The Life of the Buddha* (San Francisco: Pomegranate Communications, Inc. in association with the British Library, 2005), 21, 79.

17. William Pruitt and Peter Nyunt, "Illustrations from the Life of the Buddha," in *Pearls of the Orient: Asian Treasures from the Wellcome Library* (2003), 129, retrieved from academia.edu.

18. Christian Luczanits, "The Life of the Buddha in the Sumstek," *Orientations* 30, no. 1 (1999): 30–39, retrieved from academia.edu.

19. Ghaniur Rahman, "Iconographic Symbolism of the Prodigious Birth of the Buddha Sakyamuni," *Pakistan Journal of History and Culture*, 29, no. 1 (2008): 155–73, retrieved from academia.edu.

20. Herbert, *Life of the Buddha*, 16, 226.

21. E. H. Johnston, trans., *Asvaghosa's Buddhacarita, or Acts of the Buddha* (Delhi: Motilal Banarsidass, 1977), 23.

22. Jones, *Mahavastu*, 2:3.

23. Beal, *Romantic Legend*, 63.

24. See Garling, *Stars at Dawn*, 55–61, for a more detailed treatment of Maya's death.

25. Lozang Jamspal and Kaia Fischer, trans., "The Story of Kesini," in *The Hundred Deeds [Karmasataka]*, part 3, chap. 4 (84000: Translating the Words of the Buddha, 2020), http://read.84000.co/translation/toh340. html.

26. Trent Walker, "Saṃvega and Pasada: Dharma Songs in Contemporary Cambodia," *Journal of the International Association of Buddhist Studies* 41 (2018): 271–325. The PDF is available on trentwalker.org.

27. Trent Walker, "Introduction," in *Stirring and Stilling: A Liturgy of Cambodian Dharma Songs*, 2011, http://www.stirringandstilling.org/introduction.html.

28. Trent Walker, "Maya's Guidance for Gotami," in *Stirring and Stilling: A Liturgy of Cambodian Dharma Songs*, 2011, http://www.stirringandstilling.org/introduction.html.

## Chapter Three: Mother and Queen

1. Samuel Beal, trans., *The Fo-Sho-Hing-Tsan-King: Life of the Buddha by Ashvaghosa Bodhisattva, The Sacred Books of the East*, ed. Max Muller (Oxford: Clarendon Press, 1883), 19:23.

2. Pruitt, *Commentary*, 181n4. See also Dash, *Mahapajapati*, 43.

3. Beal, *Romantic Legend*, 52.

4. Wickremesinghe, *Biography of the Buddha*, 15n2. See also Beal, *Romantic Legend*, 57.

5. Beal, *Life of the Buddha*, 19, 20.

6. Beal, *Life of the Buddha*, 359.

7. Beal, *Life of the Buddha*, 359–60.

8. Bigandet, *Legend of Gaudama*, 49.

9. Beal, *Romantic Legend*, 63.

10. DTC, *Lalitavistara*, chap. 7. .

11. DTC, *Lalitavistara*, chap. 7.

12. Beal, *Life of the Buddha*, 355.

13. Cowell, *Buddha-Karita*, 21.

14. Beal, *Romantic Legend*, 64.

15. Beal, *Romantic Legend*, 64.

16. Sem Vermeech, "An Early Korean Version of the Buddha's Biography," *Journal of the Oxford Centre for Buddhist Studies* (2011), 1:205–6.

17. Nanamoli and Bodhi, *Majjhima Nikaya*, 1102.

18. DTC, *Lalitavistara*, chap. 8.

19. Beal, *Romantic Legend*, 65.

20. DTC, *Lalitavistara*, chap. 9; Beal, *Romantic Legend*, 65.

21. DTC, *Lalitavistara*, chap. 11.

22. John S. Strong, *The Legend of King Ashoka: A Study and Translation of the Ashokavadana* (Princeton, NJ: Princeton University Press, 1983), 247.

23. Charles Hallisey, "Devotion in the Buddhist Literature of Medieval Sri Lanka," PhD diss., University of Chicago (1988), 300.

24. Pruitt, *Commentary*, 181n4.

25. Bhikkhuni Tathaloka, e-mail message to author, February 20, 2020.

26. Reimagined from Walters, *Legends*, 4.25.

27. Alice Collett, "Therigatha: Nanda, Female Sibling of Gotama Buddha," in *Women in Early Buddhism: Comparative Textual Studies*, ed. Alice Collett (Oxford: Oxford University Press, 2014), 140–59.

28. Pruitt, *Commentary*, 107.

29. Pruitt, *Commentary*, 108.

30. Walters, *Legends*, 4.25.

31. Bode, "Women Leaders," 765.

32. Walters, *Legends*, 4.25.

33. Walters, *Legends*, 4.25.

34. Bodhi, *Anguttara Nikaya*, 111.

35. Reimagined from Walters, *Legends*, 3.13.

36. Bodhi, *Samyutta Nikaya*, 1:823n393.

37. Jones, *Mahavastu*, 2:22.

38. Linda Covill, trans. *Handsome Nanda* by Ashvaghosa, Clay Sanskrit Library (New York: New York University Press and JJC Foundation, 2007), 59.

39. Covill, *Handsome Nanda*, 59.

40. Covill, *Handsome Nanda*, 82–83.

41. Winternitz, *History of Indian Literature*, 2:264.

42. DTC, *Lalitavistara*, chap. 12. See also Beal, *Romantic Legend*, 88–92; Jones, *Mahavastu*, 2:71–72.

43. Thomas Watters, trans., *On Yuan-Chwang's Travels in India 629–645 A.D.*, ed. T. W. Rhys Davids and S. W. Bushell (London: Royal Asiatic Society, 1904; London: Forgotten Books, 2012), 2:4–5. Citations refer to the Forgotten Books edition.

44. Jones, *Mahavastu*, 2:66–69.

45. Covill, *Handsome Nanda*, 133.

46. Beal, *Romantic Legend*, 371.

47. Beal, *Romantic Legend*, 373.

48. Eugene Watson Burlingame, trans., *Buddhist Legends: Translated from the Original Pali Text of the Dhammapada Commentary*, Harvard Oriental Series, ed. Charles Rockwell Lanman (Cambridge, MA: Harvard University Press, 1921), 28:223.

49. Bodhi, *Anguttara Nikaya*, 111.

50. Jones, *Mahavastu*, 2:135.

51. Beal, *Romantic Legend*, 126.

52. Jones, *Mahavastu*, 2:130.

53. John Strong, "A Family Quest: The Buddha, Yasodhara and Rahula in the *Mulasarvastivada Vinaya*," in *Sacred Biography in the Buddhist Traditions of South and Southeast Asia*, ed. Juliane Schober (Honolulu: University of Hawai'i Press, 1997), 115.

54. Beal, *Romantic Legend*, 123.

55. DTC, *Lalitavistara*, chap. 15.

56. Beal, *Life of the Buddha*, 64.

57. Johnston, *Buddhacarita*, 85.

58. Beal, *Life of the Buddha*, 98.

59. DTC, *Lalitavistara*, chap. 15.

60. DTC, *Lalitavistara*, chap. 15.

61. Beal, *Romantic Legend*, 148.

62. Nanamoli, *Life of the Buddha*, 10.

63. Johnston, *Buddhacarita*, 115–16.

64. Except where noted, this summary is constructed from Beal, *Romantic Legend*, 366–68; Jones, *Mahavastu*, 3:126–29; and an unpublished translation (with his permission) by Charles Hallisey, September 2019.

65. Jones, *Mahavastu*, 3:127.

66. Jones, *Mahavastu*, 3:127.

67. Jones, *Mahavastu*, 3:128.

68. Beal, *Romantic Legend*, 368.

69. Beal, *Romantic Legend*, 368.

70. Jones, *Mahavastu*, 3:129.

71. Seishi Karashima and Katarzyna Marciniak, "The Story of Hastini in the Mahavastu and Fobenxingji jing," *Annual Report of the International Research Institute for Advanced Buddhology at Soka University for the Academic Year 2018* 22 (2019): 115, retrieved from academia.edu.

72. Jones, *Mahavastu*, 3:133.

73. W. H. D. Rouse, trans., "Cula-nandiya Jataka," in *The Jataka, or Stories of the Buddha's Former Births*, ed. E. B. Cowell (Cambridge, UK: Cambridge University Press, 1895), 2:140.

74. Rouse, "Cula-nandiya Jataka," 2:141–42.

75. H. T. Francis and R. A. Neil, trans., "Culladhammapala Jataka," in *The Jataka, or Stories of the Buddha's Former Births*, ed. E. B. Cowell (Cambridge, UK: Cambridge University Press, 1897), 3:117–20.

76. Masato Izumi, "Unicornis Asianus and the Sacred Eros," *Journal of Literature and Linguistics* 34, no. 3 (2004): 41, https://link.springer.com/article/10.1007%2FBF03379432. For an extensive discussion of this Jataka, see Giacomo Benedetti, "The Story of Ekasrnga in the Mahavastu with Its Parallels," *Journal of Asian Civilizations* 38, no. 1 (2015): 1–51, retrieved from academia.edu.

77. Jones, *Mahavastu*, 3:139.

78. Jones, *Mahavastu*, 3:139.

79. Anandajoti Bhikkhu, trans., "Nalinika's Story, or The Seduction of an Innocent," September 2010, https://www.ancient-buddhist-texts.net/English-Texts/Jatakas/526-Nalinikas-Story.htm.

## Chapter Four: Reunion of Mother and Son

1. Xianlin, *Fragments of the Tocharian*, 12.

2. Xianlin, *Fragments of the Tocharian*, 12.

3. Jones, *Mahavastu*, 3:116.

4. Jones, *Mahavastu*, 3:116.

5. Hardy, *Manual of Buddhism*, 203–4.

6. Jones, *Mahavastu*, 3:245–46.

7. Bhikkhu Analayo, "Gotami-sutta," in *Madhyama-agama Studies* (Taipei: Dharma Drum Publications, 2012), 470; Bigandet, *Legend of Gaudama*, 177.

8. Damcho Diana Finnegan, "'For the Sake of Women, Too': Ethics and Gender in the Narratives of the *Mulasarvastivada Vinaya*," PhD diss., University of Wisconsin–Madison (2009), 126.

## Chapter Five: Empowerment of the Sakya Women

1. Xianlin, *Fragments of the Tocharian*, 151.
2. Xianlin, *Fragments of the Tocharian*, 12.
3. Finnegan, "Ethics and Gender," 124.
4. Finnegan, "Ethics and Gender," 124.
5. Finnegan, "Ethics and Gender," 124.
6. Rockhill, *Life of the Buddha*, 58.
7. Finnegan, "Ethics and Gender," 127.
8. Finnegan, "Ethics and Gender," 127.
9. Finnegan, "Ethics and Gender," 129.
10. Xianlin, *Fragments of the Tocharian*, 151.
11. Xianlin, *Fragments of the Tocharian*, 151.
12. Xianlin, *Fragments of the Tocharian*, 12.
13. Xianlin, *Fragments of the Tocharian*, 157.
14. Xianlin, *Fragments of the Tocharian*, 157.
15. Xianlin, *Fragments of the Tocharian*, 157.
16. Pema Khandro Rinpoche, "The First Women's March," *Lion's Roar*, January 18, 2019.
17. I. B. Horner, *Women under Primitive Buddhism: Laywomen and Almswomen* (New York: E. P. Dutton, 1930; New York: Gutenberg, 2011), 98–99. Citations refer to the Gutenberg edition.

## Chapter Six: Mahaprajapati Makes a Robe for Her Son

1. Bhikkhu Analayo, "Theories on the Foundation of the Nun's Order: A Critical Evaluation," in *Chinese Buddhist Encyclopedia*, n.d., http://www.chinabuddhismencyclopedia.com/en/index.php/Theories_on_the_Foundation_of_the_Nuns'_Order_%E2%80%93_A_Critical_Evaluation.
2. Nanamoli and Bodhi, *Majjhima Nikaya*, 1102.
3. Analayo, "Theories," online section 3.
4. Beal, *Life of the Buddha*, 85, 87.
5. Jones, *Mahavastu*, 3:300; Garling, *Stars at Dawn*, 128.
6. T. W. Rhys Davids trans., *The Questions of King Milinda, The Sacred Books of the East*, ed. Max Muller (Oxford: Clarendon Press, 1894), 36:52.
7. Xianlin, *Fragments of the Tocharian*, 12–13.
8. Xianlin, *Fragments of the Tocharian*, 14–15.
9. Xianlin, *Fragments of the Tocharian*, 161.
10. Xianlin, *Fragments of the Tocharian*, 145–47.
11. Xianlin, *Fragments of the Tocharian*, 169.
12. Strong, "A Family Quest," 116–19.
13. Beal, *Romantic Legend*, 193.

14. Xianlin, *Fragments of the Tocharian*, 169.

15. Watters, *Travels in India*, 2:11.

16. Watters, *Travels in India*, 2:12.

17. Xianlin, *Fragments of the Tocharian*, 13.

18. Xianlin, *Fragments of the Tocharian*, 169.

19. Xianlin, *Fragments of the Tocharian*, 169, 173.

20. Xianlin, *Fragments of the Tocharian*, 173.

21. Xianlin, *Fragments of the Tocharian*, 13.

22. Jonathan A. Silk, *Cui Bono? Or Follow the Money. Identifying the Sophist in a Pali Commentary* (Hamamatsu, Japan: Kokusai Bukkyoto Kyokai, 2002), 130.

23. Bhikkhu Analayo, "Women's Renunciation in Early Buddhism: The Four Assemblies and the Foundation of the Order of Nuns," in *Dignity and Discipline. Reviving Full Ordination for Buddhist Nuns*, ed. Thea Mohr and Jampa Tsedroen (Boston: Wisdom Publications, 2010), 86–90. See also Garling, *Stars at Dawn*, 102–4.

24. Xianlin, *Fragments of the Tocharian*, 173–77.

25. Nanamoli and Bodhi, *Majjhima Nikaya*, 1102.

26. Charles Willemen, trans., *The Storehouse of Sundry Valuables* (Berkeley, CA: Numata Center for Buddhist Translation and Research, 1994), 112.

27. Dash, *Mahapajapati*, 62–64.

28. Padmanabh S. Jaini, "Stages in the Bodhisattva Career of the Tathagata," in *Maitreya: The Future Buddha*, ed. Alan Sponberg and Helen Hardacre (Cambridge: Cambridge University Press, 1988), 63.

29. Jaini, "Stages," 63.

30. Jaini, "Stages," 63n30.

31. Jaini, "Stages," 62.

32. Sayagyi U Chit Tin, *The Coming Buddha Ariya Metteyya*, 2nd rev. ed. (Kandy, Sri Lanka: Buddhist Publication Society, 1992), 30, https://www.bps.lk/olib/wh/wh381_U-Chit-Tin_The-Coming-Buddha-Ariya-Metteyya.pdf.

33. Etienne Lamotte, *History of Indian Buddhism: From the Origins to the Saka Era* (Louvain-la-Neuve, France: Institut Orientaliste de l'Universite Catholique de Louvain, 1988), 703–5.

34. Jaini, "Stages," 55.

35. Jones, *Mahavastu*, 1:52.

36. Jones, *Mahavastu*, 1:42.

37. Jaini, "Stages," 61, 76.

38. J. C. Wright, review of *Fragments of the Tocharian A Maitreyasamiti-Nataka of the Xinjiang Museum, China: In Collaboration with Werner Winter and*

*Georges-Jean Pinault*, by Ji Xianlin, *Bulletin of the School of Oriental and African Studies* 62, no. 2 (1999): 369.

39. H. Saddhatissa, trans. and ed., *The Birth Stories of the Ten Bodhisattvas and the Dasabodhisattuppattikatha* (London: Pali Text Society, 1975), 30.

40. Samuel Beal, trans., *Buddhist Records of the Western World: Translated from the Chinese of Hiuen Tsiang, A.D. 629* (London: Trubner, 1884; London: Forgotten Books, 2015), 2:46. Citations refer to the Forgotten Books edition.

41. Lamotte, *History of Indian Buddhism*, 703–4.

42. Beal, *Buddhist Records*, 2:47.

43. Beal, *Buddhist Records*, 2:47.

44. Saddhatissa, *Birth Stories*, 32; Watters, *Travels in India*, 51.

45. Rhys Davids, *Questions of King Milinda*, 52.

46. Jaini, "Stages," 74; Lamotte, *History of Indian Buddhism*, 701.

47. Jan Nattier, "The Many Faces of Maitreya," in *Maitreya: The Future Buddha*, ed. Alan Sponberg and Helen Hardacre (Cambridge: Cambridge University Press, 1988), 36.

48. Watters, *Travels in India*, 143.

49. Bodhi, *Samyutta Nikaya*, 1:679.

50. Bhikkhu Nanamoli, trans. *The Illustrator of Ultimate Meaning: Commentary on the Minor Readings, Part 1, by Bhadantacariya Buddhaghosa* (London: Pali Text Society, 1978), 97.

51. Samuel Beal, trans., *Travels of Fah-hian and Sung Yun, Buddhist Pilgrims from China to India (400 A.D. and 518 A.D.)* (London: Trubner, 1869), 133; Watters, *Travels in India*, 143.

52. Beal, *Buddhist Records*, 2:142.

53. Beal, *Travels*, 133.

54. Beal, *Buddhist Records*, 2:144.

55. Andy Rotman, trans., *Divine Stories: Divyavadana, Part 1* (Boston: Wisdom Publications, 2008), 126.

56. Watters, *Travels in India*, 145.

57. Rotman, *Divyavadana*, 126.

58. Beal, *Buddhist Records*, 2:144; Beal, *Travels*, 132–33.

59. Lamotte, *History of Indian Buddhism*, 207; Jones, *Mahavastu* 3:54, incl. n8.

60. Jaini, "Stages," 75.

61. Jaini, "Stages," 75.

## Chapter Seven: The Fall of Kapilavastu and Rise of the Sakya Women

1. For a discussion of the inconsistent chronology, see Bodhi, *Anguttara Nikaya*, 1801n1728, 1805n1748.

2. Udaya Prasanta Meddegama, trans., *Amavatura (The Flood of Nectar) by Gurulugomi*, Classical Sinhalese Texts Translation Series (Colombo, Sri Lanka: Central Cultural Fund Publication, Ministry of Cultural Affairs & National Heritage, 2006), 206.

3. Bhikkhu Bodhi, *The Suttanipata: An Ancient Collection of the Buddha's Discourses, Together with Its Commentaries* (Boston: Wisdom Publications, 2017), 838.

4. Hardy, *Manual of Buddhism*, 307.

5. Jones, *Mahavastu*, 3:96.

6. Hardy, *Manual of Buddhism*, 308.

7. Bodhi, *Suttanipata*, 838n1241; Dash, *Mahapajapati*, 77.

8. Bigandet, *Legend of Gaudama*, 206–9.

9. Bigandet, *Legend of Gaudama*, 207.

10. Nanamoli, *Life of the Buddha*, 77, 104.

11. Bigandet, *Legend of Gaudama*, 207–8.

12. Hardy, *Manual of Buddhism*, 341.

## Chapter Eight: Ordination of Mahaprajapati and the Five Hundred Women

1. Hardy, *Manual of Buddhism*, 309.

2. Garling, *Stars at Dawn*, 200.

3. Xianlin, *Fragments of the Tocharian*, 157.

4. Horner, *Primitive Buddhism*, 98–99.

5. Hardy, *Manual of Buddhism*, 309.

6. Foley, "Women Leaders," 346.

7. Bigandet, *Legend of Gaudama*, 209.

8. Finnegan, "Ethics and Gender," 310.

9. Bhikkhu Analayo, *The Foundation History of the Nuns' Order*, (Hamburg Buddhist Studies 6), (Bochum, Germany: Projektverlag, 2016), 208.

10. Analayo, *Foundation*, 189.

11. Analayo, *Foundation*, 191.

12. Hallisey, *Therigatha*, 11.

13. Analayo, *Foundation*, 208.

14. Bhikkhu Analayo, "The Going Forth of Mahaprajapati in T 60," *Journal of Buddhist Ethics* 23 (2016): 19.

15. Analayo, *Foundation*, 220.

16. Analayo, *Foundation*, 212.

17. Analayo, *Foundation*, 189.

18. Rockhill, *Life of the Buddha*, 60.

19. Bhikkhu Analayo, *Madhyama-agama Studies*, Dharma Drum Buddhist College Research Series 5 (Taipei: Dharma Drum Publications, 2012), 452.

20. Analayo, *Foundation*, 203.

21. Analayo, *Madhyama-agama*, 472.

22. Hardy, *Manual of Buddhism*, 310.

23. Analayo, "Mahaprajapati in T 60," 19; See also Garling, *Stars at Dawn*, 240–42.

24. Horner, *Primitive Buddhism*, 338.

25. Analayo, *Foundation*, 183.

26. Hardy, *Manual of Buddhism*, 308–9.

27. Jones, *Mahavastu*, 2:22.

28. Garling, *Stars at Dawn*, 76; Beal, *Romantic Legend*, 53.

29. Analayo, *Foundation*, 218.

30. Bigandet, *Legend of Gaudama*, 211; Rockhill, *Life of the Buddha*, 62.

31. Horner, *Primitive Buddhism*, 102.

32. Rockhill, *Life of the Buddha*, 24.

33. Rockhill, *Life of the Buddha*, 56–57.

34. Hardy, *Manual of Buddhism*, 341.

35. Hardy, *Manual of Buddhism*, 341.

36. Hardy, *Manual of Buddhism*, 341.

37. Alexander Csoma Korosi, "Notices of the Life of Shakya, Extracted from the Tibetan Authorities," *Asiatic Researches* 20 (1836): 308.

38. Cowell, "Buddha-Karita," 199–200.

39. Walters, *Legends*, 4.30.

40. Hallisey, *Therigatha*, 49.

41. Hallisey, *Therigatha*, 15, 251n15.

42. Hallisey, *Therigatha*, 250; Pruitt, *Commentary*, 20.

43. Foley, "Women Leaders," 345.

44. Analayo, *Foundation*, 54.

45. Bigandet, *Legend of Gaudama*, 209–10.

46. Hardy, *Manual of Buddhism*, 310.

47. Hardy, *Manual of Buddhism*, 310.

48. Analayo, *Foundation*, 192.

49. Analayo, *Foundation*, 192.

50. Analayo, *Foundation*, 56.

51. Analayo, *Foundation*, 56–57.

52. Analayo, *Madhyama-agama*, 469–70.

53. Analayo, *Foundation*, 203.

54. Hardy, *Manual of Buddhism*, 311.

55. Analayo, *Foundation*, 204.

56. Garling, *Stars at Dawn*, 101–5.

57. Analayo, *Foundation*, 209; Rockhill, *Life of the Buddha*, 61.

58. Analayo, *Foundation*, 193, 209, 218.

59. Analayo, *Foundation*, 64.

60. Analayo, *Foundation*, 197

61. Analayo, *Madhyama-agama*, 474.

62. Hardy, *Manual of Buddhism*, 311.

63. Analayo, *Foundation*, 204.

64. Bigandet, *Legend of Gaudama*, 210.

65. Analayo, *Foundation*, 197.

66. Bigandet, *Legend of Gaudama*, 210.

67. Hardy, *Manual of Buddhism*, 311.

68. Analayo, "Women's Renunciation," 96–97.

69. Bhikkhu Analayo, "The Validity of Bhikkhuni Ordination by Bhikkhus Only, according to the Pali *Vinaya*," *Journal of the Oxford Center for Buddhist Studies* 12 (2017): 9–25.

70. Horner, *Primitive Buddhism*, 119.

71. I. B. Horner, trans., *The Book of Discipline (Vinaya Pitaka)*, in *Cullavagga* (London: Luzac, 1963), 5:384–85.

72. Analayo, *Foundation*, 111–12.

73. Analayo, *Foundation*, 115.

74. Analayo, *Foundation*, 116.

75. Hardy, *Manual of Buddhism*, 312.

76. Analayo, *Foundation*, 190.

77. Bigandet, *Legend of Gaudama*, 210–11.

78. Analayo, *Foundation*, 216.

79. Burlingame, *Buddhist Legends*, 30:281.

80. Burlingame, *Buddhist Legends*, 30:281.

81. Burlingame, *Buddhist Legends*, 30:281.

82. Analyao, *Foundation*, 201.

83. Hardy, *Manual of Buddhism*, 312.

84. Foley, "Women Leaders," 346.

85. Analayo, *Foundation*, 206.

86. Analayo, *Foundation*, 206.

87. Damien Keown and Charles S. Prebish, eds., *Encyclopedia of Buddhism* (New York, Routledge, 2010), 119.

88. Horner, *Book of Discipline*, 401.

## Chapter Nine: Mahaprajapati: Foremost in Seniority

1. Finnegan, "Ethics and Gender," 321.

2. Bhikkhu Analayo, *Samyukta-agama Studies*, Dharma Drum Institute of Liberal Arts Research Series 2 (Taipei: Dharma Drum Publications, 2015), 181.

3. Dash, *Mahapajapati*, 108–10.

4. Analayo, *Samyukta-agama*, 198.

5. Anandajoti Bhikkhu, trans., *The Stories about the Foremost Elder Nuns* (Singapore: Kong Meng San Phor Kark See Monastery, Awaken Publishing and Design, 2017), 165.

6. Analayo, *Samyukta-agama*, 157.

7. Analayo, *Samyukta-agama*, 158.

8. Analayo, *Samyukta-agama*, 173–74.

9. *Dictionary of Pali Proper Names*, http://www.palikanon.com/english/pali_names/n/nandaka.htm.

10. Bodhi, *Anguttara Nikaya*, 1193.

11. Bodhi, *Anguttara Nikaya*, 1193.

12. Pruitt, *Commentary*, 182.

13. Bhikkhu Analayo, "*Anguttara-nikaya/Ekottarika-agama*: Outstanding *Bhikkhunis* in the *Ekottarika-agama*," in *Women in Early Buddhism: Comparative Textual Studies*, ed. Alice Collett (Oxford: Oxford University Press, 2014), 98.

14. Bodhi, *Anguttara Nikaya*, 111.

15. Analayo, "Outstanding *Bhikkhunis*," 99–100.

16. Analayo, "Outstanding *Bhikkhunis*," 101.

17. Pruitt, *Commentary*, 182.

18. Pruitt, *Commentary*, 182–83.

19. Hardy, *Manual of Buddhism*, 312.

20. Hardy, *Manual of Buddhism*, 312.

21. Hardy, *Manual of Buddhism*, 312.

22. Walters, *Legends*, 4.17.

23. Walters, *Legends*, 4.17.

24. Nanamoli, *Life of the Buddha*, 173.

25. Nanamoli and Bodhi, *Majjhima Nikaya*, 596.

26. Pruitt, *Commentary*, 195.

## Chapter Ten:  A Patchwork of Stories

1. Horner, *Book of Discipline*, 507.

2. Horner, *Primitive Buddhism*, 357.

3. F. Anton von Schieffer, trans., *Tibetan Tales, Derived from Indian Sources* (London: Kegan Paul, Trench, Trubner, 1906), 203–5.

4. Finnegan, "Ethics and Gender," 252.

5. Finnegan, "Ethics and Gender," 252.

6. Lozang Jamspal and Kaia Fischer, trans., *The Minor Points of the Monastic Discipline* (working title) [*Vinayaksudrakavastu*] (84000: Translating the Words of the Buddha, forthcoming).

7. Jamspal and Fischer, *Vinayasudrakavastu*, forthcoming.

8. Jamspal and Fischer, *Vinayasudrakavastu*, forthcoming.

9. Horner, *Primitive Buddhism*, 130.

10. Jamspal and Fischer, *Vinayasudrakavastu*, forthcoming.

11. Jamspal and Fischer, *Vinayasudrakavastu*, forthcoming.

12. Jamspal and Fischer, "The Story of She Who Gathers," in *The Hundred Deeds* [*Karmasataka*] part 1, chap. 11 (84000: Translating the Words of the Buddha, 2020), https://read.84000.co/translation/toh340.html.

13. Jamspal and Fischer, "Victory Banner," in *The Hundred Deeds* [*Karmasataka*], part 1, chap. 6 (84000: Translating the Words of the Buddha, 2020), https://read.84000.co/translation/toh340.html.

14. Jamspal and Fischer, "The Betrothal of the Bride: Two Stories," in *The Hundred Deeds* [*Karmasataka*], part 3, chap. 3 (84000: Translating the Words of the Buddha, 2020), https://read.84000.co/translation/toh340.html.

15. Jamspal and Fischer, *Vinayasudrakavastu*, forthcoming.

16. Dash, *Mahapajapati*, 114.

17. Dash, *Mahapajapati*, 116.

18. Horner, *Book of Discipline*, 95.

19. Dash, *Mahapajapati*, 112–13.

20. Jones, *Mahavastu*, 3:94.

## Chapter Eleven:  The *Parinirvana* of Mahaprajapati

1. Walters, *Legends*, 4.17.

2. Tathaloka Theri, "Lasting Inspiration," *Present: The Voices and Activities of Theravada Buddhist Women*, December 2012, http://www.bhikkhuni.net /wp-content/uploads/2013/06/Lasting-Inspiration.pdf.

3. Bhikkhuni Dhammadinna, "The *Parinirvana* of Mahaprajapati Gautami and Her Followers in the *Mulasarvastivada Vinaya*," *Indian International Journal of Buddhist Studies* 16 (2015): 30, retrieved from academia.edu.

4. Hardy, *Manual of Buddhism*, 313.

5. Dhammadinna, "*Parinirvana*," 31, 35.

6. Hardy, *Manual of Buddhism*, 313.

7. Dhammadinna, "*Parinirvana*," 31.

8. Walters, "Gotami's Story," in *Buddhism in Practice*, ed. Donald S. Lopez Jr. (Princeton, NJ: Princeton University Press, 1995), 118–19.

9. Walters, "Gotami's Story," 119.

10. Hardy, *Manual of Buddhism*, 313.

11. Walters, "Gotami's Story," 119.

12. Walters, "Gotami's Story," 120.

13. Walters, "Gotami's Story," 120.

14. Walters, "Gotami's Story," 121.

15. Bhikkhu Analayo, *Miracle-Working Nuns in the* Ekottarika-agama (Taipei: Dharma Drum Institute of Liberal Arts, 2015), 10.

16. Hardy, *Manual of Buddhism*, 313.

17. Walters, "Gotami's Story," 121–22.

18. Walters, "Gotami's Story," 122.

19. Hardy, *Manual of Buddhism*, 313.

20. Hardy, *Manual of Buddhism*, 313.

21. Pruitt, *Commentary*, 191.

22. Hardy, *Manual of Buddhism*, 313–14.

23. Walters, "Gotami's Story," 124.

24. Pruitt, *Commentary*, 191.

25. Walters, "Gotami's Story," 125.

26. Walters, "Gotami's Story," 126.

27. Pruitt, *Commentary*, 187.

28. Walters, "Gotami's Story," 126.

29. Hardy, *Manual of Buddhism*, 314.

30. Pruitt, *Commentary*, 192.

31. Pruitt, *Commentary*, 193.

32. Pruitt, *Commentary*, 194.

33. Pruitt, *Commentary*, 191.

34. Walters, "Gotami's Story," 132.

35. Walters, "Gotami's Story," 133.

36. Hardy, *Manual of Buddhism*, 314.

37. Pruitt, *Commentary*, 198.

38. Walters, "Gotami's Story," 134.

39. Walters, "Gotami's Story," 135.

40. Hardy, *Manual of Buddhism*, 314.

41. Pruitt, *Commentary*, 186.

42. Walters, *Legends*, 4.17.

43. Bhikkhuni Dhammadinna, "The Funeral of Mahaprajapati Gautami and Her Followers in the *Mulasarvastivada Vinaya*," *Indian International Journal of Buddhist Studies* 17 (2016): 26–27, 30–31, retrieved from academia.edu.

44. Dash, *Mahapajapati*, 141–42.

45. Pruitt, *Commentary*, 199.

46. Dhammadinna, "Funeral," 38n25.

47. Dhammadinna, "Funeral," 31.

48. Walters, "Gotami's Story," 136.

49. Dhammadinna, "Funeral," 38.

50. Dhammadinna, "Funeral," 27, 31.

51. Dash, *Mahapajapati*, 144–45.

52. Bigandet, *Legend of Gaudama*, 1:208–9.

53. Hardy, *Manual of Buddhism*, 315.

54. Hardy, *Manual of Buddhism*, 313.

55. Walters, "Gotami's Story," 121.

56. Walters, "Gotami's Story," 137–38.

## Epilogue: Her Story Continues

1. Andrew Olendzki, "What's in a Word? Nirvana," *Tricycle: The Buddhist Review*, Spring 2019, https://tricycle.org/magazine/what-is-nirvana-in -buddhism.

2. Jan D. Willis, "Tibetan Buddhist Women, Past and Present," in *Buddhist Women Across Cultures, Realizations*, ed. Karma Lekshe Tsomo (Albany, NY: State University of New York Press, 1999), 146–47.

3. Bunno Kato, Yoshiro Tamura, and Kojiro Miyasaka, trans., *The Threefold Lotus Sutra* (Tokyo: Kosei, 1987), 216.

4. Kato, Tamura, and Miyasaka, *Lotus Sutra*, 217.

5. Thomas Cleary, *The Flower Ornament Sutra: A Translation of the Avatamsaka Sutra* (Boston: Shambhala Publications, 1993), 1395.

6. Cleary, *Flower Ornament Sutra*, 1384–97. With many thanks to Professor Robert Thurman for his kind assistance reviewing this passage with the author, in an e-mail exchange, February 10, 2019.

# BIBLIOGRAPHY

Alabaster, Henry, trans. *The Wheel of the Law: Buddhism Illustrated from Siamese Sources*. London: Trubner, 1871.

Analayo, Bhikkhu. "*Anguttara-nikaya/Ekottarika-agama*: Outstanding Bhikkhunis in the *Ekottarika-agama*." In *Women in Early Buddhism: Comparative Textual Studies*, edited by Alice Collett. Oxford: Oxford University Press, 2014.

———. *The Foundation History of the Nuns' Order*. Hamburg Buddhist Studies 6. Bochum, Germany: Projektverlag, 2016.

———, trans. "The Going Forth of Mahaprajapati in T 60." *Journal of Buddhist Ethics* 23 (2016): 1–33.

———. *Madhyama-āgama Studies*. Dharma Drum Buddhist College Research Series 5. Taipei: Dharma Drum Publications, 2012.

———. *A Meditator's Life of the Buddha, Based on the Early Discourses*. Cambridge, UK: Windhorse Publications, 2017.

———. "Miracle-Working Nuns in the *Ekottarika-āgama*." *Indian International Journal of Buddhist Studies* 16 (2015): 1–27.

———. *Samyukta-agama Studies*. Dharma Drum Institute of Liberal Arts Research Series 2. Taipei: Dharma Drum Publications, 2015.

———. "Theories on the Foundation of the Nun's Order—A Critical Evaluation," section 4. *Chinese Buddhist Encyclopedia*. http://www.chinabuddhismency clopedia.com/en/index.php/Theories_on_the_Foundation_of_the_Nuns'_Order_%E2%80%93_A_Critical_Evaluation.

———. "The Validity of *Bhikkhuni* Ordination by *Bhikkhus* Only, According to the Pali *Vinaya*," *Journal of the Oxford Center for Buddhist Studies* 12 (2017): 9–25.

———. "Women's Renunciation in Early Buddhism: The Four Assemblies and the Foundation of the Order of Nuns." In *Dignity and Discipline: Reviving Full Ordination for Buddhist Nuns*, edited by Thea Mohr and Jampa Tsedroen. Boston, MA: Wisdom Publications, 2010.

Bays, Gwendolyn, trans. *The Voice of the Buddha: The Beauty of Compassion*. 2 vols. Berkeley, CA: Dharma Publishing, 1983.

Beal, Samuel, trans. *The Fo-Sho-Hing-Tsan-King: Life of the Buddha by Ashvaghosa Bodhisattva.* Vol. 19 of *The Sacred Books of the East.* Edited by Max Muller. Oxford: Clarendon Press, 1883.

———, trans. *The Romantic Legend of Sakya Buddha: From the Chinese Sanscrit.* London: Trubner, 1875.

———, trans. *Si-Yu-Ki: Buddhist Records of the Western World.* Translated from the Chinese of Hiuen Tsiang, Delhi: Oriental Books Reprint Corporation, 1969.

———, trans. *Travels of Fah-hian and Sung Yun, Buddhist Pilgrims from China to India (400 A.D. and 518 A.D.).* London: Trubner, 1869.

Bhikkhu, Anandajoti. "Nalinika's Story, or The Seduction of an Innocent." September 2010. https://www.ancient-buddhist-texts.net/English-Texts/Jatakas/526-Nalinikas-Story.htm.

———, trans. *The Stories about the Foremost Elder Nuns.* Singapore: Kong Meng San Phor Kark See Monastery, Awaken Publishing and Design, 2017.

Bigandet, Paul, trans. *The Life or Legend of Gaudama, the Buddha of the Burmese.* London: Kegan Paul, Trench, Trubner, 1911–12.

Blackstone, Kathryn R. *Women in the Footsteps of the Buddha: Struggle for Liberation in the Therīgāthā.* Delhi: Motilal Banarsidass, 2000.

Bode, Mabel. "Women Leaders of the Buddhist Reformation (from the *Manoratha Purani*, Buddhagosha's Commentary on the *Anguttara Nikaya*)." *Journal of the Royal Asiatic Society* 25, no. 3 (1893): 517–66, 763–98.

Bodhi, Bhikkhu, trans. *The Connected Discourses of the Buddha: A New Translation of the Samyutta Nikaya.* 2 vols. Boston, MA: Wisdom Publications, 2000.

———, trans. *The Numerical Discourse of the Buddha: A Translation of the Anguttara Nikaya.* Boston: Wisdom Publications, 2012.

———, trans. *The Suttanipata: An Ancient Collection of the Buddha's Discourses, Together with Its Commentaries.* Boston, MA: Wisdom Publications, 2017.

*Buddhist Dictionary of Pali Proper Names.* http://www.palikanon.com/english/pali _names/dic_idx.html. (Website note: Most of the entries have been taken from the *Dictionary of Pali Names* by G. P. Malalasekera [1899–1973], which is available as printed version from the Pali Text Society, London.)

Burlingame, Eugene Watson, trans. *Buddhist Legends: Translated from the Original Pali Text of the Dhammapada Commentary.* Vols. 28 and 30. Harvard Oriental Series. Edited by Charles Rockwell Lanman. Cambridge, MA: Harvard University Press, 1921.

Buswell, Robert E., and Donald Lopez, eds. *The Princeton Dictionary of Buddhism.* Princeton, NJ: Princeton University Press, 2014.

Caplow, Florence, and Susan Moon, eds. *The Hidden Lamp: Stories from Twenty-Five Centuries of Awakened Women.* Boston, MA: Wisdom Publications, 2013.

Chit Tin, Sayagyi U. *The Coming Buddha Ariya Metteyya*. With the assistance of William Pruitt. 2nd rev. ed. Kandy, Sri Lanka: Wheel Publication No. 381/383, 1992. https://www.bps.lk/olib/wh/wh381_U-Chit-Tin_The-Coming-Buddha-Ariya-Metteyya.pdf.

Chogyel, Tenzin. *The Life of the Buddha*. Translated with introduction and notes by Kurtis R. Schaeffer. New York: Penguin, 2015.

Clarke, Shayne. *Family Matters in Indian Buddhist Monasticisms*. Honolulu: University of Hawai'i Press, 2014.

Cleary, Thomas, trans. *Entry into the Realm of Reality*. Boston, MA: Shambhala Publications, 1989.

———, trans. *The Flower Ornament Sutra: A Translation of the Avatamsaka Sutra*. Boston, MA: Shambhala Publications, 1993.

Collett, Alice, ed. *Women in Early Buddhism: Comparative Textual Studies*. Oxford: Oxford University Press, 2014.

Covill, Linda, trans. *Handsome Nanda,* by Asvaghosa. Clay Sanskrit Library. New York: New York University Press and JJC Foundation, 2007.

Cowell, E. B., trans. "The Buddha-Karita of Ashvasghosha." In *Buddhist Mahayana Texts*. Vol. 49 of *The Sacred Books of the East*. Edited by Max Muller. Oxford: Clarendon Press, 1894.

———, ed. *The Jātaka, or Stories of the Buddha's Former Births*. 6 vols. Cambridge, UK: Cambridge University Press, 1895–1907.

Csoma Korosi, Alexander. "Analysis of the Dulva: A Portion of the Tibetan Work Entitled the Kah-Gyur." *Asiatic Researches* 20 (1836): 41–93.

———. "Notices of the Life of Shakya: Extracted from the Tibetan Authorities." *Asiatic Researches* 20 (1836): 285–317.

Cueppers, Christoph, Max Deeg, and Herbert Durt, eds. *The Birth of the Buddha: Proceedings of the Seminar Held in Lumbini, Nepal, October 2004*. Lumbini, Nepal: Lumbini International Research Institute, 2010.

Dash, Shoba Rani. *Mahaprajapati: The First Bhikkhuni*. Seoul: Blue Lotus Books, 2008.

Dhammadinna, Bhikkhuni. "The Funeral of Mahaprajapati Gautami and Her Followers in the *Mulasarvastivada Vinaya*." *Indian International Journal of Buddhist Studies* 17 (2016): 25–74. Retrieved from academia.edu.

———. "The Parinirvana of Mahaprajapati Gautami and her Followers in the *Mulasarvastivada Vinaya*." *Indian International Journal of Buddhist Studies* 16 (2015): 29–61. Retrieved from academia.edu.

———. "The Upasampada of Mahaprajapati Gautami in the *Mulasarvastivada Vinaya* and a Sutra Quotation in the Samathadeva's Abhidharmakosopayikatika." *Journal of Buddhist Studies* 13 (2016): 91–122. Retrieved from academia.edu.

Dharmachakra Translation Committee, trans. *The Play in Full* [*Lalitavistara*]. 84000: Translating the Words of the Buddha, 2013. https://read.84000.co/translation /UT22084-046-001.html.

Durt, Hubert. "The Meeting of the Buddha with Maya in the Trayastrimsa Heaven: Examination of the Sutra of Mahamaya and Its Quotations in the Shijiapu, Part 1." In *Journal of the International College for Postgraduate Buddhist Studies 11* (2007).

Edwardes, Michael, ed. *A Life of the Buddha from a Burmese Manuscript.* London: The Folio Society, 1959.

Eichenbaum Karetzky, Patricia. *The Life of the Buddha: Ancient Scriptural and Pictorial Traditions.* Lanham, MD: University Press of America, 1992.

Finnegan, Damcho Diana. "A 'Flawless' Ordination Some Narratives of Nuns Ordination in the *Mulasarvastivada Vinaya*." In *Dignity and Discipline: Reviving Full Ordination for Buddhist Nuns,* edited by Thea Mohr and Jampa Tsedroen. Boston, MA: Wisdom Publications, 2010.

———. "'For the Sake of Women, Too.' Ethics and Gender in the Narratives of the *Mulasarvastivada Vinaya*." PhD diss., University of Wisconsin–Madison, 2009.

Foley, Caroline A. "Women Leaders of the Buddhist Reformation, as Illustrated by Dhammapala's Commentary on the *Therigatha*." In *Transactions of the Ninth International Congress of Orientalists.* Vol. 1: *Indian and Aryan Sections.* Edited by E. Delmar Morgan. London: Committee of the Congress, 1893.

Foucher, A. *The Life of the Buddha According to the Ancient Texts and Monuments of India.* Abridged translation from the French by Simone Brangier Boas. Middletown, CT: Wesleyan University Press, 1963.

Francis, H. T., and R. A. Neil, trans. "Culladhammapala Jataka." In *The Jataka, or Stories of the Buddha's Former Births,* edited by E. B. Cowell. Cambridge, UK: Cambridge University Press, 1897.

Garling, Wendy. *Stars at Dawn: Forgotten Stories of Women in the Buddha's Life.* Boulder, CO: Shambhala Publications, 2016.

Geiger, Wilhelm, trans. *The Mahavamsa, or The Great Chronicle of Ceylon.* London: published for the Pali Text Society by Henry Frowde, Oxford University Press, 1912.

Gombrich, Richard. "Feminine Elements in Sinhalese Buddhism." *Wiener Zeitschrift fur die Kunde Sudasiens* 16 (1972): 67–93.

Hallisey, Charles. "Devotion in the Buddhist Literature of Medieval Sri Lanka." PhD dissertation, University of Chicago, 1988.

———. "Roads Not Taken in the Study of Theravada Buddhism." In *Curators of the Buddha: The Study of Buddhism under Colonialism,* edited by Donald S. Lopez Jr. Chicago: University of Chicago Press, 1995.

———, trans. *Therigatha: Poems of the First Buddhist Women.* Murty Classical Library of India Vol. 3. Cambridge, MA: Harvard University Press, 2015.

Hardy, R. Spence, trans. *A Manual of Buddhism in Its Modern Development*. London: Partridge and Oakey, 1853.

Herbert, Patricia. *The Life of the Buddha*. San Francisco: Pomegranate Communications in association with the British Library, 2005.

Horner, I. B., trans. *The Book of Discipline (Vinaya Pitaka)*. In *Cullavagga*, vol. 5. London: Luzac, 1963.

———. "Women in Early Buddhist Literature: A Talk to the All-Ceylon Buddhist Women's Association." Access to Insight (Legacy Edition). Kandy, Sri Lanka: Buddhist Publication Society. Last revised November 30, 2013. http://www.accesstoinsight.org/lib/authors/horner/wheel030.html.

———. *Women under Primitive Buddhism: Laywomen and Almswomen*. New York: E. P. Dutton, 1930. Facsimile reprint, New York: Gutenberg, 2011.

Izumi, Masato. "Unicornis Asianus and the Sacred Eros," *Journal of Literature and Linguistics* 34, no. 3 (2004): 41–59. https://link.springer.com/article/10.1007%2FBF03379432.

Jaini, Padmanabh S. "Stages in the Bodhisattva Career of the Tathagata." In *Maitreya: The Future Buddha*, edited by Alan Sponberg and Helen Hardacre. Cambridge: Cambridge University Press, 1988.

Jamspal, Lozang, and Kaia Fischer, trans. *The Hundred Deeds [Karmasataka]*. 84000: Translating the Words of the Buddha, 2020. http://read.84000.co/translation/toh340.html.

———, trans. *The Minor Points of the Monastic Discipline* (working title) [*Vinaya-ksudrakavastu*]. 84000: Translating the Words of the Buddha, forthcoming. http://read.84000.co/translation/toh6.html.

Jayawickrama, N. A. *The Sheaf of Garlands of the Epochs of the Conqueror: Being a Translation of Jinakalamalipakaranam of Ratannapanna Thera of Thailand*. London: Published for the Pali Text Society by Luzac, 1968.

Johnston, E. H., trans. *The Buddhacarita, or Acts of the Buddha by Ashvaghosa*. Delhi: Motilal Banarsidass, 1977.

Jones, J. J., trans. *The Mahavastu*. 3 vols. London: Luzac, 1949–56.

Karashima, Seishi, and Katarzyna Marciniak. "The Story of Hastini in the Mahavastu and Fobenxingji jing." *Annual Report of the International Research Institute for Advanced Buddhology at Soka University for the Academic Year 2018* 22 (2019): 115. Retrieved from academia.edu.

Karetzky, Patricia Eichenbaum. *The Life of the Buddha: Ancient Scriptural and Pictorial Traditions*. Lanham, MD: University Press of America, 1992.

Kato, Bunno, Yoshiro Tamura, and Kojiro Miyasaka, trans. *The Threefold Lotus Sutra*, with revisions by W. E. Soothill, Wilhelm Schiffer, and Pier P. Del Campana. Tokyo: Kosei, 1987.

Keown, Damien, and Charles S. Prebish, eds. *Encyclopedia of Buddhism*. New York, Routledge, 2010.

Khandro Rinpoche, Pema. "The First Women's March." *Lion's Roar*, January 18, 2019.

Kosambi, D. D. *Myth and Reality: Studies in the Formation of Indian Culture.* Mumbai: Popular Prakashan, 2013.

Lamotte, Etienne. *History of Indian Buddhism: From the Origins to the Saka Era.* Louvain-la-Neuve, France: Institut Orientaliste de l'Universite Catholique de Louvain, 1988.

Lopez, Donald S., Jr., ed. *Curators of the Buddha: The Study of Buddhism under Colonialism.* Chicago: University of Chicago Press, 1995.

Luczanits, Christian. "The Life of the Buddha in the Sumstek." *Orientations* 30, no. 1 (1999): 30–39. Retrieved from academia.edu.

Meddegama, Udaya Prasanta, trans. *Amavatura (The Flood of Nectar) by Gurulugomi.* Classical Sinhalese Texts Translation Series No. 2. Colombo: Central Cultural Fund Publication, Ministry of Cultural Affairs and National Heritage, 2006.

Mitra, R. L., trans. *The Lalita-Vistara: Memoirs of the Early Life of Sakya Sinha (Chs. 1–15).* Delhi: Sri Satguru Publications, 1998. First published in 1877.

Mohr, Thea, and Jampa Tsedroen, eds. *Dignity and Discipline: Reviving Full Ordination for Buddhist Nuns.* Boston, MA: Wisdom Publications, 2010.

Monier-Williams, Monier. *A Sanskrit English Dictionary.* Delhi: Motilal Banarsidass, 1974.

Muldoon-Hules, Karen. *Brides of the Buddha: Nuns' Stories from the Avadanasataka.* Lanham, MD: Lexington Books, 2017.

Murcott, Susan. *First Buddhist Women: Poems and Stories of Awakening.* Berkeley, CA: Parallax Press, 2006.

Nanamoli, Bhikkhu, trans. *The Illustrator of Ultimate Meaning: Commentary on the Minor Readings, Part 1 by Bhadantacariya Buddhaghosa.* From *The Minor Readings: The First Book of the Minor Collection.* London: Pali Text Society, 1978.

————. ed. and trans. *The Life of the Buddha According to the Pali Canon.* Onalaska, WA: BPS Pariyatti Editions, 1992.

Nanamoli, Bhikkhu, and Bhikkhu Bodhi, trans. *The Middle Length Discourses of the Buddha: A New Translation of the Majjhima Nikaya.* Edited and revised by Bhikkhu Bodhi. Boston: Wisdom Publications, 1995.

National Geographic Society. "Archaeological Studies Confirm Early Date of Buddha's Life," November 25, 2013. https://phys.org/news/2013-11-archaeological -discoveries-early-date-buddha.html.

Nattier, Jan. "The Many Faces of Maitreya." In *Maitreya: The Future Buddha*, edited by Alan Sponberg and Helen Hardacre. Cambridge: Cambridge University Press, 1988.

Obeyesekere, Ranjini, trans. *Portraits of Buddhist Women: Stories from the Saddharma-ratnavaliya.* Albany, NY: SUNY, 2001.

Ohnuma, Reiko. *Ties That Bind: Maternal Imagery and Discourse in Indian Buddhism*. Oxford: Oxford University Press, 2012.

Oldenberg, Hermann. *Buddha: His Life, His Doctrine, His Order*. Translated by William Hoey. London: William and Norgate, 1882; reprint, London: Forgotten Books, 2012.

———, trans. and ed. "The Bhikkhuni Lineage." Chap. 18 in *Dipavamsa [The Chronicle of the Island]: An Ancient Buddhist Historical Record*. February 2019. https://www. ancient-buddhist-texts.net/Texts-and-Translations/Dipavamsa/index.htm.

Olendzki, Andrew. "What's in a Word? Nirvana." *Tricycle: The Buddhist Review*, Spring 2019.

Paul, Diana. *Women in Buddhism: Images of the Feminine in the Mahayana Tradition*. Berkeley, CA: University of California Press, 1985.

Pradhan, Bhuwan Lal. *Lumbini-Kapilavastu-Dewadaha*. Kathmandu: Tribhuvan University, 1979.

Pruitt, William, trans. *The Commentary on the Verses of the Theris, by Acariya Dhammapala*. Bristol, UK: Pali Text Society, 2017.

Pruitt, William, and Peter Nyunt. "Illustrations from the Life of the Buddha." In *Pearls of the Orient: Asian Treasures from the Wellcome Library*. n.d., 123–49. Retrieved from academia.edu.

Rahman, Ghaniur. "Iconographic Symbolism of the Prodigious Birth of the Buddha Sakyamuni." *Pakistan Journal of History and Culture* 29, no. 1 (2008): 155–73. Retrieved from academia.edu.

Reynolds, Frank E. "Rebirth Traditions and the Lineages of Gotama: A Study in Theravada Buddhology." In *Sacred Biography in the Buddhist Traditions of South and Southeast Asia*, edited by Juliane Schober. Honolulu: University of Hawai'i Press, 1997.

Rhys Davids, C. A. F., and K. R. Norman, trans. *Poems of Early Buddhist Nuns (Therigatha)*. Oxford: Pali Text Society, 1989.

Rhys Davids, T. W., trans. *Buddhist Birth Stories (Jataka Tales): The Commentarial Introduction Entitled "Nidanakatha, The Story of the Lineage."* Rev. ed. London: George Routledge & Sons, 1908.

———. *The Questions of King Milinda*. Vol. 36 of *The Sacred Books of the East*. Edited by Max Muller. Oxford: Clarendon Press, 1894.

Rhys Davids, T. W., and William Stede, eds. *The Pali Text Society's Pali-English Dictionary*. London: Cheapstead, 1921–25.

Rockhill, W. Woodville, trans. *The Life of the Buddha and the Early History of His Order*. London: Trubner, 1884.

Rogers, H. T., trans. *Buddhaghosa's Parables*. London: Trubner, 1870.

Rotman, Andy, trans. *Divine Stories: Divyavadana, Part 1*. Boston: Wisdom Publications, 2008.

Rouse, W. H. D., trans. "Cula-nandiya Jataka." In *The Jataka, or Stories of the Buddha's Former Births*, edited by E. B. Cowell. Vol. 2. Cambridge: Cambridge University Press, 1895.

Saddhatissa, H., trans. and ed. *The Birth Stories of the Ten Bodhisattvas and the Dasabodhisattuppattikatha*. London: Pali Text Society, 1975.

Schober Juliane, ed. *Sacred Biography in the Buddhist Traditions of South and Southeast Asia*. Honolulu: University of Hawai'i Press, 1997.

Silk, Jonathan A. *Cui Bono? Or Follow the Money: Identifying the Sophist in a Pali Commentary*. Hamamatsu, Japan: Kokusai Bukkyoto Kyokai, 2002.

Skilling, Peter. "Nuns, Laywomen, Donors, Goddesses: Female Roles in Early Indian Buddhism." *Journal of the International Association of Buddhist Studies* 24, no. 2 (2001): 241–74.

Strauch, Ingo. "The Bajaur Collection of Kharosthi Manuscripts: Mahaprajapati Gautami and the Order of Nuns in a Gandharan Version of the *Daksinavibhangasutra*." In *Women in Early Buddhism: Comparative Textual Studies*, edited by Alice Collett. Oxford: Oxford University Press, 2014.

Strong, John S. *The Buddha: A Short Biography*. Oxford: Oneworld, 2002.

———. "A Family Quest: The Buddha, Yasodhara and Rahula in the *Mulasarvastivada Vinaya*." In *Sacred Biography in the Buddhist Traditions of South and Southeast Asia*, edited by Juliane Schober. Honolulu: University of Hawai'i Press, 1997.

———. *The Legend of King Ashoka: A Study and Translation of the Ashokavadana*. Princeton, NJ: Princeton University Press, 1983.

Theri, Tathaloka. "Lasting Inspiration." *Present: The Voices and Activities of Theravada Buddhist Women*, December 2012. http://www.bhikkhuni.net/wp-content/uploads/2013/06/Lasting-Inspiration.pdf.

Thomas, Edward J. *The Life of the Buddha as Legend and History*. Delhi: Motilal Banarsidass, 1977. First published in 1927.

Tsomo, Karma Lekshe, ed. "Mahaprajapati's Legacy: The Buddhist Women's Movement: An Introduction." In *Buddhist Women Across Cultures: Realizations*. New York: SUNY Press, 1999.

Vermeech, Sem. "An Early Korean Version of the Buddha's Biography." *Journal of the Oxford Centre for Buddhist Studies* 1 (2011): 197–211.

Von Schiefner, F. Anton, trans. *Tibetan Tales, Derived from Indian Sources*. Translated with an introduction by W. R. S. Ralston. London: Kegan Paul, Trench, Trubner, 1906.

Walker, Trent. "Samvega and Pasada: Dharma Songs in Contemporary Cambodia." *Journal of the International Association of Buddhist Studies* 41 (2018): 271–325. (The PDF is available at trentwalker.org.)

———. *Stirring and Stilling: A Liturgy of Cambodian Dharma Songs* (2011). http://www.stirringandstilling.org/introduction.html.

Walshe, Maurice, trans. *The Long Discourses of the Buddha: A Translation of the Digha Nikaya*. Boston: Wisdom Publications, 1995.

Walters, Jonathan S. "Apadana: Theri-apadana, Wives of the Saints: Marriage and *Kamma* in the Path to Arhantship." In *Women in Early Indian Buddhism: Comparative Textual Studies*, edited by Alice Collett. Oxford: Oxford University Press, 2013.

———. "Gotami's Story." In *Buddhism in Practice*, edited by Donald S. Lopez, Jr. Princeton, NJ: Princeton University Press, 1995.

———, trans. *Legends of the Buddhist Saints: Apadanapali*. Walla Walla, WA: Whitman College, 2018. http://apadanatranslation.org.

———. "Stupa, Story, and Empire: Constructions of the Buddha Biography in Early Post-Asokan India." In *Sacred Biography in the Buddhist Traditions of South and Southeast Asia*, edited by Juliane Schober. Honolulu: University of Hawai'i Press, 1997.

———. "A Voice from the Silence: The Buddha's Mother's Story." *History of Religions* 33, no. 4 (1994): 358–79.

Watters, Thomas, trans. *On Yuan-Chwang's Travels in India 629–645 A.D.* 2 vols. Edited by T. W. Rhys Davids and S. W. Bushell. London: Royal Asiatic Society, 1904; reprint, London: Forgotten Books, 2012.

Wickremsinghe, K. D. P. *The Biography of the Buddha*. Colombo, Sri Lanka: published by the author, 1972.

Willemen, Charles, trans. *The Storehouse of Sundry Valuables*. Taisho vol. 4, no. 203. Translated from the Chinese of Kikkaya and Liu Hsiao-piao (compiled by T'an-yao). Berkeley, CA: Numata Center for Buddhist Translation and Research, 1994.

Willis, Jan D. "Tibetan Buddhist Women, Past and Present." In *Buddhist Women Across Cultures, Realizations*, edited by Karma Lekshe Tsomo. Albany, NY: State University of New York Press, 1999.

Winternitz, Maurice. *A History of Indian Literature. Buddhist Literature and Jaina Literature*. 1927. Translated by S. Ketkar and H. Kohn. New Delhi: Oriental Books Reprint Corporation, 1977.

Wright, J. C. Review of *Fragments of the Tocharian A Maitreyasamiti-Nataka of the Xinjiang Museum, China. In Collaboration with Werner Winter and Georges-Jean Pinault*, by Ji Xianlin. *Bulletin of the School of Oriental and African Studies* 62, no. 2 (1999): 369.

Xianlin, Ji, trans., ed. *Fragments of the Tocharian A Maitreyasamiti-Nataka of the Xinjiang Museum, China*, in collaboration with Werner Winter and Georges-Jean Pinault. Berlin: Mouton de Gruyter, 1998.

# CREDITS

Every effort has been made to contact rightsholders. Grateful acknowledgment is made to the following institutions and publishers for citations included in this book:

Excerpts from "Legends of the Buddhist Saints," copyright © 2018 Jonathan S. Walters. Published by Jonathan S. Walters and Whitman College. http://www.apadana translation.org. Reprinted with permission of the author.

Excerpts from *The Commentary on the Verses of the Theris by Achariya Dhammapala* by William Pruitt, copyright © 2017 by the Pali Text Society. Reprinted with permission.

Excerpts from the *Damamuka-nidana-sutra*, from *Fragments of the Tocharian A Maitreyasamiti-Nataka of the Xingjiang Museum, China*, by Ji Xianlin, copyright 1998, republished with permission of Walter de Gruyter and Company; permission conveyed through Copyright Clearance Center, Inc.

Excerpts from "'For the Sake of Women, Too': Ethics and Gender in the Narratives of the *Mūlasarvāstivāda Vinaya*" PhD diss., copyright © 2009 by Diane Damchö Finnegan. Reprinted by permission of the author.

Excerpts from *Foundation History of the Nuns' Order,* copyright © 2016 by Bhikkhu Analayo. Reprinted with permission of the author.

Excerpts from "Gotami's Story" by Jonathan Walters in *Buddhism in Practice*, edited by Donald S. Lopez, copyright © 1995. Reprinted by permission of Princeton University Press.

Excerpts from *Handsome Nanda,* copyright © 2007 by Linda Covill. Reprinted by permission of New York University Press.

Excerpts from the *Lalitavistara*, reprinted from *The Play in Full*, © Dharmachakra Translation Committee and used with permission of 84000: Translating the Words of the Buddha (84000.co). The words and views in this book regarding the *Lalitavistara* are entirely the present author's and are not necessarily endorsed by 84000 or the Dharma Translation Committee.

Excerpts from *The Middle Length Discourses of the Buddha: A New Translation of the Majjhima Nikâya*, translated by Bhikkhu Nanamoli, edited and revised

# INDEX

# ABOUT THE AUTHOR

WENDY GARLING is a writer, mother, independent scholar, and authorized dharma teacher with a BA from Wellesley College and a MA in Sanskrit language and literature from the University of California, Berkeley. She is the author of *Stars at Dawn: Forgotten Stories of Women in the Buddha's Life* (2016, Shambhala Publications), a groundbreaking new biography of the Buddha that relates his journey to awakening through the stories of Buddhism's first women.

For many years Wendy has taught women's spirituality with a focus on Buddhist traditions, while also pursuing original research into women's stories from ancient Sanskrit and Pali literature. From 1991–92 she coordinated the Georgia chapter of the International Year of Tibet, helping to bring many Tibetan cultural and dharma events to Atlanta, UGA, and Emory University. As a freelance writer and editor, she was on the editorial team at the Boston Women's Health Collective for the 2005 edition of *Our Bodies Ourselves*, and wrote business articles for The Palladium Group, published through Harvard Business Publishing.

A Tibetan Buddhist practitioner, Wendy has studied with teachers of different schools and lineages, foremost her refuge lama His Holiness the 16th Karmapa (who gave her the name Karma Dhonden Lhamo), her kind root lama, the late Sera Je Geshe Acharya Thubten Loden, and His Holiness the Dalai Lama whom she first met in India in 1979. Pilgrimage has played an important role in Wendy's life: in 2007 she journeyed to the sites of women saints in Tibet, and in 2012 and 2018 to sacred sites of the Buddha in India. Her dream is to bring back the stories of Buddhism's first women, reawaken their voices, and ensure that they are not just remembered, but valorized as integral to the roots of Buddhism. Wendy lives in Concord, Massachusetts, and can be reached at wendy.garling@yahoo.com.